Jacob Udo-Udo Jacob
Convincing Rebel Fighters to Disarm

Jacob Udo-Udo Jacob

Convincing Rebel Fighters to Disarm

UN Information Operations in the Democratic
Republic of Congo

DE GRUYTER
OLDENBOURG

ISBN 978-3-11-061259-2
e-ISBN (PDF) 978-3-11-047189-2
e-ISBN (EPUB) 978-3-11-046977-6

Library of Congress Cataloging-in-Publication Data
A CIP catalog record for this book has been applied for at the Library of Congress.

Bibliographic information published by the Deutsche Nationalbibliothek
The Deutsche Nationalbibliothek lists this publication in the Deutsche Nationalbibliografie;
detailed bibliographic data are available on the Internet at http://dnb.dnb.de.

© 2018 Walter de Gruyter GmbH, Berlin/Boston
This volume is text- and page-identical with the hardback published in 2017.
Cover illustration: akg-images/Horizons/Ton Koene
Typesetting: Konvertus, Haarlem
Printing and binding: CPI Books GmbH, Leck

♾ Printed on acid-free paper
Printed in Germany

www.degruyter.com

To Professor Philip M. Taylor
(1954–2010)

Table of Contents

List of Tables and Figures

List of Abbreviations

ADF NALU	Allied Democratic Forces/National Army for the Liberation of Uganda
AFDL	Alliance des Forces Démocratiques pour la Libération du Con go – Zaïre
AG	Armed group
ALC	Armée de Libération du Congo
ALiR	Armée de Libération du Rwanda or Rwandan Liberation Army
AMDI	African Media Development Initiative
AMISOM	African Union Mission in Somalia
ANC	Armée Nationale Congolaise (the army of the RCD, 1998–2003)
ANR	Agence National de Renseignements (intelligence agency of the GoDRC)
AU	African Union
BBC	British Broadcasting Corporation
BINUB	United Nations Integrated Office in Burundi
CBO	community based organisation
CEI	Commission Electorale Indépendante (of the DRC)
CFA	comprehensive cease-fire agreement
CIAT	Comité International d'Accompagnement de la Transition
CNDD/FDD	Conseil National pour la Défense de la Démocratie / Forces de Défense de la Démocratie CNS Conférence Nationale Souve raine (Zaïre/DRC)
COB	company operational base
CoFS	combatants on foreign soils
CONADER	Commission Nationale de la Démobilisation et Réinsertion (DRC)
CRAP	Commando de Recherche et d Action en Profondeur
DC	demobilisation centre
DCAF	Geneva Centre for the Democratic Control of Armed Forces
DDA	Department for Disarmament Affairs (UN)
DDR	Disarmament, Demobilisation and Reintegration
DDRRR	Disarmament, Demobilisation, Repatriation, Rehabilitation and Reintegration
DFID	United Kingdom Department for International Development
DPA	Department of Political Affairs (UN)
DPKO	Department of Peacekeeping Operations (UN)
DRC	Democratic Republic of Congo
D&R	Disarmament & Repatriation
EU	European Union
EUPOL	European Union police mission, "EUPOL-Kinshasa"
FAB	Forces Armées Burundaises
FAC	Forces Armées Congolaises
FAR	Forces Armées Rwandaises
FARDC	Forces Armées de la République Démocratique du Congo
FAZ	Forces Armées Zaïroises
FCO UK	Foreign and Commonwealth Office
FDD	Forces pour la Défense de la Démocratie
FDN	Forces de le Défense Nationale
FNL	Forces Nationales pour la Libération
FDLR	Forces Démocratiques pour la Libération du Rwanda
FOCA	Forces Combattants Abacunguzi (military wing of the FDLR)
FRODEBU	Front pour la démocratie au Burundi
FROLINA	Front de Libération Nationale

GoB	Government of Burundi
GoDRC	Government of the DRC
GoR	Government of Rwanda
GoU	Government of Uganda
HRW	Human Rights Watch
ICD	Inter-Congolese Dialogue
ICG	International Crisis Group
ICGLR	International Conference on the Great Lakes Region
ICTR	International Criminal Tribunal for Rwanda
IDP	internally displaced persons
IO	Information Operations
IRC	International Refugee Committee
ISP	internet service providers
ISPA	Internet Service Providers' Association
ISS	Institute of Security Studies
JCC	Joint Ceasefire Commission
JED	Journaliste en Danger (Journalist in Danger)
JPHR	Journalists for the Promotion of Human Rights
JPT	Joint Protection Team
JVM	joint verification mechanism
KFOR	NATO-led Kosovo Force
LRA	Lord's Resistance Army
MDRP	Multi-Country Demobilisation and Reintegration Programme
MDTF	Multi Donor Trust Fund
MICAH	International Civilian Support Mission in Haiti
MICIVIH UN-OAS	International Civilian Mission in Haiti
MINURCA	United Nations Mission in the Central African Republic
MINUSTAH	United Nations Stabilisation Mission in Haiti
MIST	Military Information Support Team
MLC	Mouvement pour la Libération du Congo
MOD	UK Ministry of Defence
MONUC	United Nations Mission in the DRC
MOPAP	Mobilisation, Propagande et animation Politique
MPR	Mouvement Populaire de la Révolution
MR	military region
MRP	Mouvement de la Résistance Populaire
NALU	National Army for the Liberation of Uganda
NCD	National Disarmament Commission
NCL	Non-Conventional Logistics (Logistique Non Conventionnelle)
NGO	non-governmental organisation
NSS	National Security Strategy
OMGUS	Office of Military Government US
ONUB	United Nations Mission in Burundi
ONUC	United Nations Operations in the Congo
OHCHR	Office of the United Nations High Commissioner for Human Rights
OSCE	Organization for Security and Co-operation in Europe
OZRT	Office Zairois de Radio Television
PALIPEHUTU	Parti pour la Libération du Peuple Hutu
PALIR	Peuple Armé de Libération du Rwanda

PBSO	Peacebuilding Support Office
PCRU	The Post-Conflict Reconstruction Unit
PIO	public information operations
PNDR	Programme National pour la Démobilisation et la Réintégration (GoDRC)
PPRD	Partie du Peuple pour la Reconstruction et la Démocratie
PSO	peace support operations
QIPs	quick impact projects
RCD	Rassemblement Congolais pour la Démocratie
RCD-ML	Rassemblement Congolais pour la Démocratie – Mouvement de Libération
RCD-N	RCD National
RDF	Rwandan Defence Forces (name of the army of the GoR since 2002)
RDR	Retour Démocratique au Rwanda (predecessor of ALIR and FDLR before 1996)
RDRC	Rwandan Demobilisation and Reintegration Commission
RFI	Radio France Internationale
RTLM	Radio Télévision Libre des Mille Collines
RTNC	Radio Télévision Nationale Congolaise (Congolese National Radio and Television)
RPA	Rwandan Patriotic Army (name of the army of the GoR from 1994–2002)
RSF	Reporters Sans Frontières
RUD	Raliement Pour Unité et la Democratie or Rally for Unity and Democracy
SALW	small arms and light weapons
SCR	Security Council Resolution
SC	UN Security Council
S/CRS	Department of State – the Office of the Coordination for Reconstruction and Stabilization
SSR	Security Sector Reform
SPLA	Sudan People's Liberation Army
TG	Transitional Government (DRC)
TNC	transnational corporations
TOB	temporary operational base
TPP	Tri-Partite Plus Commission
TPVM	Third Party Verification Mechanism
UBU	Umugambwe wa'Bakozi Uburundi (Burundian Workers Party)
UFLD	Union of Forces for Liberation and Democracy
UN	United Nations
UNAMSIL	United Nations Mission in Sierra Leone
UNDP	United Nations Development Programme
UNESCO	United Nations Educational, Scientific and Cultural
UNHCHR	United Nations High Commissioner for Human Rights
UNHCR	United Nations High Commissioner for the Refugees
UNIOSIL	United Nations Integrated Office for Sierra Leone
UNMIBH	United Nations Mission in Bosnia Herzegovina
UNMIH	UN Mission in Haiti
UNMIK	United Nations Interim Administration Mission in Kosovo
UNMIL	United Nations Mission in Liberia
UNMIS	United Nations Mission in the Sudan
UNMISET	United Nations Mission of Support in East Timor
UNMIT	United Nations Integrated Mission in Timor-Leste

UNOB	United Nations Office in Burundi
UNOCHA	United Nations Office for the Coordination of Humanitarian Affairs
UNPROFOR	United Nations Protection Force
UNSC	United Nations Security Council
UNSCR	United Nations Security Council Resolution
UNSOA	United Nations Support for AMISOM
UNTAC	United Nations Transition Authority in Cambodia
UNTAET	United Nations Transitional Administration in East Timor
UNTAG	United Nations Transition Assistance Group (Namibia)
UNTMIH	United Nations Transition Mission in Haiti
UPDF	Ugandan People's Defence Forces
UPRONA	Union pour la Progrès Nationale
VOA	Voice of America
WNBF	West Nile Bank Front

Preface

While there have been increasing interests on the role of communications in transforming conflicts in crises states, actual contents and impacts of UN Information Intervention activities in ongoing conflicts have remained under-studied. This book explores the Information Operations activities of one of the largest and most complex UN peacekeeping missions in history – the UN Mission in the Democratic Republic of Congo *(MONUC)*. In addition to dealing with one of the worst humanitarian disasters in human history, the UN Mission is tasked with the mandate of disarming and repatriating foreign combatants. The most problematic of the armed groups has been the Forces Démocratiques pour la Libération du Rwanda (FDLR) made up mainly of Rwandan Hutu militants and former members of the Hutu Interahamwe militia – accused of leading the 1994 genocide. In addition to disarmament, demobilization, repatriation, resettlement and reintegration (DDRRR), MONUC was also saddled with the responsibility of stabilizing the country, providing protection to civilians, supporting the country's key institutions of government and disarming, demobilizing and integrating militants of several fractious indigenous armed groups particularly in the eastern part of the country into a unified Congolese national army.

In addition to leaflet drops, strategically located Quick Impact Projects, Direct Sensitization Programmes and Direct Phone Calls to Commanders of Armed Groups (AGs), a critical element of MONUC's IO is Radio Okapi – operated by Swiss-based Hirondelle Foundation. The UN's Department of Public Information is prohibited from engaging in "Propaganda" (General Assembly resolution 13 (I), of February 1946); however, when the UN is involved in a significantly complex mission, what role does Information Operations play in its operations? What kind of Communication activity should the UN be involved in as it battles multiple enemies most of which are embedded among civilian populations and in extremely difficult terrains. Importantly, what Messages or Narratives should be projected by the UN as it seeks to convince foreign combatants to voluntarily disarm and return to their home countries. This work contributes significantly to a debate that is becoming increasingly contentious if not raucous within the UN system about what approach or combination of approaches to Information Operations really works during peace support operations – the *Information Approach* that provides objective information without any embellishments or the psychological operations (Psyops) approach defined by the US Military as planned operations to "convey selected information and indicators to foreign audiences to influence emotions, motives, objective reasoning" with the intention of inducing or reinforcing foreign attitudes and behaviour favourable to the originator's objectives (Joint Publications 3–13.2). Moreover, there is an ever increasing need for an empirically sound knowledge base on the nature of impacts of various Peace Support Information Operations approaches particularly in an era when the UN and Western Militaries are increasingly outsourcing or contracting information support and strategic communications functions to private consulting companies.

What obtains at the moment is a tendency for procurement specialists to award strategic communications contracts based on military experience of Consultants. At Field Mission level, there is an emerging proclivity to hire Military Information experts as consultants to design and implement IO programmes. The likely consequence is that techniques of military information activities (such as Deception Operations) are used as a strategy. The danger is that IO and its various assemblages run the risk of being perceived locally as an external propaganda tool meant to serve the interests of its foreign originators. This work hopes to stimulate debates on UN IO particularly relating to whose right or duty it is to project and impart information in a crises society when Information becomes a humanitarian need or a key element of strategy; the nature of messages and narratives that should be projected to rebel groups embedded in civilian populations; and how to assess the effectiveness of IO approaches.

This book takes the debate to the jungles of the DRC drawing on interviews and focus group comments of former armed combatants of the FDLR, Hutu civilians and Congolese autochthons in South Kivu Province of Eastern DRC and UN Public Information staff. By investigating the nature, components and impacts of the UN Mission's Information Operations, the book hopes to provide instruments with which the UN's Public Information professionals, Military Information experts, operational researchers and scholars can compare predictions and rationalize impacts as they happen in future conflicts. For Communications scholars, this work is a significant advancement on contemporary understanding of the relative importance of communication models and their interactions within conflict settings particularly in situations where the media become a part of a conflict either as an instrument for multiplying or transforming the conflict.

1 From Peace Propaganda to Information Intervention

The atrocities of the 1990s in the Balkans and Rwanda generated a consensus among a section of communication and conflict scholars that preventing genocide which can result from hate speech, ethno-nationalist propaganda and information deprivation in conflict areas are justifications for "information intervention". Metzl (1997a) has argued for an information intervention mechanism within a UN rapid deployment force to counter "situations where media activities incite mass violence". Price and Thompson (2002) have significantly built on Metzl's work on Information Intervention. They define information intervention as "the extensive external management, manipulation or seizure of information space in conflict zones" (2002, 8). In their introduction to *Forging Peace: Intervention, Human Rights and the Management of Media Space,* Monroe Price and Mark Thompson (2002) write eloquently on the rationale for a form of humanitarian intervention that involves the use of information. They see information intervention, not necessarily as a quick-fix media intervention programme but as an intervention architecture that involves several mechanisms and actors – undertaken by states or IGOs in response to misuse of mass communication especially when there is potential for mass violation of human rights. Strategies can range from providing counter information that opposes harmful incitement to proscribing or suppressing the medium of harmful incitement itself. The legal framework surrounding information intervention with coercive powers such as jamming without the consent of the home state remains debated (Price and Thompson 2002).

Information Intervention has not featured prominently on any specific UN mandate or recommendations of any high-level panel of the UN. Although *The Responsibility to Protect* document of the ICISS notes the role of information in conflicts, it does not see information intervention as a stand-alone intervention mechanism but as an arm of a comprehensive or multidimensional humanitarian intervention. Section 7.37 of the document states that "operational planning for an operation to protect should contain a fairly sub-concept for public information". The document adds that the proper conduct of an appropriate information campaign is not only critical to maintaining public support for an intervention but also to maintaining the cohesion of the coalition. The document, subtly supporting any kind of necessary media intervention, stresses that "appropriate information campaign" must aim to erode to all extents possible "the support the opposing leader may enjoy with his or her own people or with allies". Achieving this would involve perception management activities aimed at affecting or manipulating the psychological disposition of specific audiences using the tools of psychological operations or psyops. The question of whether the UN should use the tools of psyops in its peace operations has occupied the attention of several blue ribbon and high-level review panels of the United

Nations ever since its creation. The August 2000 (Brahimi) report on UN Peacekeeping Operations, for instance, has made interesting recommendations for the involvement of the media in peace operations. The document emphasized the imperatives of designing a public information campaign strategy particularly for key aspects of a mission's mandate as part of the first elements of deployment in a new peace support mission. However, the major failing of the report in terms of public information is that it did not provide a clear framework for mission public information operations. Moreover, it failed to include media restructuring as an element of post-conflict peacebuilding. Also its recommendations were mostly structural or administrative, and not doctrinal. But the document did criticize the DPI's Peace and Security Section as having "little capacity to create doctrine, strategy or standard operating procedures for public information functions in the field other than on a sporadic and ad hoc basis" (United Nations 2000, par. 235). This seems to be a major problem with the UN doctrines – absence of a clear framework. For instance, UN doctrine on Information Operations recommends the use of the most appropriate media of reaching specific target audience in a conflict area, but it also fails to provide a clear framework for operationalization. Spotting this gap, Peter Krug and Monroe Price in Price and Thompson (2002) recommend a pre-packed toolkit or "module" with a self-contained set of formal rules and procedures for conflict zones (p. 148). They have suggested a module for peacekeeping-related information intervention that comprises a self-contained set of mechanisms. While accepting the need to have a universal set of agreed objectives for information intervention, it is important to be wary of self-contained information intervention modules that import a set of standards and measurements of practice. An effective information intervention plan needs to be "home-grown" and participatory. It may be necessary to involve local communities and local journalists in the identification and design of communication strategies and indicators for assessing outcomes. A successful use of this strategy may involve the use of participatory field-based visualization techniques, interviews and focus groups to generate information for the design of communication strategies, and media messages. A lot more will be discussed on this later in the book.

1.1 Information Intervention in History

Information Intervention is not new. It can be traced back to the *Entnazifizierung* processes of the Allied Occupational Forces after WWII. According to Thompson and Price (2002), the de-Nazification programmes of the Allied Occupational Forces remain the prototype of post-conflict information management. It involved "wholesale attempts to empty the information space of its previous political content and recast its relationship to executive government" (Thompson and Price 2002, 4). Different approaches were adopted by the four occupying powers (the US, Britain, Soviet Union and France) in their zones of control. The American zone provided a classic example of the application of Foucauldian concepts of governmentality and disciplinarity in information intervention processes. The US Army and the Office of Military Government US (OMGUS) exercised a complex and firm control over the information space to prevent any form of Nazi propaganda and pursued a "collective guilt" and "collective responsibility" campaign agreed upon by the Allied powers. Between 1945 and 1949, the Americans effectively shaped the content of information in their zone (Goldstein 2008; Ziemke 1990).

In the American zone, the Information Control Division headed by General Robert McClure eased the information campaign programme into three functional phases. The first phase involved a total blanking of the Nazi Information space. To this end, German newspapers, radio stations, theatres, moving picture houses and concert halls were shut down. The intention was to restrict the information space and ensure a total control thereof. Information for Germans was completely controlled, and it all came from *Die Mitteilung*, Radio Luxemburg and other US Army newspapers. After a total blackout of Nazi information, the second phase of the intervention involved a psychological reconditioning of Germans to "maintain and deepen the mood of passive acquiescence (to the occupation), to encourage food production; and to arouse a sense of collective responsibility for Germany's crimes" (Ziemke 1990, 368). The third phase involved selecting and licensing "disciplined" German editors and journalists to operate newspapers. Goldstein (2008) writes that by mid-1946 press licences had been given to 73 Germans drawn from fairly heterogeneous ideological leanings, including 29 Social Democrats, 17 Christian Democrats and 5 Communists. There was a pre-publication censorship until August 1946 when it was switched to post-publication censorship. After 1946, with the start of the cold war, both the US and the Soviets started using the German publications in their zones to attack the other's policies and spread propaganda (Goldstein 2008). In March 1946, OMGUS took over the editorial of *Neue Zeitung*, the major newspaper in its area of control, to counteract Soviet propaganda.

1.2 Metzl's Concept of Information Intervention: Clearing Conceptual Landscapes

Metzl first used the term *Information Intervention* in 1997. Since then, the term has attracted interests from Communications scholars interested in media interventions in crises societies. In an interview with Mark Thompson in October 2000 contained in Price and Thompson (2002), Metzl describes information intervention as "a soft form of humanitarian intervention" (p. 41) involving the use of information in an aggressive manner when it is justified on strong human rights grounds. The core of Metzl's thinking on information intervention is the role information plays in situations of conflict where "humanitarian intervention" might be necessary. He argues that all the major humanitarian crises and human rights conflicts over the past century began with a propaganda phase involving a control of the means of mass communication by extremists and using them as an instrument of incitement against other groups. A major case in point is Rwanda where Hutu extremists used RTLM to organize the extermination of Tutsis and moderate Hutus. He believes that if information intervention had been applied in Rwanda, genocide could possibly have been avoided (Metzl 1997). As a counter strategy information intervention seeks to

> *address those patterns of misuse of mass communications, and asks how we can use a more aggressive form of information related action, first to provide counter-information that opposes harmful incitement and second to proscribe or suppress the latter in extreme circumstances.* (Metzl interview in Thompson 2002, 42)

Beyond these two functional scopes of information intervention which I will describe as Reactionary Information Intervention, Metzl also talks of a broader use of information by the UN in its peace support operations which he terms "Phase II" – coming after the international community has established itself in a conflict area. Phase II and reactionary information intervention both demand a totally different legal and political framework and will demand different strategies. In both cases however, Metzl argues, the most important and most sustainable objective is to empower voices of moderation and reason within the crises society; where this is unachievable, the next objective of information intervention is to bring in news and information from outside the society to create objectivity. The third objective and likely the most controversial is an aggressive interference with negative media activity in the crises society which may involve jamming of incendiary media broadcasts. But this would always have to be a last resort after pre-agreed thresholds have been crossed. One of his recommendations in this regard is the formal introduction of an information intervention component in Chapter VII of the UN Charter. A Chapter VII mandate implies a tacit acceptance of the need for reactionary information intervention to deal with threats to international peace and security (Blinderman 2002). This would, of course, demand the UN developing an enhanced capacity to monitor provocative propaganda, reporting an occurrence, supporting independent media and engaging in peace broadcast of reliable news in conflict areas even in situations where there are no full-fledged peacekeeping deployments. This, Metzl believes, would place a huge functional demand on the UN in terms of how it addresses pre-conflict propaganda and how it utilizes information tools in peacekeeping and other operations. Of particular interest is his call for a cohesive unit within the UN that brings together best practices, develops guidelines, trains and maintains a database of skills and equipment while serving as a focal point for information intervention activities. This is essential to avoid the problem of interveners having to reconstitute themselves for each conflict and the "ad hoc syndrome" which has been the feature of most UN Public Information activities.

For Metzl, Information Intervention is not sporadic, it should involve careful planning – an understanding of how people in the conflict society obtain their information, the sort of information they trust, how they process it, how they think about their problems and why they think the way they do. Fundamental to Metzl's doctrine on Information Intervention is an awareness of how people get information because "bombarding a country with radio broadcasts doesn't achieve anything if people don't get their information from radio" (Thompson 2002, 44). Moreover, he reasons, people need to feel they are involved in some form of dialogue because people tend to develop their ideas and opinions through dialogue. A dialogue model of Information Intervention according to Metzl enables audiences to form their own opinions based on multiple and reliable information. Metzl does acknowledge that his proposed Dialogue Model is more complicated and difficult to manage than the traditional propaganda methods of leaflet dropping. Essentially, Information Intervention is not merely reactionary or always coercive but a long-term well-planned process of media development in crises states. Metzl's framework of information intervention involves three goals:

1. Media intervention: a clear explanation of the models used, the resources available and a plan of how interveners and local actors would work together.
2. Establishment of an effective Mouthpiece of the International Community with a transparent structure.
3. A responsible environment where all actors act responsibly "explaining that different models and frameworks have been used successfully elsewhere in the world to develop media responsibility, with a system of sanctions for those who don't abide by minimum standards" (Ibid, 52).

Doubtless, as a concept, information intervention is not new. As a form of practice, though suffering from a crisis of terminology, information intervention has proliferated. In many parts of the world, particularly in Africa, several NGOs, Church organizations, foreign governments, etc are involved in producing radio programmes and in some cases running radio broadcast stations intended to inform and change the attitude of people in divided societies and in some respects build a culture of peace. Moreover, the concept, according to Price and Thompson, "has not yet congealed to the point where analysts can get to work" (Ibid, 3), and according to Kyrke-Smith (2007) on key issues, the debate is stale and remains unresolved. However, there is yet a clearly defined framework of specific and time-referenced actions as well as a detailed evaluation of a specific information intervention mechanism to understand areas of success and areas of failures for each conflict phase. Price and Thompson have divided information intervention into three temporal phases: pre-conflict, mid-conflict and post-conflict. Approaches they rightly reason, should be defined by the phase of the conflict. But fundamental to their strategy in all phases is counter information and suppression of harmful information where necessary.

1.3 Reactionary and Developmental Information Intervention

Based on contemporary works on information intervention so far, two streams of activities have emerged and deserve conceptual distinction:

1. Information intervention activities aimed at enhancing public affairs and media relations (or public diplomacy) that seek to project a certain message at a certain audience either with or without the sovereign's consent. The intention usually is to influence opinion or action. (Reactionary Information Intervention)

2. Media development activities carried out by foreign state or non-state actors that aim to assist in building a democratic media sphere within a crises state. (Developmental Information Intervention)

The two streams, it must be noted, are not mutually exclusive; indeed, they could be complementary. The danger though is in the application of techniques of military information activities such as Deception Operations in information intervention efforts particularly with the expanding usage of the term "psyops" (Taylor 2002). Taylor has drawn conceptual lines of comparison between techniques of information intervention and techniques of cyber warfare, noting that both approaches emphasize the importance of information to strategy during times of conflict. "Cyberwar and information intervention are, in this sense, related phenomena" (Ibid, 313), when information becomes an element of strategy in a post-conflict situation, and not merely an undifferentiated product of public sphere, it becomes difficult if not hypocritical to apply traditional thinking on free expression and human rights (Ibid). Using examples from NATO information campaigns in Kosovo aimed at transforming ethnic hatred, Taylor argues that "information warfare and techniques used in information warfare are slowly becoming part of the arsenal used during post-conflict information interventions" (Ibid, 317). It is propelled by a new sensitivity to the imperatives of adopting effective communication strategies in supporting mission objectives – ranging from prevention of ethnic clashes to transforming ethnic hatred in divided societies. Somehow the two streams of information intervention seem to have managed to find a confluence, in terms of techniques of implementation. But Taylor warns it is essential to delineate the boundaries however conceptually similar they seem. The broadening definition of psyops has tended to merge its focus with media operations. However, it is essential to differentiate between both doctrines. According to Taylor

> It is essential for psyops and Media Operations to be kept as completely separate, albeit co-ordinated, activities; a press conference is not, and never should be, a psychological operation in the strictest sense. (Ibid, 321)

The problem of information intervention particularly when it is supported or mounted by powerful states in the global North, or executed by the military such as the MIST in the UN Mission in Haiti, is that it runs the risk of being perceived as an external propaganda tool meant to serve the interests of its originators. In such circumstances, there is the danger of information interveners wittingly or unwittingly becoming a part of the conflict they seek to transform. Moreover, any corresponding media development effort would be viewed with suspicion with a huge consequence on the credibility of the entire peace operation. To avoid this, Price and Thompson (2002) and Price (2000) argue for the involvement of NGOs in information intervention either as partners or as watchdogs. It is not just about the purveyor of the information intervention programme but the resonance of content across the parties or networks involved in the conflict and how the entire intervention programme is perceived including the development elements by the parties to the conflict. In Rwanda, for instance, it is hard to argue that development information intervention activities by the weak UN Mission would have countered the propaganda messages of RTLM well enough to prevent the genocide. An element of reactionary information intervention involving coercive action such as jamming and/or using techniques of psyops designed primarily to transform ethnic tensions between Hutus and Tutsis could probably have been more impactful. The major letdown in UN efforts in Rwanda was that its public information attempts were feeble if not completely lacking. Also, some development information activity involving broadcast of reliable information could have saved lives and reduced the humanitarian catastrophe. For instance, during the advancement of the Rwandan Patriotic Front (RPF), RTLM had broadcast that the RPF were killing everyone on their way into Kigali and that there was no Hutu left alive in RPF's areas of control. As a result, huge Hutu populations fled the RPF advance and within two weeks over one million Hutus had fled alongside retreating Rwandan Government Forces into the Democratic Republic of Congo. RTLM's strategy was to create panic, cause huge populations to move in order to create a human shield for the defeated Rwandan Armed Forces (FAR) and the Interahamwe as they retreated into the DRC to regroup. If the UN had had a strong and credible information presence, they would have dispelled RTLM's propaganda and the false rumours that swirled at the time. An objective development information intervention presence could have proven that the RPF were not killing civilian Hutus as falsely reported. The consequence of this lack of true and objective information was overcrowded refugee camps with subhuman conditions in the eastern DRC; an outbreak of cholera that killed thousands and international aid agencies having to undertake the daunting task of distributing 30 million litres of drinking water and 1000 tons of food daily. Moreover, although the DRC was already sleep-walking towards the precipice, the so-called first Congo war (November 1996 – May 1997), which has killed millions ever since, was a direct result of the influx of Hutu combatants into the country from Rwanda, sandwiched among millions of displaced civilians. The lessons of Rwanda give expression to proponents of both reactionary and development information intervention to prevent genocide and humanitarian catastrophes. Developmental information intervention or Media Development is more longer term and according to Metzl sounds more palatable as a term than Information Intervention.

Indeed, "Intervention" as a term is controversial basically due to the potential breadth of activities it could involve. At one extreme, it could include military intervention and in the case of Information – there is the potential to expand it to include Deception Operations. On the other extreme, it could be seen as any kind of pressure on a state including World Trade Organisation policies and concerning information it could involve the hegemony of transnational media networks such as the BBC, RFI and/or the VOA and the public diplomacy objectives of their sponsors. Some other schools of thought are inclined to see intervention as any kind of non-consensual operation carried out within a state by another state or non-state actor, such as provision of direct emergency relief to disaster affected populations, economic sanctions, arms embargo, diplomatic or military threats and international prosecutions such as the recent genocide charges filed against Sudan's President Omar Hassan al-Bashir by the Chief Prosecutor of the International Criminal Court. Not only is "intervention" contested, the word(s) preceding "intervention" is also as contested. For instance, the term "humanitarian intervention" has been used by the media, academics and government functionaries to refer to military interventions including the American-led invasion of Iraq much to the opposition of humanitarian agencies and workers (please see HRW, January 2004). Humanitarian organizations insist that the phrase "humanitarian intervention" should be distinctly used to describe interventions undertaken "for the stated purpose of protecting or assisting people at risk". Moreover, "humanitarian" tends to prejudge the intervention as being defensible (ICISS 2001, 9).

Information intervention encompasses the two streams identified earlier – Reactionary Information Intervention and Developmental Information Intervention. It involves the use of techniques of psyops to achieve predefined effects – it could be as routine as convincing farmers in Shabunda in Eastern DRC that it is safe to travel to Goma in North Kivu to sell their produce or as complicated as persuading Hutu combatants in the Kivus to lay down their arms and join MONUC's DDRRR programme and repatriate to Rwanda. Both ways, Information Intervention involves the use of the media by International actors including IGOs and NGOs and/or a collaboration of both in promoting reconciliation, providing news and information in crises states where such was limited or threatened due to conflict. The purpose of information intervention would be to create an enabling socio-political environment for conflict transformation processes to be achieved. In the past decade, the UN has worked to enhance its capacity in this regard by developing partnerships with NGOs and other organizations to provide credible information in crises states and seek to transform ethnic discourses. The intention, according to Kofi Annan (2000), is to use communication as a "source of leverage" for achieving peace. Essentially, Information Intervention as a concept and a sphere of enquiry in this book explores the broader role of the media and other public diplomacy activities in the hands of international actors to transform patterns of conflict and build a local culture of peace in divided borderland societies.

1.4 "Phase II" Information Intervention in the DRC

MONUC's Public Information Operations (PIO) in the DRC, aimed at persuading rebel fighters to disarm, fit into what Metzl describes as Phase II information intervention – or "a broader use of information by the international community in its peacekeeping operations" (Price and Thompson 2002, 42). Of crucial importance to this work is what Information tools MONUC has used to transform conflict in a country divided by ethnicity, where opinions are so easily formed from socially transmitted information or *Radio Trottoir*, torn apart by Mao-styled guerrilla insurgents and transnational ethnic networks with shadow economic objectives. A key information intervention challenge in the DRC was the ability of MONUC to integrate the very diverse and ethnically coloured views of the country into a viable narrative framework for sustainable conflict transformation. Unlike in Bosnia where information intervention was carried out solely by inter-governmental agencies or Liberia where it was mounted by an NGO, in the DRC, we see a collaboration of an IGO with an NGO. This is novel and fits into Price's prescription of an alliance between NGOs and IGOs to achieve media restructuring in post-conflict states (Price, 2000). In the case of the DRC, Radio Okapi is run by Swiss-based Hirondelle Foundation but the programmes are under the general authority of the UN Secretary General's Special Representative in the DRC. Radio Okapi offers a refreshing model for post-conflict information intervention because of its unique IGO/NGO collaboration. Its mission is also different from previous UN Mission radio stations. UNPROFOR Radio service in the former Yugoslavia, for instance, had the main objective of explaining the mandate of the mission. UNTAC and UNTAG radio missions in Cambodia and Namibia, respectively, both had the mission of educating voters about upcoming election processes. Moreover, these radio stations were solely a part of the UN peacekeeping missions in those countries. But Radio Okapi's objectives are designed to fit into a model of Radio as a social developer and a peacebuilder (Betz 2004). In an interview with Radio Netherlands, David Smith, then MONUC chief of Information, set out the mission of Radio Okapi thus:

> *This radio project will allow people in rebel held territories to speak to people in government-controlled territories for the first time since the war broke out. A big role of the radio will be to convince people that it's in their interest to lay down their arms, and either be repatriated to their home country, if they come from somewhere else, or to find ways to join civil society and leave the war behind.*[1] (Radio Netherlands 25-02-2002)

This seems rather a tall objective, but essentially it highlights the unique expectations from Radio Okapi. A distinguishing element in the nature of information intervention in the DRC has been the intensity, magnitude and indeed the novel collaboration

---

[1] This interview was accessed on the internet: Radio Netherlands Media Network Dossier: Peace Radio: Democratic Republic of Congo, www.rnw.nl/realradio/dossiers/html/congo-p.html (date accessed 5 February 2006).

between the UN and a "foreign" and very unique NGO and the challenges of such partnerships. In the DRC, radio okapi is the largest radio station and has the widest reach.
It is also the largest radio mission ever operated by the United Nations. Radio Okapi's
mix of information, education and entertainment programmes across its vast network
of transmitting and relay stations are designed to achieve specific mission objectives
and to create localized cultures of peace in communities across the country. Radio
Okapi has however had an immensely difficult time in the DRC, with two of its journalists killed[2] and several others intimidated by armed gangs.[3] In the eastern region
of the country, Radio Okapi has faced the ever present allochthony/autochthony (foreigner /local) crises in terms of questions of foreign content and ownership in a region
where citizenship and nationality are contested issues. Though the station has an
array of programmes (which will be discussed later in this book) aimed at various networks and actors in the DRC conflict, there is the potential risk of a crisis of message –
what message for whom and with what effects on other groups? Besides, although
Radio Okapi is directly run by Swiss based Hirondelle Foundation, it is joined at the
hip with the UN and is subject to reservations local folks have about UN peacekeepers.
In its almost 10 years in the DRC, MONUC has had to deal with various controversies
regarding its Peacekeepers – ranging from accusations of rape, arms dealing, trade
in conflict diamonds and coltan, negation of their responsibility to protect civilians
under threat of violence from rebel groups and MONUC's support to the Congolese
army FARDC in the controversial Kimia II operation in the Kivus aimed at rooting out
FDLR elements. MONUC's credibility burdens have the potential of weighing down
the credibility of its mouthpiece – Radio Okapi. Moreover, there is the issue of frames
and discourses in Radio Okapi's programme content. The impression is that conflict
interveners are overlooking or in some cases totally ignoring local crises situations
as irrelevant to the national peace process. In South Kivu, for example, a canvas of
Rwandan Hutus and autochthons in some communities have attempted to forge a
life together through inter-marriage, but tensions remain with the Tutsi Banyamulenges; in North Kivu, there are lines of division between Rwandan Banyarwandas
and autochthons; however, MONUC's message on its flagship programme *Gutahuka*
remained the same: "Hutus, go back home to Rwanda". A seeming crisis of message
in terms of blanket messages targeted at Hutu populations despite the delicate differences would call to question the depth of the UN's knowledge of its target audiences.
Media ideology or ethics is critical particularly in cases of crises, where the overall
intention is not only to inform but also to build the peace. These and others are issues
discussed in the following chapters.

---

2 Radio Okapi Journalist Didace Namujimbo was shot dead in Bukavu in November 2008 by unknown
gunmen; 17 months after, another Radio Okapi Journalist Serge Maheshe was also killed in Bukavu.
3 The most recent being the brutal beating on 7 August 2009 of Paulin Munanga, Radio Okapi's Provincial Correspondent in Lubumbashi, by security agents of Agence Nationale des Renseignements
(ANR) while covering a demonstration by human rights activists in Katanga.

2 A Foucauldian View of UN Information Intervention

Information Operations and indeed Information Intervention as a function of humanitarian intervention has remained under-theorized and restricted mostly to operational level discourses and practice borne out of expediency. This chapter draws on Foucauldian concepts of disciplinary power, biopolitics and governmentality to deconstruct the concept of information intervention.

A lot of studies have applied Michael Foucault's concepts of governmentality, biopolitics and disciplinarity to international affairs (see, for example, Campbell 2005; Duffield and Waddell 2004; Huysmans 2004; Larner and Walters 2004a, 2004b; Larrinaga and Doucet 2008; Lipshutz and Rowe 2005; Perry and Maurer 2003; Merlingen and Ostranskanite 2006; Walters and De Haar 2005; Zanotti 2006, 2008). In his work *The History of Sexuality Volume I* (1998), Foucault charts the course of transformation from the classical age to the modern age where sovereignty progressively made way for a government that had as its chief concern the life and health of the population. Prior to this shift, the ancient Sovereign had the power to "foster life or disallow it to the point of death" (Foucault 1998, 138). This power went through two stages of evolution: first the disciplinary stage and second the biopolitics stage. Disciplinary stage was concerned with the individual as an object and sought to modify and socially control the "individual" including the deviant elements in the society. Beginning from the mid-eighteenth century after the emergence of institutional structures that could support medicine, punishment, education, etc., a new form of power emerged that referenced citizens no longer as objects or "machines" but as species – humans. This new calibration of citizens was based, not on individuality, but on communality with citizens as aggregates of population or "biopolitics of the human race" (Foucault 2003, 243). Duffield and Waddell write that in Foucauldian terms, the previous construct of the "individual" as an object was based on a wrong premise because the "multiple social, economic and political factors that aggregate to establish the health and longevity of a population appear at the level of the individual as chance" (Duffield and Waddell 2004, 4). But at the population level "they reveal themselves in terms of constants, probabilities and trends" (Ibid, 4). This made possible the formation of a biopolitical power that relied on institutions to control populations, to make forecasts, proffer solutions and "intervene at the level of their generality" (Foucault 2003, 246). For Foucault, *biopolitics* adopts a regulatory framework to foster stability and security at the level of populations, while *disciplinarity* seeks to train individuals to be socially productive. Though these two technologies developed at different periods, they were not meant to remain mutually exclusive. Rather they were merged or superimposed to be mutually re-enforcing – rules and monitoring mechanisms were developed to punish, to reward and to make individual citizens socially productive members of the society. In Foucault's view, relating biopolitics or technology of life to security "around the random element in a population" is essential "to optimize a state of life" (2003, 246). In their analysis of the Foucauldian view of security, Duffield and Waddell (2004) write that for Foucault, security is inalienably linked to "securing populations against the contingent and aleatory nature of existence through risk assessment, modifying environments or compensation" (p. 5).

In a typically genealogical method, Foucault demonstrates how techniques of normalization and disciplinarity evolved along discursive trajectories to create the modern system of disciplinarity seen in schools, prisons, hospitals, factories and ultimately for control of the society. At the core of disciplinarity is a power technique that domesticates and transforms individuals to make them responsible, productive and responsive. Fundamental to Foucault's thinking on disciplinary power are three core systems of control: hierarchical observation, normalization and examination. Control can be achieved through observation – as in Jeremy Bentham's Panopticon where a guard sees everything, not literally but through a "relay" of hierarchically ordered observers – where the observed data moves from realms of lower power to realms of higher power. In the Panopticon, the intention is to achieve conformed behaviour by introducing a mental state of being observed on the inmate. "Hence the major effect of the Panopticon", Bentham writes in his letters, is "to introduce in the inmate a state of consciousness and permanent visibility that assures the automatic functioning of power" (Bentham 1995). Foucault's thesis on Panopticonism sees Jeremy Bentham's Panopticon prison as the ideal architectural model of modern disciplinary power (Foucault 1995; Dobrzeniecki 2008). The Prison's central tower may not necessarily observe all inmates all the time, but inmates have the awareness that they are being observed. The consciousness of being watched makes inmates behave as if they are on a *Big Brother* or reality show. They thus subject themselves to their own internal control.

The chief concern of disciplinary control is training individuals to meet set standards or to correct deviant behaviour (Foucault 1995). This is achieved by hierarchal observation to ensure normalization or imposition of norms or acceptable standards of behaviour. "Examination" combines hierarchical observation with "normalizing judgement" in a power-knowledge mix by eliciting and reporting the true state of inmates while controlling their behaviour to meet "normalized" standards. For Foucault, the power-knowledge mix is more intimate than Francis Bacon's calibration of the linkages between the two concepts. For Bacon, knowledge is required to increase power, and knowledge is empowering. But for Foucault, it is about power creating a hegemony of knowledge through which societies and or individuals are trained to conform to normalized codes of behaviour. In knowing, power controls, and in controlling, power knows.

Foucault and Humanitarian Intervention

The post–cold war era has seen increasing shifts from geopolitics or the security of states to biopolitics or the security of life. Biopolitics would involve interventions at the aggregate level of population aimed at managing or compensating for the contingent and unpredictable nature of existence which may be created by conflicts. The biopolitical privileging of populations over sovereignties has been obvious at the supranational realm since the UN's first military intervention in the former Zaire in 1960. The United Nations Operation in the Congo (Opération des Nations Unies au Congo, or ONUC) was established to assist the newly independent Congolese government to protect its populations, to maintain law and order and to provide technical assistance in areas of governance and security. Since ONUC, the international community has intervened in several politically dysfunctional states to achieve normalization – Haiti, Rwanda, Bosnia, Ivory Coast, Liberia, Sierra Leone, etc. Zanotti (2006) writes that following Foucauldian doctrines, international organizations have attempted to "tame unpredictability, cast light onto obscure borderlands and promote the transformation of abnormal states into ... productive members of the 'international community'" (p. 152). But biopolitical intervention has not been limited to situations of conflict. Campbell (2005) writes that biopolitical interventions have also been obvious "in domains other than extreme cases of violence and war" (p. 950) such as humanitarian support to countries suffering from natural disasters, for example the 2004 Tsunami in South East Asia and the 7.0 magnitude earthquake in Haiti in early 2010. Such humanitarian biopolitical responses by foreign states working alongside non-state actors (such as humanitarian agencies) seek to relieve affected populations of suffering from unpredictable natural disasters when national governments cannot on their own provide the succour their citizens require. Even in countries facing diplomatic sanctions, the biopolitical privileging of populations has been evident in the international community's willingness to provide assistance to citizens facing suffering. For example, during the 2008 cyclone Nargis in Myanmar where over 80,000 people were killed, various state and non-state actors offered assistance despite the sanctions then and the unfriendliness of the country's military leaders. The overriding interest in the Myanmar case was the desire to provide succour to Myanmar citizens that suffered the effects of the cyclone irrespective of international reservations against a dictatorial and reclusive national government. This kind of biopolitical intervention however has not usually been the case in situations where the media is used or allowed by the state to be used to propagate genocide such as the case of RTLM in Rwanda in 1994. RTLM actively mobilized Hutus to kill Tutsis after an orchestrated campaign of dehumanization. Also, in the Democratic Republic of Congo, during the twilight of the Mobutu era the media was used by political bigwigs to incite groups and populations against other ethnic groups. Following the election of opposition leader Etienne Tshiesekedi (from Kasai Province) to the post of Prime Minister by Zaire's National Conference, Mr. Gabriel Kumwanza, the Governor of Katanga Province, home state of the previous Prime Minister Nguza Karl-I-Bond, used the media to mobilize thousands of his party youths to embark on a well-planned ethnic cleansing of over 100,000 Kasains (Masoka 2006).

Such cases and more potently, lessons from misuse of information as a tool for genocide in Rwanda and the Balkans in the 1990s justified arguments by scholars and international policy analysts for a biopolitical privileging involving an international intervention mechanism to protect populations against the use of the media for dehumanization and genocide (see, for example, Metzl 1997a, 1997b; Carruthers 2000; Howard 2001; Melone, S. D., Terzis, G., & Beleli, O., 2002; Price and Thompson 2002; Kirschke 1996; Price and Krug 2002; Allen and Stremlau 2005; Bratic 2008; Kyrke-Smith 2007).

3 The Liberal Institutionalist Foundations of Post–Cold War UN Information Operations

Since the end of the cold war, potential sources of international or regional instability have shifted from threats of nuclear catastrophe to more unpredictable and diffused forms of threats. Insurgency, dysfunctional states, hate media, women and minority rights, amongst others which hitherto were confined to domestic politics have shifted into the mainstream of international politics. During the cold war, such issues and any other internal challenges to states were seen by the two dominant powers in zero-sum terms either as an opportunity to weaken the other power's influence or as a threat to the patronizing power's influence. Conflicts even in so-called third-world countries were in most cases fostered and exacerbated by outside powers for the purpose of exerting influence or reducing the other power's influence. Generally, internal causes of civil conflicts such as hate media, socio-economic alienation of minority groups or dictatorial governments were, more often than not, overlooked mainly for the purpose of maintaining the status quo. International interests in internal political affairs of countries (including human rights and media regulation) were almost non-existent.

The role of intergovernmental organizations in this regard has equally intensified. The United Nations in particular has been more engaged in states. Liberal Institutionalism or governments working alongside international organizations to achieve normalization have increasingly redefined international relations. Several blue ribbon committees and high level panels were set up to review and recommend ways and means to make the UN more effective, notable among these was the high level Panel on UN Peacekeeping Operations, chaired by former Algerian Foreign Minister Mr. Lakhdar Brahimi, to present a clear set of specific, concrete and practical recommendations to enhance the UN's intervention mechanism. There were also the High Level Panel on Threats, Challenges and Change; high level panel on system-wide coherence across development related agencies, funds and programmes of the UN in areas relating to humanitarian assistance, environmental activities and development, among others. In addition to UN reforms, there were also a range of new institutional actors and mechanisms that introduced new voices, perspectives and new monitoring and regulatory landscapes within the international community, including the UN High Commissioner for Human Rights, the International Criminal Tribunal for the former Yugoslavia and sister tribunals for Rwanda and Sierra Leone. Significantly, there has also been an increase in the number of NGOs involved in global issues as well as transnational media networks purveying and reporting violence and conflicts real time. The interplay of these new actors introduced a different playing field for states and the UN. In response to the increasingly intricate interaction and interdependencies of state, non-state and institutional actors, the UN has become more active and more exploratory in its reforms and operations. Greater access has also been granted for NGOs to the international forum, so they can engage with issues of humanitarianism, environment, development, conflict transformation and peacebuilding. This was a vindication for Liberal Institutionalists such as Robert Keohane, who saw international institutions as capable of creating "a more loosely coupled system at the global level" that achieves the same major objectives achievable by liberal democracies in crisis states (Keohane 2001). However, to achieve the cooperation and development within states, international institutions needed to develop additional communication capabilities that would enable them to obtain spontaneous accent in the societies they sought to transform. The problem, as Duffield (2001) aptly observed however, was that international intervention institutions become more "directly concerned with trying to change the way people think and what they do" instead of building or redistributing resources (Duffield 2001, 312). But for Keohane, persuasive communication aimed at making people change the way they think and behave is an essential element in liberal institutional intervention. Since global institutions do not have the coercive powers of states, they will have to exercise legitimate influence through communication and persuasion if they must achieve voluntary cooperation (Keohane 2001). Unsurprisingly, communications increasingly became a key element of UN strategy. In 1997, Secretary General Kofi Annan set up a nine-member task force on the Reorientation of United Nations Public Information Activities to review and make appropriate recommendations on ways and means to enhance the UN communications strategy. The task force was also mandated to examine possible ways and means through which the DPI could reorient its work to convey UN communications more strategically, "to greater effect". The panel's 34 page report, "Global Vision, Local Voice: A Strategic Communications Programme for the United Nations", released in August 1997 maintained that the fundamental principles of UN Communications needed a complete turn-around obviously from its original stance against "Propaganda". The UN, the panel stressed, needed to be more assertive in its communications. It further recommended that the DPI must use "strategic communications" and "public diplomacy" to achieve UN objectives. According to Mark Alleyne (2005), who has researched the UN extensively, it marked a turning point in UN Public Information.

There were further radical reforms in UN strategic communications in 2002. The United Nations Communications group was created to enhance inter-agency coordination in public information and communication. It was tasked with the responsibility of researching new and creative ways to show how UN programmes are delivering results and promoting a coherent image of the United Nations.

Also, at mission level, the UN was learning to broaden its use of the media in its Missions information and education programmes. In Cambodia, for instance, the UN Transition Authority in Cambodia (UNTAC) actively used its mission radio service to dispel rumours and rebel propaganda. Notably, UNTAC dispelled the Khmer Rouge's propaganda that the ballot-marking pencils contained radio beacons that can reveal votes to the Khmer Rouge and make voters targets for reprisal attacks (Lindley 2004).

Ingrid Lehmann quotes Tim Carney, UNTAC's Advisor on Information, to the Special Representative of the Secretary General as acknowledging "the vital, central role of information" to UNTAC which he treated "imaginatively" (Lehmann 1999, 60). Information operations became an essential part of UN peace support operations. The intention was to achieve specific educational objectives as an integral function of the UN Peace Missions. Public Information, like other areas of humanitarian responses, drew on all assets of the intervention mission to achieve results. The Information programme of UN Mission in Haiti (UNMIH), for instance, was remarkably enhanced by the military. The Military Information Support Team (MIST) had the key objective of enhancing public support for UNMIH, set conditions for successful elections; enhance popular support for democracy and for the Haitian National police while working to reduce local violence (Lehmann 1999).By October 1995, MIST had distributed close to 3 million handbills and 500,000 copies of 55 different posters; developed 88 radio messages; and broadcast nearly 10,000 radio spots. 8000 of these spots were in support of electoral issues with 14 different messages and an additional 15 video messages, among other information campaign materials. Among its programmes was Crime reporting hotline and a weapons turn-in programme which MIST vigorously publicized (Lehmann 1999; Avruch et al. 2000). MIST had a total staff of 104 (including 21 Haitian language linguists) located across UNMIH's six zones of deployment. The size of MIST demonstrated the importance of their function to the Mission.

But UN Public Information Operations were not restricted to only countering rebel propaganda. Communications increasingly became a tool for *influencing* rebel fighters to voluntarily disarm, convince citizens to support nascent democratic processes, vote in elections, and welcome peacekeepers, among others. Essentially UN mission operations and other humanitarian interventions acquired the added dimension of stability including changing local attitudes and beliefs.

The Responsibility to Protect bases of UN Information Intervention

The 2001 Report of the International Commission on Intervention and State Sovereignty (ICISS), *The Responsibility to Protect,* defines sovereignty aptly as implying two core responsibilities: *externally* – to respect the sovereignty of other states, and *internally* – to respect the dignity and basic rights of everyone within the state (ICISS 2001). Within contemporary context of international human rights covenants, the UN and in state practice, sovereignty is seen as fundamentally composed of these two responsibilities. The ICISS report redefined sovereignty not necessarily in terms of the Westphalian principles of territorial integrity, border inviolability and supremacy of the state but in terms of the dual responsibility which has become "the minimum content of good international citizenship" (ICISS 2001, 8). This modern meaning of sovereignty is critical to the concept of information intervention.

A key element informing the new conceptualization of sovereignty has been the evolving system of international norms, standards and laws particularly relating to human right issues and access to social and economic rights particularly by minority groups and women as well as the evolving concept of human security which I will deal with in more detail later. Furthermore, there have been a range of new and more effective international institutions, NGOs and an increased co-operation by states to monitor and implement standards in human rights and international humanitarian law. Indeed, human rights during the past two decades have evolved into a mainstream part of international law and a key subject in international relations. Though mechanisms such as Universal Declaration of Human Rights, the Geneva Conventions and the Additional Protocols on international humanitarian law in armed conflict; the Convention on the Prevention and Punishment of the Crime of Genocide; the 1966 covenants on civil, political, social, economic and cultural rights, etc. have existed for decades past, they have found greater implications and implementations in the post–cold war era. The universal jurisdiction of these instruments demands of all state parties to bring to trial any person found contravening those rights. The arrest in Nigeria and trial of former Liberian President Charles Taylor at the Special Court for Sierra Leone (SCSL) sitting in The Hague, for war crime offences and crimes against humanity during the Liberian and Sierra Leonian civil war, among several other cases demonstrate the increasing strength of these instruments.

Moreover, the evolving concept of human security or biopolitics has placed greater expectations on states concerning how they treat their own citizens. Underlying the sovereignty and intervention debate has been a fundamental shift in our understanding of the "subject" and "object" of security. Human security has emerged as a new securo-development paradigm – shifting attention, as it were, from securitization of the state or sovereign to securitization of the subject or individual. The UNDP's 1994 Human Development Report laid the foundation for human security by arguing that insuring "freedom from want" and "freedom from fear" for all persons is the best approach in tackling the problem of global insecurity. To buttress this argument, Secretary General Kofi Annan at the 54th session of the UN General Assembly in 1999 spoke eloquently on the prospects for human security and intervention against the background of UN failures in Rwanda and Kosovo. He reflected on the "collective conscience of humanity" and the need for the "defence of our common humanity". Common humanity and human security seemed to be a threat to traditional notions of state sovereignty, but in his millennium report Annan streamlined the argument more logically:

> ... if humanitarian intervention is, indeed an unacceptable assault on sovereignty, how should we respond to a Rwanda, to a Srebrenica – to gross and systematic violations of human rights that offend every precept of our common humanity? (Quoted in ICISS 2001, 2)

Indeed in situations of conflicts where vulnerable civilians are deliberately targeted, deliberately displaced, or as in the case of the Democratic Republic of Congo where women are systematically raped by ethnic militias so they can give birth to their kind (who would eventually take up the "struggle"), and in cases where governments launch a campaign of terror against its citizens like in Darfur, there has been an increasing consensus that intervention is appropriate to ensure that "deviant" states conform to international norms and uphold their responsibility to the international community and the laws thereof as well as to their own citizens.

The 2004 Report of the Secretary-General's High Level Panel on Threats, Challenges and Change, *A More Secure World: Our Shared Responsibility* set the tone for an intervention architecture to intervene within "deviant" states when it declared that "there is a growing recognition that the issue is not the 'right to intervene' of any state, but the 'responsibility to protect' of *every* state" (par. 201, p. 65) – to protect people suffering from avoidable disaster within states that refuse or are unable to uphold their responsibilities. The panel agreed that there is a collective international "responsibility to protect" during threats of genocide and other large-scale killing or serious violations of international humanitarian law which sovereign governments have been unable or unwilling to prevent. Information intervention emerged from this backdrop – the responsibility of the international community to intervene in sovereign states when the media is used as a tool for genocide. Information intervention would involve "the extensive external management, manipulation or seizure of information space in conflict zones" (Price and Thompson 2002, 8). In the DRC, for instance, this is manifested with the creation, management and sponsorships of radio stations and programmes not just by the UN's Peacekeeping Mission in the DRC (MONUC) but also by development NGOs, with funding from bilateral and multilateral donor communities most of them working coherently to develop information programmes targeting the Congolese population.

The points of contact between sovereignty and humanitarian intervention and the overarching concept of security have occupied the attention of policy analysts and International Relations scholars since the end of the cold war. Moreover, the constructivist slant in security studies has birthed an open arena for discussion of issues of identity, meaning and as earlier noted, not only the subject of security but also the object thereof. The result has been the emergence of a new understanding of state interests, identity and security as "socially constructed" (Varadarajan 2004; Booth 1991; Buzan 1991; Weaver et al. 1993; Campbell 1994; Katzenstein 1996; Krause and Williams 1997; Weldes, Laffey, Gusterson and Duvall 1999; Dillon 2004; Dillon & Reid (2001); Duffield 2001). The underlying current of constructivist scholars' view of International Relations has been an understanding of security from a transnationalized perspective. Intervention, whatever the form, leaks the state's central political authority to supra-state, sub-state and/or non-state actors and also to global civil society (Lipschutz 1992). Moreover, information flow, international trade and globalization have fundamentally deterritorialized and in many respects reterritorialized political authority typical to sovereign states in the new global institutional order. Non-state regulation of commerce, shadow transborder trade, transnational ethnic networks, international media, etc. have created what Saskia Sassen describes as a "new geography of power" resulting in "strategic complexes" of state, sub-state and non-state actors including IGOs and NGOs and Transnational Corporations (TNCs) (Sassen 1996; Duffield 2001). Essentially, while these do not in any way signal the end of sovereignty or statehood, they do usher in a new globalized era where states have to function within a broader transnational space – with greater discursive bases of power. These new power bases which include non-state actors (such as international NGOs; TNCs; Consulting Companies working on subcontracted projects for IGOs, foreign governments and their militaries; terrorist organizations; smugglers; private military companies; transnational ethnic networks; shadow/parallel economic networks dealing in raw materials from crises states, among others) intervene either directly or indirectly in the affairs of states. This new intervention by new transnational actors has created a new paradigm based on global collective conscience on issues of governance – ranging from humanist to environmental conservation. Of course, the non-territoriality of political authority has also resulted in the emergence of illicit trade channels and increasingly powerful shadow economies of transborder trade, piracy and illicit dealing on drugs, arms and raw materials. These non-state actors all combine to present new forms of challenges to the authority and sovereignty of states, particularly weak states. One of the outcomes has been the emergence of new forms of conflicts impelled by illicit trading networks in arms and raw materials, transnational ethnic networks and private military companies operating within and around states. The resulting "new wars" according to Duffield (2001) are fought by networked complexes working beyond the territorial and/or political competence of states.

In attempting to restore normalization in states weakened by so-called new wars and to prevent a total breakdown from challenges from illicit non-state actors, humanitarian assistance has evolved from merely "helping" or providing "aid" to crises states to supporting and strengthening instruments of governmental authority. Inevitably, development and security have increasingly intertwined. These all figure in the new nature of intra-state wars in the post–cold war era. Unlike during the cold war era, conflict or intra-state wars are no longer seen in zero-sum terms of super-power rivalry but as symptoms of dysfunctional statehood with potential consequences for the international community. The new security paradigm therefore links stability or normalization to effective statehood that is capable of delivering on development needs of its citizenry, access to human rights as well as social and economic rights. Development is thus seen as a corollary of stability.

The increasingly interweaving roles of IGOs such as the UN, the EU, etc. and development NGOs in developing instruments of normalization, governmentality and disciplinarity (including media intervention) in crises states underlie Duffield's (2001) claim of a radicalization of the politics of development in which development is synonymous with managing chaos or preventing insecurities. To transform conflicts or "tame chaos" (Zanotti 2006) in developing states, multilateral and bilateral donor communities have sought coherence between aid and development. Moreover, underdevelopment has been recalibrated in terms of the danger it poses – this time not merely for citizens in the underdeveloped states but also and more importantly the risk they pose for Western developed countries either through illicit migration or terrorism. The outcome has been the inter-knitting of IGOs, aid organizations, Western Governments, NGOs, etc. into a transnational network of global governance administered from the global North. Essentially in the post–cold war security environment, both the subject and object of security have transformed fundamentally from being concerned with the complex war machines of the world's super-powers to underdevelopment in some of the world's poorest states.

The increasingly converging lines of functionality between stabilization, humanitarian and development interventions make humanitarian intervention and all its offshoots, including information intervention, to be seen as an extension of a security strategy derived from state/supra-state institutions of global governance to tackle and, if need be, quarantine conflicts in crises states, and by such means have an architecture to *discipline* citizens to be productive members of their *own* societies. For Duffield (2001), the radicalization of the politics of development denotes a commitment to transforming conflict societies as a whole – including attitudes and beliefs of members or a process of disciplinarity in Foucauldian terms. More so, it involves the rerouting, as it were, of development resources to change beliefs and attitudes in violent or potentially violent borderlands in order to achieve normalization or stabilization. For the UN, it reorients the rationale for its PIO as a function of information intervention, from being only a humanitarian mechanism to prevent genocide (as reasoned by Metzl) to a radicalized politics of development where it operates as a function of stabilization or normalization of fragile states to tame ungoverned areas.

4 Between Propaganda and UN's Public Information Operations

Since Harwood Child's (1937) thesis on public opinion and peace, there has not been much scholarly analysis of peace propaganda as a problematique. Child's justification for peace propaganda is still as justifiable as it was when he argued some 80 years ago that "the presentation of peace depends upon the maintenance of a state of public opinion favourable to peace". Child's pre–World War II thesis was based on his belief that peace propaganda can help prepare public opinion psychologically for peace.

But Propaganda has never been a good word. Or more appropriately, it's a good word that went bad. Pope Gregory XV established the *Congregatio de Propaganda Fide* (Congregation for the Propagation of the Faith), made up of respected Cardinals to help spread the Roman Catholic doctrine in the missions and to counter the raging Protestantism movement. Propaganda, over the years, has acquired a rather dishonest or negative connotation. As Jowett and O'Donnell (1999, 3) have observed, words frequently used as synonyms for propaganda include lies, distortion, deceit, manipulation, etc. And more recently, the euphemism "spin" has been used for propaganda. Just as propaganda, spin is associated with the deliberate manipulation of political information. Government information/press officers involved in co-ordinated efforts of this nature to minimize negative information while presenting a negative story as a positive one have earned the name "spin doctors" – probably a politically correct variant of "propagandists". But contemporary scholars are increasingly seeing propaganda outside of a stereotyped negative box, hence making it possible to consider positive purposes for the tools of propaganda. Philip M. Taylor has written exhaustively on propaganda and its history. He uses botanical lenses to conceptualize this diversely defined concept. Taylor (2003) sees propaganda firstly as a *process*, connoting essentially that propaganda is not an end – but a means – a continuous means "for sowing, germination and cultivation of ideas" (2003, 2). The definition thus lays a foundation for understanding propaganda from a neutral perspective. Taylor further argues that propaganda can be used to service the objectives of a pluralistic democracy since democracy relies on popular consensus – which can be earned through the tools of propaganda. Also justifying the use of propaganda as a key element in a pluralistic democracy, B. S. Murty writes that it can be used for the purpose of peace. "In situations where it is necessary to express an international consensus that a particular conduct is a threat to peace, propaganda should be available to articulate the condemnation" (Murty 1989, xxxviii). Debating the involvement of democratic governments in Information Operation Campaigns, Taylor argues that peace propaganda is as important as war-time propaganda.

> When a nation goes to war, even a democratic nation, there is a tendency to accept the need to conduct propaganda. What is less well recognized is that when a nation conducts peace, there is equally a need to conduct propaganda on behalf of that peace. (Taylor 2002, 439)

Logical. However, when attempting to use propaganda as a tool for creating a local culture of peace in a divided society, contentious questions emerge such as who defines the peace? On whose terms? And who pays the highest price for the peace? In societies violently divided along ethno-nationalist, political, regional, religious or socio-economic cleavages, sustainable peace would involve a lot of conciliation, redefinition of power relations and attitudinal re-orientation. "Sowing, cultivating and germinating" ideas of peace can be challenging in terms of creating a consensus especially when it is developed from top to bottom. This thesis will seek to broaden this discourse by understanding the inhibitions to developing a local culture of peace in a divided society within the context of the DRC. Understanding such "road blocks" can help develop an information intervention agenda. This in turn can help inhibit the social construction and deepening of divisions and conflict even in a divided society.

4.1 The UN "Propaganda" Doctrine

It is pertinent to examine closely the objectives of the UN PIO during Peacekeeping Operations. The *Handbook on UN Multidimensional Peacekeeping Operation* (2003) identifies six primary objectives of UN Peacekeeping Operation's (PKO) Public Information programme. These include:
–   ensuring the peacekeeping operation's mandate and responsibilities are fully and widely understood;
–   promoting all aspects of the work of the PKO;
–   implementing a communications strategy that actively supports the PKO's objectives;
–   advancing the peace process through the creation of timely and relevant information products;
–   defend and protect the PKO from unjustified criticism and misinformation; and finally,
–   counter propaganda, false information and hate messages that are harmful to the objectives of the UN and the peace process.

The UN PKO Public Information strategy recommends the identification and usage of the most appropriate medium to reach each target audience. It lists radio, television, print, theatre, dance and music performances, town criers, etc.

A comprehensive strategy for executing these objectives would demand techniques that are psychosocial in nature if not outrightly propagandistic. But "propaganda", no matter the definition is a word the UN would rather not be identified with. They would rather use surrogates.

4.2 Outsourcing "Peace Propaganda": UN Partnership with NGOs

The United Nations maintains a very strong collaborative relationship with NGOs in various elements of its functions. In the DRC, the UN has forged a strong relationship with Hirondelle Foundation – a Swiss-based NGO. An understanding of the relationship between the two organizations will illuminate contemporary debates on the increasingly inter-weaving roles of IGOs, NGOs and foreign governments in information and other humanitarian interventions within crisis states in an evolving system of global governance. Of specific interest is the factors that led to the collaboration in the first instance, and being a novel collaboration, the UN's expectations from the partnership and Hirondelle Foundation's lessons so far.

Aside from the operational details of the collaboration between the two organizations, there are questions of possible clashes of media doctrines. Hirondelle Foundation, being a Western NGO, would be expected to frame its media doctrine along Western libertarian model of the press with its inherent Lockean underpinnings, whereas communities in the DRC, divided by years of conflict, may be in better need of a Communitarian media regime which fundamentally departs from the self/community dichotomy upon which the Libertarian press doctrine is based.

5 A Brief History of Ethnicity, Conflicts and Crisis of Citizenship in the DRC

This Chapter demonstrates that conflict in the DRC, particularly in the Kivus, is a unique example of Africa's so-called modern wars or "new wars" – the aim in most cases is not necessarily to check an enemy advancement but to inflict the most pain on *perceived* "enemies" while also achieving economic objectives through illicit extraction of mineral resources and sustenance of transborder shadow trading networks.

5.1 The Roots, Tactics and Ethnic Motivations of the "First DRC War"

Before looking at the war that ousted the totalitarian regime of Mobutu Sese Seko, it is essential to first briefly examine the factors that have created ethnic divisions in the Great Lakes region over the years.

The boundaries of today's Burundi, Rwanda, eastern DRC, southwest Uganda and northwest Tanzania were not in existence before the boundary delineation of the Berlin Conference in 1884. At the conference, the European powers recognized Belgian King Leopold's claim to the Congo basin. In 1891 and 1894, the Belgians conquered and annexed neighbouring kingdoms – first Katanga, then eastern Congo was wrested from the control of Swahili-speaking East African Arabs. As a result, the kingdoms of "Ruanda" (modern day Rwanda) and "Urundi" (modern day Burundi) were reduced to tiny landlocked entities. Substantial numbers of Tutsis and Hutus were left in the various states that were either created by the Berlin Conference or annexed by King Leopold.

The result has been an intricate mix of ethnic groups in the region. In both Rwanda and Burundi, the ethnic distribution is approximately 85% Hutu, 14% Tutsi and 1% Twa. There are two million of an estimated 15 million Hutus and Tutsis in countries surrounding Burundi and Rwanda. About 400,000 Tutsis have ancestral links to either eastern North Kivu Province (known there as the Banyarwandas) or in South Kivu Province (known there as the Banyamulenges). In the Tanzanian border with Rwanda and Burundi, there are between 750,000 and one million Hutus. There are also tens of thousands of Hutus and Tutsis in the Kisoro district of Uganda. The distribution of ethnic Tutsis and Hutus across five countries and the animosity between the two groups has at various times created tension in the countries. But the main problem besides the transnational scattering of the Hutu and Tutsi ethnic groups has been access to economic and political resources – including land, water and power. Access to resources has been ethnically defined between the two groups since pre-colonial era. The Hutus, who were predominantly farmers, had settled among indigenous hunter–gatherer Twa communities in the fifteenth century, afterwards Tutsi cattle herders – taller, lighter skinned and more slender in physique – arrived in the sixteenth century. On arrival they adopted the language and customs of the Hutus but retained their caste as warriors whose responsibility was to protect their Hutu hosts from the Arab marauders. After over four centuries of living together, tensions between the two groups started when German and Belgian colonizers arrived and introduced ethnic divisions by favouring the Tutsis with greater access to educational opportunities and positions in the local administration. The Hutus continued as farmers but under the supervision of Tutsis in the tea and coffee plantations. With the partitioning of Africa, the two groups were scattered into different countries under different colonial masters. Tensions between the two groups continued and culminated in the crises of the 1990s in the Great Lakes region.

5.2 Rwandan Roots of the Congolese Conflict

The divisions continued in Rwanda into the post-colonial period and resulted in the genocide of 1994 of ethnic Tutsis. When the Rwandan Patriotic Front (RPF), a Tutsi militant group, led by Paul Kagame, the present Rwandan president, ousted the genocidaires, millions of Hutus accompanied by those that were involved in the genocide and members of the defeated Rwandan Armed Forces (FAR) moved into the eastern DRC. At this time, the DRC was also dealing with its own ethnic and political crises.

Mass refugee movements into the Kivus completely destabilized the Mobutu government as more than one million people fleeing from Rwanda for fear of reprisals from the Tutsi-led RPF swarmed into eastern DRC. Among the refugees were over 50,000 ex-FAR elements and the Interahamwe militia that were mostly responsible for the massacre of Tutsis in Rwanda. Further complicating the situation, at the same time, there was a conflict going on in Burundi also between Tutsis and Hutus. Burundi's Hutu rebel armed group, Forces for the Defence of Democracy FDD (the military wing of the National Council for the Defence of Democracy, CNDD), joined in the refugee camps. The camp was without any external monitoring, as it was left to aid agencies to provide food and water to the refugees. The camp was overcrowded, filled with arms and with young men that were ready to bear them. There was also cash – treasury loots by fleeing government and security agents of the fallen Rwandan government. All these groups were camped along with refugees in the DRC, and before long they started roaming away from the camps and conducting guerrilla raids on Rwanda and Burundi.

In September 1996, Katanga-born Laurent Kabila, a hardened guerrilla tactician with experience of working with the South American Marxist revolutionary, Che Guevera, organized several militias to form the *Alliance des Forces Démocratiques pour la Libération du Congo-Kinshasa* (AFDL) to launch a military campaign against the government of Mobutu Sese Seko whose political authority had weakened.

Mobutu's inability or unwillingness to deal with the problem of armed groups operating within the refugee camps in the then Zaire had infuriated the new government in Rwanda. Hence, Kabila's military challenge of Mobutu's regime was welcome news for the Rwandans. Also, a few years earlier, Mobutu had set up a commission to identify "non-Congolese" in the regions of North and South Kivu and Maniema. Mobutu's intention was to persecute and de-citizenize the Banyamulenges and Banyarwandas (ethnic Tutsis that migrated from Rwanda in the nineteenth century and the 1960s, respectively).

With support from Rwanda and Burundi, the AFDL started its incursion towards Kinshasa. To deal with the AFDL threat, Mobutu aligned with Hutu armed groups to fight the AFDL. Another motivation for the Rwandan and Burundian Hutu armed groups against the AFDL was that most of AFDL's fighters were Banyamulenges and Banyarwandas. Other autochthonous groups in eastern DRC opposed to the Tutsis also formed military alliances to resist the AFDL. So the AFDL and its allies were pitted against the Congolese Armed Forces, Hutu ex-FAR, Interahamwe, FDD and indigenous militia (Mai Mai) groups. In addition to fighting the AFDL, Rwandan Hutu militias intensified their attacks against Banyamulenge and Banyarwanda civilians in the Kivus. Exasperated with it all, radical Congolese autochthons formed the Bangilima militia to chase out both the Hutus and Banyarwandas from their midst. Hundreds of Congolese Tutsis fled to neighbouring Uganda to escape attacks by the Bangilima militiamen – composed of Bahunde (Hunde), Batembo (Tembo), Banande (Nande), Banyanya (Nyanya) and Bakobo (Kobo) autochthons.

On 7 October 1996, Deputy Governor of South Kivu, Lwasi Ngabo Lwabanji, ordered ethnic Tutsis to leave the province. At the national level, the government had denied both ethnic Tutsis and Hutus in Congo citizenship rights based on increasing resentments against them by autochthonous Congolese communities. With all the ethnic divisions, poverty and increasing threat to land and water resources, the stage was set for a complex ethnic conflagration involving Tutsi, Nande, Bashi Babwari, Maluba and Kasaï ethnic groups against Hutu, Bufalero, Warega, Tembo, Hunde and Babembe ethnic groups. But the critical element in the mix was Kabila's AFDL which was at the time the most organized of all the groups. While the other groups were not making any advancement but bent on inflicting the most casualty or damage on opponents, the AFDL were more strategic in their military assaults and targets. They steadily pursued their objective of invading the capital Kinshasa to topple the Mobutu regime. This, in most part, could be attributed to Kabila's experience in guerrilla movements. He had previously headed a Marxist organization, the People's Revolutionary Party, between 1964 and the 1980s during which time he ruled an enclave among the Bembe people in eastern Kivu Province and worked with Guevara. With the support from Rwanda and Burundi, the AFDL made a steady progress towards Kinshasa. By this time, the conflict had assumed an international dimension as the Congolese government accused the Rwandan government of arming the AFDL and other Tutsi ethnic armed groups in eastern Congo.

While the Congolese government dithered on how to deal with the ethnic crises that had engulfed the country, Kabila continued his push through the east. Pushing from the Mulenge Mountains, the AFDL successfully routed the Congolese army and went on to break up the huge refugee camps harbouring Hutu militias. Hundreds of thousands of refugees as a result returned to Rwanda and some others crossed into Tanzania and Burundi, while others (mostly Interahamwe militia and ex-FAR) moved westward deeper into the forests of eastern DRC.

On 24 October 1996, the AFDL captured the gold-rich town of Uvira in South Kivu, and six days later, they captured provincial capital Bukavu. In the weeks that followed, they consolidated their territorial gains and advanced transversely – northward towards the Ugandan border up to the Sudan border and westward towards the strategic town of Kisangani, to control the mouth of the Congo River which is the DRC's main navigable waterways. Tactically, the AFDL with the full backing of the Rwandan Patriotic Army (RPA) were making important gains and by December were in control of eastern Congo. By this time, the Congolese army was falling apart and Mobutu was ill – suffering from cancer. The major military challenge the AFDL faced was the Bangilima and Mai Mai militia in the Kivus who have always been opposed to the presence of Banyarwandas in the Congo which were the main components of the AFDL.

With their control of the resource-rich east, the AFDL dug in and started trading the gold, timber, coltan and other mineral resources in the region to markets in Eastern Europe and Asia. Another economic treat for the AFDL came on 5 April 1997 when they captured Mbuji-Mayi in Kasai Province – the diamond mining centre of Congo. With significantly increased income and more sophisticated weaponry, the AFDL went on to capture the lucrative Shaba Province, the country's wealthiest with its port, airport and railway stations. The fall of Shaba Province to the AFDL was the biggest indication that Mobutu's 32-year dictatorship was on the decline and the seriousness of Kabila's group. Up to that moment, the international community was treating the AFDL as one of the ethnically motivated armed groups in Kivu. But with the AFDL's strategic ascendance, the international community was forced to take the group more seriously.

Aside from Rwanda and Burundi, the AFDL also had support from Uganda, whose president, Yoweri Museveni, had Tutsi ancestry. Besides, Uganda had strategic interests in the AFDL operations because they were also fighting the West Nile Bank Front (WNBF) – a Ugandan rebel armed group that was operating from the Congo and Sudan. Aware of his enhanced international standing, Kabila gave the UN 60 days to repatriate all Hutu refugees. But by this time the whereabouts of the armed Hutus were unknown as they had moved deeper into the forests in South Kivu. With the successes of Kabila, it became apparent that the Mobutu era had come to a most undignified end. So on 17 May 1997, Kabila declared himself President and after taking office on 29 May, he changed the country's name from Zaire to the Democratic Republic of Congo. However, as Kabila was celebrating his military success in Kinshasa, the ex-FAR and Interahamwe were regrouping in the forests of eastern Congo. Other indigenous Congolese armed groups were becoming uncomfortable with the ethnic Tutsi's increasing dominance in the government of Kabila, and in August 1997, the Democratic Resistance Alliance was formed in eastern DRC with the aim of "liberating" the area. This was the first of several rebel movements that would emerge to challenge the authority of the Kabila government. To assuage internal discomforts about his government's closeness to Tutsis and the Rwandan government, President Kabila started winding down his close relationship with Rwanda and gradually disposed of the services of the Tutsi aids that had fought to bring him to power. This pitted him against the Rwandan government and the Banyamulenges of South Kivu.

On 2 August 1998, ethnic Tutsis in Goma with support from the Rwandan government formed a well-armed rebel group – Rally for Congolese Democracy, (RCD). Banyamulenges in South Kivu immediately joined the group, and with support from Uganda and Rwanda, they quickly took control of the Kivus – and the mineral resources thereof.

To resist the Tutsi-dominated RCD, President Kabila tapped into Hutu reservations against Tutsis and enlisted the support of Hutu militants in eastern Congo that had fled from Rwanda. Hutus and Congolese autochthons were mobilized to attack Tutsis across South Kivu. This was not helped with the announcement by the Rwandan government at this time that a substantial part of eastern DRC was historically Rwandan. The Congolese felt this was a sign that the Rwandan Tutsis were intent on invading and annexing their country. This led to an alliance of Congolese autochthons with Hutus to fight the ethnic Tutsis. The autochthon–Hutu alliance was not borne out of any long-term strategic or cultural accords but was a case of "an enemy of my enemy is my friend". But the RCD was increasing in strength with several Congolese army units mutinying. With increasing support from Rwandan and Ugandan soldiers, RCD quickly took control of key towns in eastern DRC and made three strategic captures – the Inga hydroelectric station that provided power to Kinshasa; Port Matadi through which most food and other agricultural products entered Kinshasa; and the diamond centre of Kisangani.

With the increasing capitulation of his soldiers, Kabila sought help from other African countries. Also, by this time, various other armed groups were springing up in various parts of the country. Key among them was the Movement for the Liberation of Congo (MLC), covertly supported by the Ugandan government. The country at this point was at a boiling point, and Kabila's regime was experiencing a near-death situation. What has become known as the Second Congo War was in full swing.

5.3 The FDLR

The FDLR is an offshoot of the Rwandan Liberation Army (ALiR); hence, it is regarded as being made up of genocidaires. ALiR was created by former Governor of Kigali,

Colonel Tharcisse Renzaho, and ex-FAR Lieutenant Colonel Paul Rwarakabije. The group attempted a number of times to make incursions into Rwanda but was each time repelled by the Rwandan Army and left with heavy casualties. With relatively low military successes, the ALiR was restructured into two groups, ALIR 1 (based in Masisi, North Kivu and Shabunda in South Kivu) and ALIR 2 (based in Kinshasa alongside Laurent Kabila's soldiers). In 2000, ALIR 1 and 2 came together to form the FDLR which was then envisioned to be a politico-military organization. Paul Rwarakabije was made the Commander in Chief of the group. Politically, their intention has been to replace the Paul Kagame government in Rwanda, and they claim the military component is to protect Hutu refugees in the DRC from Tutsi attacks. Over the years, it has received support from the Congolese government both under Laurent Kabila and Joseph Kabila. The group was used as a proxy force to fight foreign armies, particularly the RCD and the Rwandan forces in the east. It has since fallen out of favour with the Joseph Kabila government and is under heavy military and political pressures to disarm and return to Rwanda. Although it is not certain the number of fighters in the ranks of the FDLR at the moment, in 2002, they numbered between 15,000 and 20,000 units. At the time of writing this chapter, they constituted the main armed group still operating in the eastern DRC.

5.4 South Kivu: *Autochtonie* and the Crises of Citizenship

In eastern DRC, the Native Authority oversees issues of ethnic identity and make recommendations for issuance of certificates of origin. In South Kivu, it is a very important institutional authority because ethnic identity since colonial times grants or bars access to land resources, political participation, social inclusion and other "customary" rights. It is only autochthonous ethnic groups that have the right to a full Native Authority. Native Authority in South Kivu has three hierarchies. The lowest authority is the Chief of the locality followed by the *Chef de Groupement,* and then the highest authority the *Mwami* of the *Collectivité.* Foreigners or *allochthons* in the Kivus have the lowest Native Authority – Chief of the locality who answers to the higher authorities. Only autochthons have the right to second and third tier native authorities – the *Chef de Groupement* and the *Mwami.* Indeed this is where customary power lies. The *Chef de Groupement* and the *Mwami* have the power to confirm ethnic identity and issue identity cards, oversee local administration, allocate customary land for farming, hold tribunals through which customary justice is meted out, run local markets and collect tributes and levies. The exception, though, is that in North Kivu Banyaruchurus and Banyamasisis (predominantly Rwandan Hutus) are entitled to higher tiers of Native Authority as they are considered indigenous, but in South Kivu the Banyamulenge (predominantly Tutsis) are considered foreign. The Kirundi-speaking immigrant minority in the Ruzizi Valley are considered autochthons. The other immigrant minority are the Banyamulenges who are mainly Tutsis. Some of them arrived in the 1880s while others arrived in 1959–1960.

Banyamulenges are still seen as foreigners or allochthons in South Kivu, and their chiefs have been confined to the first tier, the Chief of the locality. To have access to land, they would need to pay homage to higher order chiefs. Though the Banyamulenges have existed in South Kivu for over a century, they have not been integrated with the autochthonous groups and are still classed as foreigners. In many respects, there have been conflicting legislations regarding their status. The 1972 Citizenship Decree extended citizenship to Rwandan Tutsis that arrived in 1959–1960. Then in 1981 the law was changed. The 1981 law restricted citizenship to only those persons who could demonstrate an ancestral connection to the population residing in 1885 in the territory then demarcated as Congo. This was upheld by the Sovereign national conference in 1991. In 2006, due to international pressure, the new constitution granted automatic citizenship to persons whose ancestors were resident in the DRC as at independence in 1960.

One of the factors that make citizenship such a contested issue in the DRC and in South Kivu, in particular, is the rights and access it brings. Another factor is the influx of refugees. Hutu and Tutsi refugees have come to South Kivu from Tanzania, Burundi and Rwanda at various points in history and have settled with their families. Autochthons do not want the refugees to be granted citizenship so that they do not have to compete with them for customary rights, land, water and other resources. But despite these, autochthons in South Kivu have always been more comfortable with Hutu refugees than their Tutsi cousins. And when Hutus were scattered from their camps in Mugunga after attacks by Tutsi-dominated AFDL, most autochthons in South Kivu felt it was alright to take the Hutus in. The media was an instrument in generating public opinion in favour of the Hutus despite the fact that many among them were accused of genocide. In December 1997, "Voice of the Patriot", a radio station of the *L'union de Forces pour Libération et la Démocratie* (or Union of Forces for Liberation and Democracy, UFLD), urged "true" Congolese to oust the Tutsis and protect the Hutus. The following is the BBC's transcript of the broadcast:

> *We have been telling you since yesterday that we have an enemy whom you know very well. However, we would like to remind you that the enemy is gearing up to harm you...These Tutsi killers who invaded our country continue to prepare themselves to plant their flags on both sides so that Bukavu town can become theirs... You know the cunning of those people, they claim to be Congolese. First of all, the Banyamulenge tribe does not exist here. We have a map of the tribes but there is no Banyamulenge tribe on that map. They come with guns, they kill us, and after killing us they call upon us, the survivors, to accept them as Congolese. Who are they that we should accept them?... We urge you citizens, if you see our soldiers, give them food. If you see a Hutu soldier, give him food. These Hutus have suffered a lot. And, these Hutus are our brothers. Let no one deceive you that a Hutu is a Tutsi...But these stupid people [Tutsis], these lazy people, we have accommodated them since 1958 when they arrived here. They were our servants. Today they have turned against us saying that the country has become theirs.* (BBC Transcript of broadcast on 11 December 1997 quoted in Minorities at Risk Project 2004).

The autochthones of South Kivu responded and took in the Hutus. The Mai Mai militia, a nationalist Congolese government reserve created to face rebellions and occupations by foreign armies, were called in to protect the Rwandan Hutus. Mai Mai has a strong presence in Walungu and has since been fighting side by side with Hutu FDLR. The Mai Mai has also helped non-combatant Hutus to settle into community life in villages in South Kivu. Although they have been welcomed in South Kivu, Hutus do not have the citizenship that accords them customary rights and access to land resources.

Mai Mai militants see Rwandan Tutsis as the root of Congo's many problems. Their alliance with the FDLR is another case of "the enemy of my enemy is my friend" than any common ideology or history. In South Kivu, many households have voluntarily given their children to fight for the Mai Mai as an act of patriotism, not necessarily to their country but to their ethnic identity.

5.5 Brief Notes on Key Flash Points in the DRC

South Kivu

South Kivu is one of the provinces in the DRC. It is located in the eastern part of the country and has its provincial capital in Bukavu. South Kivu is bordered to the north by North Kivu Province, to the west by Maniema Province and to the South by Katanga Province. The eastern part of the province shares international boundaries with Rwanda, Burundi and Tanzania. In addition to provincial capital Bukavu, there are other important *Territoires* and towns in South Kivu. These include Baraka, Fizi, Kabare, Katana, Kaziba, Lemera, Mwenga, Nundu, Nyangezi, Shabunda, Uvira and Walungu. South Kivu has a population of approximately 2.4 million. Along with North Kivu, it has been the centre of conflict since 1994 when millions of Rwandan refugees and combatants crossed into the DRC from Rwanda and Burundi. Although the FARDC has a major base in South Kivu, the province is reputed for high rates of sexual violence against women since the war started.

South Kivu is made up of various autochthonous tribes – the Legas, the Bashis, the Bwaris, the Viras, the Bafuleros, the Shis, the Baregas, the Barundis, the Banyindus, the Babembes, the Havus and the Tembos, among other smaller tribes. They all have dialects with relative lexical similarities. Approximately 95% of the population speak Swahili – the regional language. There is also the Banyamulenges – the Tutsis of South Kivu. Most South Kivu indigenes consider the Banyamulenges to be allochthons because they are "recent arrivals". Although the Banyamulenges arrived towards the end of the nineteenth century even before independence (Weis 1959; Turner 2007), they are generally seen and treated by South Kivusians as cultural outsiders. The Banyamulenges along with Hutus in South Kivu speak Kinyarwanda.

Because of years of interaction between the groups, most people in South Kivu under-stand Kinyarwanda.[4]

Fizi

Fizi is a town and also a *Territoire* in South Kivu Province. It is located west of Lake Tanganyika. *Collectivities* within Fizi include N'gangya, Lulenge, M'tambala, Yan-gani'a and Itombwe. As with other research sites, the *lingua franca* is Swahili. Fizi is the birthplace of President Joseph Kabila and has a high number of Rwandan Hutus living side by side with Congolese indigenes.

Mwenga

Mwenga is a town and also a *Territoire* in South Kivu. It is the insurgents' paradise. The vast jungles and forests make this town and indeed the entire *Territoire* an ideal operational base for armed groups. It is also rich in mineral resources. Located south-west of provincial capital Bukavu, it has been one of the territories that have suffered most from the war. Since 1996, there have been thousands of abuctions, rapes, loot-ings and killings in Mwenga. The FDLR has had a strong foothold in Mwenga mainly because of the terrain and access to gold, cassiterite, coltan and wolframite mines.

Uvira

Uvira is a gold-rich town and *Territoire* in South Kivu. It is located at the north of Lake Tanganyika. There is also Lake Kalundu, south of the town. These lakes provide transport links to Kalemie and Kigoma in Tanzania and Bujumbura in Burundi. There is also a road network linking Uvira to Bukavu and to Bujumbura (Burundian capital). Citizens of Uvira are mostly Roman Catholics and are relatively more literate than citizens in neighbouring towns mainly because of exposure to trade and communica-tions from Bukavu, Tanzania, Burundi and Rwanda. Historically, Uvira has had a high number of political and economic elites. This is because prior to the creation of South Kivu Province, Uvira was the capital of South Kivu sub-region which was then part

---

4 Because of years of animosity between Congolese autochthons and the Banyamulenges, Kinyar-wanda is seen by several Congolese as the enemy's language and because of that they claim to be unable to speak the language, whereas, in fact, most South Kivusians do understand and can speak Kinyarwanda almost fluently.

of Kivu Province. As provincial capital, it had more access to economic and political resources.

Walungu

Walungu is about 80 kilometres southwest of Bukavu. It is a town and a *Territoire*. Peopled by the Bashis, Walungu is organized within a fairly decentralized feudal system where each household owns a portion of land for residence and for agricultural purposes. Folks here depend solely on their farms for food and living. During the war, several people in Walungu abandoned their farmland and fled. When they returned, months and years later, they found that their lands and homes had been taken over by Hutu militants and refugees. Both the FDLR and Mai Mai have strong presence in Walungu.

6 From *Authenticity* to *Governmentality*: A Brief History of the Media in the DRC

This chapter explores the media landscape of the DRC from the era of Marshal Mobutu Sese Seko to the intervention era. An awareness of the media history in the DRC, the role of the media in shaping the country's national discourse and its relationship with the politics of the country is essential in understanding the context of UN's Information Operations in the DRC. The history of the media and government/press relations has been as chequered as the political history of the country itself. History of the Congolese media is complicated and accentuated by its political crises. The media has often been used by political elites as a propaganda tool and a means of oppression. To situate the state of the DRC's media prior to intervention in the proper context, I have classified its history into four phases:

1. Mobutu Phase I (Pre-1990) – Era of the *Authentic* Media
2. Mobutu Phase II (Post-1990) – Era of *Débrouillez-vous*
3. Kabila I Phase – Era of Official Silence, Repression and *Coupage* (1997–2001)
4. Regulation & Intervention Phase – Era of Governmentality

6.1 Era of the "Authentic" Media

President Mobutu Sese Seko was the head of the republic and "Founder-President" of the only political party in the country – the *Mouvement Populaire de la Revolution* (MPR). Mobutu's era is divided into two parts – pre-1990 and post-1990. A number of factors determined this categorization. As I will later explain, the end of the cold war redefined politics in the DRC.[5] It resulted in the dearth of super-power patronage and the security it guaranteed, and in the DRC it marked a shift of seismic proportions in Mobutu's totalitarian government. On 20 October, 1990, Mobutu made a landmark speech lifting the ban on political parties and granting the newly recognized parties access to the media. Prior to this time, the media was part of the country's single party. This turning point from a one party state to a multi-party state marked a key moment for DRC's media. This part explores the state of the media and nature of politics prior to 20 October 1990.

The media in the pre-1990 era represented Mobutu's voice of dominance. The government-controlled *Office Zairois de Radio Television* (OZRT) and a handful of private publications owned by Mobutu's cronies worked as the government's mouthpiece. In Kinshasa where there is a highly literate population, *Salongo* and *Elima* were the two main newspapers and their responsibility was to spread the government's propaganda messages. Each of the other regions had a newspaper also owned directly

---

5 For the purpose of this report, DRC and Zaire are used interchangeably to refer to the country during the Mobutu era when it was officially named Zaire.

by the government. In Bukavu there was *Jua*; *Mjumbe* in Lubumbashi and *Bayoma* in Kisangani. There were a few private publications that were authorized, but they were systematically starved of funding, as organizations that depended on government patronage were warned off advertising on the publications. As a result, most of the private papers were very irregular and subsequently went out of publication. The only non-government media that thrived were the religious media – primarily those of the Catholic Church. But they were warned to remain politically neutral. Journalists were generally warned that their reports should not explicitly or implicitly, directly or indirectly implicate the head of state.

In addition to reporting the government's programmes, the OZRT worked to smear Mobutu's political opponents, distort information and help create a cult figure of Marshal Mobutu. In May 1990, for instance, when protesting students of the University of Lubumbashi were massacred by government troops, *Voix du Zaire*, part of the OZRT media network, reported a lower number of casualties than the number that were actually killed in the clash and blamed the students for their fate. Concerning the same event, the government-owned agency *Agence Zairose de Presse* (AZAP) reported that the deaths resulted from a fight between the students for tribal causes and justified government's intervention to prevent the tribal war from escalating. According to Braekman (1996) and Frère and Marthoz (2007), this version of the story was with the intention of reinforcing Mobutu's claim to being the guarantor of National Unity and the only person capable of preventing a re-occurrence of the inter-tribal wars that killed thousands soon after independence.

The media under the OZRT fell within the ambits of Mobutu's absolute power. To understand the role of the media in the DRC and how it has affected the peacebuilding processes today, it is imperative to understand the nature of Mobutu's propaganda in the pre-1990 era.

The information terrain in this era was not a given, it was articulated and reiterated through various typologies of forms – including dance, songs, unique musical accompaniments; media including government news agencies, government paid journalists, national symbols, songwriters, traditional dance troupes, newspapers, broadcast media, etc; and cultural institutions like theatre, cinema, music production outfits, literature on traditional folklores etc. Mobutu mobilized these three elements (Agents, Brokers and Institutions) in propagating a large-scale campaign of *Authenticite*. To achieve a deeper awareness of the context of information in the DRC, a detailed understanding of Mobutu's authenticity ideology, its agents, brokers and institutions is essential.

Authenticity: The Making of a Politico-cultural Propaganda System

Mobutu's propaganda efforts were achieved through a policy he interestingly named "authenticity". It was a propaganda model based on cultural and political nationalism.

The Office of *Mobilisation, Propagnde et animation Politique* (MOPAP) was created to manage the highly complex "authenticity" campaign. MOPAP's mandate was to mobilize wholesale support for Mobutu's regime using cultural forms such as traditional songs, folk tales, dance and cultural nationalism. The media was at the fundamental core of the "authenticity" campaign. Ikambana's (2007) self-described "afrocentric analysis" of Mobutu's authenticity philosophy locates it within a political system that sought to redress the dignity of the Zairian after centuries of colonial domination. He writes:

> Mobutu's policy of authenticity assumed that the Zairian people should rebuild their own culture and erase the scars left by decades of colonial rule…. Authenticity was a cultural renaissance, a return to the wisdom of the African ancestors that would have allowed the Zairian people to rediscover themselves without foreign influence. (p. 24–25)

Indeed, as a political philosophy, authenticity was overtly intended to recover the pride and cultural values of the Zairian. But I will later argue that it was a complex politico-cultural propaganda machinery to entrench Mobutu's regime on the political and cultural sub-consciousness of the country. Between late 1960s and late 1980s, authenticity became the dominant politico-cultural discourse in Zaire and was framed within a coherent cultural propaganda form with the media working as agents. Philip M. Taylor has defined cultural propaganda as:

> The promotion and dissemination of national aims and achievements in a general rather than specifically economic or political form although it is ultimately designed to promote economic and political interests. (1981, 125–126).

For Mobutu's Zaire, cultural propaganda stretched this definition. It went beyond "promotion and dissemination of national aims and achievements" to a mental, socio-cultural and political re-engineering. It was institutionalized and represented in all facets of national life. Political and cultural propaganda techniques were very shrewdly merged. In this chapter, I will describe how the media was used as a tool for political and cultural propaganda. I will argue that in addition to the media, various other institutions of state were skillfully used to execute Mobutu's propaganda campaign. It needs re-emphasizing that an understanding of the depth of Mobutu's authenticity campaign is essential to a contextual understanding of the information terrain of the DRC and the *autochthony/allochthony* divide that still plague the country years after Mobutu.

Between Authenticity and Mobutism

The essence of Zairian public cultural policy was Mobutism as encapsulated in the doctrine of the MPR and expressed in the ideology of authenticity. Mobutu's authenticity campaign demanded citizens and state to be directly involved in the creation, presentation and promotion of the country's cultural heritage. Four Congolese languages were selected as national languages instead of only French as it was before: Kikongo, Lingala, Swahili and Tshiluba. One of the objectives of authenticity was to forge a form of national cultural consciousness which had been lacking among the 250 tribes of the Congo. Mobutism as a politico-cultural philosophy, according to Botombele (1975), was a philosophy of cultural authenticity to form the basis of the country's political, social, economic and cultural activities. According to him, Mobutism "is a form of humanism seeking the fullest expression of the total Zairian personality" (p. 50). Soon, Mobutuism was used inter-changeably with authenticity and what was originally cultural propaganda framed as an instrument of African renaissance became an instrument of Mobutu's personality cult. Again, the media played a vital role in this regard. The national newspaper, *Salongo,* in its editorial of 22 March 1974 proclaimed "it is correct to speak of 'Mobutuism' as authenticity since he is its inspiration and incarnation". The media became a tool for Mobutu's cultural renaissance drive, and discourse of citizenship or Zairanization. Mobutu and other government ministers were routinely addressed by the title of "Citizen". Through the media, Mobutu led a campaign of name changing – from Western sounding names to Zairian names. In a speech to a congress of the MPR in 1972, Mobutu articulated the concept of authenticity thus: "we advocate the return of authenticity in order to make it clear that we should interpret the concept of development in the light of our own system of thought and our own scale of values." And in his preface to Cornet's (1971) *The Art of Black Africa in the Land of the River Zaire,* he wrote: "one of our prime concerns must be the restructuring of our glorious past with its balance, harmony and cultivation". The concept of authenticity was, according to Botombele, a policy of the mind and the media's role in the campaign was critical. In a 1975 report published by UNESCO, he wrote:

> to put this vast programme of cultural promotion into operation, no better means exist than the mass media. Use of them has enabled the cultural revolution to be consolidated and the aim is to inculcate in Zairians the ideals of the MPR. (Botombele 1975, 75)

The heavily funded MOPAP was responsible for mass mobilization for "authenticity" and Mobutism which had become the dominant ideology of the MPR. Agencies other than the traditional media were used to propagate the Mobutist ideology such as "patriotic songs", traditional singing and dancing in the praise of the Founder-President – Mobutu and the Congolese establishment. To fulfil its responsibilities, MOPAP received greater state funding than the Ministries of National Economics and Social Affairs put together (Masoka 2006). The recurring phrase in the national media in this era was "nous les Zairos authentiques" (we the authentic Zairians), indexing as it were, the historical past (cultural authenticity) and a conceptualized present-future of national identity (White 2008). In a speech to the UN General Assembly in 1974, Mobutu explained the concept of "authenticity" thus:

Authenticity is the realization by the Zairian people that it must return to its origins, seek out the values of its ancestors to discover those which contribute to its harmonious and natural development. It is the refusal to blindly embrace imported ideologies. It is, in short, the affirmation of mankind in its place, as it is, with its mental and social structures.

"De-culturalization", New Names and the Deification of Mobutu

The state-controlled media was at the forefront of the massive public campaign that accompanied authenticity. Congo was re-named Zaire, and the national currency, towns and cities, streets, waterways and building names were all given new names. The national anthem and flag were also changed. The statues of Belgian King Leopold, Stanley and King Baudoin were all toppled. People that bore French, Belgian or Christian names changed their names to Congolese ones. Mobutu himself led the way. He changed his name from Joseph-Desire Mobutu to Mobutu Sese Seko. The media also led the campaign in replacing the reference terms "Monsieur" and "Madame" with "Citoyenne" and "Citoyen", respectively. European suits were replaced with "abacost", a high collared jacket created by Mobutu. Newscasters on national television were among the first to adorn the new brightly coloured jackets.

Authenticity as a propaganda architecture was aimed at deconstructing the Belgian colonial context of "de-culturalization". The central argument that MOPAP put forward was that the Belgian colonialists had stripped the Congolese of their culture and socio-communal values handed down by their ancestors. Authenticity was a reaction, a strategy of fighting back the long-term ideological and material de-culturalization of the Congolese during the long colonial period. Embedded in popular songs, poems, artwork, dance, signposts and literature, authenticity became the lingua-franca of Zaire. Larry Devlin, (in)famous CIA Chief of Station in the DRC at the time, quoted in Wrong (2000), said the campaign "did make Zairians feel they were something special" (p. 91).

Wrong corroborates that "authenticity" swiftly snowballed into Mobutism – an extravagant personality cult created by Mobutu's Chief Propagandist and head of MOPAP, Sakombi Inongo. The propaganda approach was holistic. This era was marked by very innovative use of propaganda that cut across cultural and political spectra. An indigenous propaganda system called "animation" was introduced to enhance the propaganda effort. Animation, according to Adelman (1975), involved "changing the words of traditional songs and chants so as to praise the President and the national party" (p. 135). Through "animation", Mobutu mobilized not only the media but also songs, poems, folk tales, etc. "to preserve the cultural heritage of the major tribal groups while, at the same time, furthering national unity under the President" (Ibid, 135). Various institutions other than the media were used in the authenticity campaign. One of the main institutions was the government-funded Lokole Publishing House.

Politico-Cultural Propaganda Activities of Lokole Publishing House

Officially under the Department of Culture and the Arts, Lokole Publishing House was an important arm of "Citizen" Mobutu's politico-cultural propaganda campaign. It had three sections: Directorate General, Financial Section that dealt with the sale and distribution of "authenticity" books, photographs, records and other merchandize as well as a Technical Section that primarily oversaw the media coverage of official or private cultural events, publication of news and production of patriotic songs. One of its most popular materials was *Animation in the Revolution* – A collection of Patriotic songs of the MPR (1974). The songs promoted "authenticity" as a policy and magnanimously praised Mobutu. An example of one of such songs is Mambe Imolinga's *Ibala* (meaning Marriage). *Ibala*, a very popular song in Kinshasa in the early 1970s, hailed what it called "marriage" between the people and their Guide, Mobutu. Here are the lyrics in Lingala:

'Ibala'

Mobutu na bana ba Zaire ibala oh	*Translation*
	Marriage between the Zairians and
Elima bom'onka nsongo OO ibala oh	Presiding spirit, spouse of Nsongo
Mobutu ngana onka mama Yemo	Mobutu, *son* of Mama Yemo
Afrique euma iboke ibala oh	Mobutu
Kuku Ngbendu nd'ilombe ou ibala	(goddess)
Equateur, Kivu, Bas-Zaire ibala	All of Africa united
Biomba is'oya papa ibala oh	Marriage of Kuku Ngbendu
Mbda nkama ya bokonzi ibala	With the Equator, with Kivu, with
Bayeyeleke, bayeyeleke	The economy in Zairian hands
ibala oh bayeyeleke, bayeyeleke	Mobutu one hundred years in power.
oh bayeyeleke (3X)	

(Translation in Botombele 1976)

Other songs extolled Mobutism as an ideology and sought popular support for the Mobutist work ethic. An example is Makonka's *Sese Seko Bukatele* (The Instructions of Sese Seko).

'Sese Seko Bukatele'

Ta Mobutu bukatele!	*Translation*
	People of Zaire, not one of you
	Is ignorant of the key word
Tuenda sadi salongo	Of Guide Sese Seko Kuku Ngbendu
Sese Seko bukatele!	W a Za Banga who
Tuenda sadi salongo	Asks us to apply the
Kuku Ngsendu bukatele	Spirit of salongo so that
Tuenda sadi salongo	W e can eat our fill.

W a Za Banga bukatele	And we the Zairian people
Tuenda sadi salongo	Have answered his call
Yaye yaye betompe tutambudi	And have taken up our
Nguba zeto na masangu beto	Implements to cultivate the
mosi tuakuna zo	Earth, which will yield
Beto pe bana samu watutambudi	In abundance earthnuts, maize and
Beto pe bana ngolo zatusongele	other crops.
Bapangi dimba (bis)! Yalutela	Brothers and sisters, let us
Buna tuayaula nsatu a mayska!	All respond to that call!
ma kuaku	He who does not shall die
Tanda mu mua mpidi e eh	Of hunger by his own fault,
	For man to eat must work.

(Translation in Botombele 1976)

There were also songs like Ludala Mundoloshi's *Tuvua Tutendela Nzambi* from Western Kasai that extolled the authenticity ideology.

'Tuvua Tutendela Nzambi'

Bangabanga ne batoks tuvua	Translation
	Before the whites came
tutendelela Nzambi,	Our ancestors knew God
Mu miakulu yetu Nzambi utuitaba	And adored Him in their fashion
Kadi pakalua Belge e kulua kutukandika	This those whites condemned as pagan
ditendelela	belief
Nzambi mu dina dia bankambua betu	They imposed on us their foreign names
Belge et kutuinika mena a famille	like Désiré-Joseph and
Yabo	Marie-Antoinette.
Désiré- Joseph ne Marie-Antoinette	Since his advent, Mobutu
Kadi pakalua Mobutu, wakalua	Has rescued us from this
kutuk andika	Mental alienation,
Mena a bena Yuda a bilongo ne	Prohibiting these Jewish names
mitshi	Intended for the trees of Europe.
Kadi tuitabayi mena a bankambua	Let us take again *the* names
betu	Of our ancestors
Bu mudi Mobutu Sese Seko Kuku	Like Mobutu Sese Seko Kuku
Ngbendu W a Za Banga.	Ngbendu W a Za Banga.

(Translation in Botombele 1976)

Such songs, with their spectacularly rhythmic gusto, were constantly played on state-controlled radio and television stations across the country. Bob White has written exhaustively on the politics of music and dance in Mobutu's Zaire; he affirms that song and dance and other cultural instruments were an integral part of Mobutu's complex propaganda architecture. It was a means of showing support for the "Founder-President". Indeed, "song and dance would become an integral part of Mobutu's elaborate propaganda machine, one that relied on the power of public spectacle as a means of mobilizing support for the state" (White 2008, 69). Authenticity, through a complex politico-cultural propaganda system, dominated the information terrain of Zaire during the period. Trado-modern Zairian music was hugely funded by the state. To motivate musical artists to sing "authentic" songs, Mobutu established the Mobutu Sese Seko Fund for Artists and Writers under Decree No. 72/022 of 28 March 1972 to provide "material assistance" to Zairian artists and writers registered on its list. Registration involved an agreement in principle to write and sing songs that glorified Mobutuism. During this period, musical production boomed. Quoting figures from SONECA, Botombole (1976) writes that between 1970 and 1973 a total of 6,114,213 records were produced. Doubtless, as Olema (1997) has maintained, Mobutu showed particular interest in musicians at the critical points in his regime, but White (2008) argues that such interests were not always wholesome. According to him, Mobutu's interest stemmed from his recognition that the participation of popular musical stars was necessary to sustain an appearance of legitimacy for his regime. Participation included popular musicians warming up the crowds before any of Mobutu's mass rallies. "The Presence of musicians and music constituted an important part of constructing an illusion of consensus" writes White (2008, 80). The songs played a critical role in the propagation of Mobutu's political ideologies. They provided the vector for Mobutu's political propaganda. Botombele (1976) writes that it was Mobutist authenticity that made musicians to be aware of their role as spokesmen and as educators so they can "play an active part in the cultural revolution, helping to make the people more receptive to revolutionary ideas" (p. 35). Authenticity and Mobutism were grafted into each other to drive the argument that African ancestral values demanded unmitigated loyalty to the authority. Indeed, crafters of Authenticity realized the enormous impact music could have for Mobutism and the mass mobilization its multi-dimensional implementation would require. The Congolese naturally love rhythmic music and the dance; hence, building the Congolese popular culture into Authenticity campaign would create enormous boost for the political objectives of its planners. This is reflected by Botombele (1976): "in our cultural revival the musician is the most effective agent for the glorification of our ancestral values, such as respect for authority, solidarity for the people with their leader and respect for women" (p. 35). The issue of respect or loyalty for authority and solidarity with the political leader became the driving message of Mobutuism – the political by-product of Authenticity. Mobutu was glorified in songs as The Guide, The Helmsman, and Father of the Nation, among several other glorifying titles. The daily television news broadcast started with an image of Mobutu descending God-like from heaven and was received with rhythmic singing, drumming and dancing. His picture adorned not only the covers of the national and regional newspapers but also walls of government and business offices in Kinshasa while his glorification in the national media reached messianic proportions.

The brain behind Mobutu's propaganda machinery was Sakombi Inongo, a brilliant power player who has remained a constant in the DRC's political vagaries even beyond the Mobutu era. As Head of MOPAP, Inongo created a personality cult of Mobutu. Aside from titles such as *Mulopwe* (God-King), pronouns referring to Mobutu in the state controlled newspapers and in government press releases were capitalized. Mobutu was renowned for appointing and dismissing officials without much ado,[6] but Inongo lasted in government for about two decades and was re-appointed as Information Minister by Laurent-Desire Kabila – the rebel leader that ended Mobutu's rule.

Authenticity and the Rise of Pan-African Nationalism

During this era, taking a cue from the success of Mobutu's authenticity campaign, pan-Africanist ideologies raved through the newly independent countries of Africa. On its merits, *Authenticity* compared with the philosophies of other Africanist philosophers such as Ghana's Kwame Nkrumah, Nigeria's Nnamdi Azikiwe, Tanzania's Julius Nyerere and Kenya's Jomo Kenyatta. But where they differed fundamentally was in the underlying political intentions and modes of implantation of each philosophy. Nkrumah, for instance, concerned about the negative impact of colonialism on the learning experience of African youths particularly as it relates to African orientation, identity and language, sought to reverse the distorted ideas about Africa as a people without culture and history by creating an Institute of African Studies dedicated to producing an extensive and diversified library of African classics and oral history. These included literary forms and oral history from all parts of Africa passed on from generations to generations – including folk tales and epics. For Nkrumah and other Africanists at the time, any discourse on African cultural renaissance transcended mere political content or statements. Nkrumah articulated his ideology of African Personality as:

> *Cultural and social bonds which unite African nations and is not associated with a particular state, language, religion, political system or colour of the skin. For those who project it, it expresses identification not only with African historical past, but with the struggle of the African people in the African revolution to liberate and unify the continent and to build a just society.* (Nkrumah 1973a, 205)

African Personality demanded that African people be treated as agents and not as spectators in the international community (Botwe-Asamah 2005). It was a call for a pan-African awareness that "we are all African people" (Hagan 1991b, 18). Nkrumah linked African Personality to specific cultural characteristics that cut across the African experience. These according to Botwe-Asamah included attributions to

---

6 Most of the Ministers, regional administrators and heads of government departments only occupied their positions for less than a year.

"communalistic social values, efficient institutional structures and a humane attitude to all humans" (2005, 78). Diape's (1970) argument that Mobutu's ideology of authenticity was at par with Nkrumah's African Personality (also expounded by Jomo Kenyatta, Nnamdi Azikiwe), Fanon's ideology of "National Consciousness", Nyerere's "Ujama" philosophy or Toure's "Africanity" is inaccurate if not politically misleading. Indeed, Mobutu's expression of "authenticity" as evident in his "Zairanization" and "radicalization" economic policies, the legacy of "debrouilez-vous" and the institutions created for Authenticity were aimed at perpetuating his dictatorship and mobilizing the Congolese people towards this end. The *Authentic* propaganda model deliberately used African traditional metaphors of kinship and chiefly authority to legitimize Mobutu's totalitarian rule (White 2008; Schatzberg 1993). Indeed, as Botwe-Asamah (2005) has argued, *Authenticity* was philosophically and ideologically at variance with the Africanist philosophies of Nkrumah, Kenyatta, Azikiwe, etc. Authenticity represented Mobutu's voice of dominance expressed in his cult political philosophy – Mobutuism. The media for two decades were wholly part of the campaign. It is worth noting that the instruments of Mobutu's authenticity campaign were far-reaching and ubiquitous and not limited to the media. As earlier noted, it involved very innovative use of politico-cultural propaganda to link traditional Zairian music and dance with nationalism and obedience to the Chief – Mobutu.

In summary, Mobutu era (part I) saw the media working in tandem with other state institutions to propagate Mobutu's policy of *Authenticity* and its offspring Mobutuism under a one-party totalitarian regime. Today the Congolese still believe that if there was any enduring legacy Mobutu bequeathed to them, it was the restoration of their love of their own very peculiar brand of music and a collective sense of nationalism. But the nationalistic fervour created by *Authenticity* was not without its side effects. As we shall see in subsequent sections of this work, it alienated "foreigners" particularly the Tutsi Kinyarwandas and the Banyamulenges. Citizenship became a contested issue and laid the groundwork for the divisions and conflicts in the Kivus that continue till today.

6.2 Era of Débrouillez-vous (1990–1997)

On 20 October 1990, President Mobutu Sese Seko delivered a very important address to the nation. He announced an end to the one party system that had been in place since he took over government in 1965. By this announcement, other political parties were allowed to register and operate in the country. This marked a new era in the country's media history because the new political parties either created their own media houses or won the support of already existing media organizations. Until this era, the media was regulated by Decree 70/057 of 28 October 1970 and later modified by Decree 81/011 of 2 April 1981. The 1981 variant of the law decreed that all journalists were "militants" of the Mouvement Populaire de la Revolution (MPR) and thus responsible for spreading the party's ideals. With the liberalization of the media and the political space, the Zairian National Conference, set up to make political reforms in the country, made various recommendations to reform communication structures and principles to be more democratic. The Conference's Information, Press and Audio-Visual Commission denounced the government's repressive media laws. In 1995, the *Etats Generaux de la Communication* (or Communications Convention) revised the texts of the earlier decrees. An unprecedented liberal media law was promulgated in 22 June 1996. Article 8 of the law states:

> *Everyone has the right to freedom of opinion and expression. By 'freedom of expression', this law means the right to inform, to be informed to have opinions and feelings and to communicate them without hindrance, whatever the medium used on condition that the law, public order, other people's rights, and accepted standards of behaviour are respected.* (Congo Press Law 1996 [Article VIII])

This new law fundamentally ended the state's monopoly on the country's information space, at least on paper. The liberalized political and information space opened up a breadth of arena for greater political activity and greater participation by the media. The new political parties created radio stations, newspaper publications and television stations. Within five years, a total of 638 press titles were authorized and over 400 political parties were formed (Frère and Marthoz 2007).

Frère and Marthoz (2007) write that the media organizations that emerged generally fell into two groups: those that supported Mobutu and those that supported the radical opposition. Although he authorized the emerging media pluralism, Mobutu continued to repress the press this time through intimidation and violence. Most of the frenetic media boom in this era was in the newspaper sector. Privately owned radio stations started emerging in 1992. *Radio Maendeleo* was created in Bukavu, *Radio Zenith* in Lubumbashi, *Radio Amani* in Kisangani; others were *Raga FM, Radio Television Kin-Malebo* and *Malebo Broadcast Channel* (MBC), among others. There were also private television stations set up in Kinshasa – *Antenne A* was set up in 1991, other stations soon joined – *Canal Kin 1 & 2, Raga TV, Tele Kin Malebo* and *Tropicana TV*, among several other television stations. These stations reflected the increasingly discursive power bases in the country. Politico-religious radio stations also emerged and added to the mix. The Catholic Church, which remains the most influential non-political organization in the country, created *Radio Elikya* in Kinshasa. The protestant community created *Radio Sanyo Malamu*. Not to be left behind, Evangelical Christian religious groups also joined the frenzy and several evangelical radio stations were created – *Radio Television Puissance, Radio Television Armee de l' Eternal, Radio Television Message de Vie, Amen Television, Radio Television Sentinelle,* and *Radio Tele Kintuadi*, among others. The unprecedented and sudden media boom of the early 1990s had its adverse effects. Rigorous investigation of reports made way for sensationalism. During this feverish climate, "the media often paid scant respect to professional ethics and lapsed into many abuses" (Frère and Marthoz 2007, 45).

It's Boom Time! Let the Party Begin

The media boom was attended by a similar boom in political party activities during the political liberalization era. The new media organizations quickly aligned themselves to either Mobutu or any of the "radical opposition" parties. The opposition media were mainly occupied with the "failings" of the Mobutu regime and called for democratic reforms. The major problem of the newly created media organizations that set themselves against the government was money. Pro-government media had steady access to government patronage and the financial rewards it brought but the opposition did not. According to Frère and Marthoz (2007), "as they were progressively confronted with problems of financial survival, the newspapers became more dependent on political support" (p. 47). The religious media, sponsored by the different faith groups they represented, also jostled to contribute to the political discourse. In addition to broadcasting religious programmes, the religious media also reported the news, and with the private media, they challenged state-owned media's dominance over public discourse and sought to neutralize some of the government's media propaganda. For example, in 1991 when students of Lubumbashi University were massacred by government troops, the pro-government media had unquestioningly reported the government's side of the story. The new private and religious media re-investigated the incident and later disproved the government's earlier version that the shootings were as a result of "clashes between students for tribal causes" (Braekman 1996).

During this era, the media was used by political bigwigs to incite groups and populations against the other and in Katanga genocide was arguably committed. Following the election of opposition leader Etienne Tshiesekedi (from Kasai Province) to the post of Prime Minister by Zaire's National Conference, Mr. Gabriel Kumwanza, the Governor of Katanga Province, home state of the previous Prime Minister Nguza Karl I Bond, used the media to mobilize thousands of his party youths to embark on a well-planned ethnic cleansing of over 100,000 people from Kasai Province (Masoka 2006). Over a million others were displaced in towns surrounding Lubumbashi. Pro-government newspapers *Le Lushois* and *Le Liberateur-Ujamaa* among others led the incitement campaign by stirring Katangans to expel Kasaian population from Katanga. *Ujamaa*, one of the many titles that backed Governor Kumwanza, ran the headline: "The Kasains must leave" and "These dogs without collars" (Frère and Marthoz 2007). In August 1992, *La Cheminee* wrote on its editorial of Kasains:

> They are thieves, liars, sorcerers, braggarts, flatterers, profiteers.... They live in total and primitive promiscuity in very large families and share their house with sheep, chickens and dogs in unsupportable hygienic conditions, they make too much noise because of their big mouths.

The *Daily Salongo* in early September ran the headline "What if the Balubas were hunted everywhere?" (RSF 1995). The Balubas are inhabitants of the Kasai region.

Kinshasa-based opposition press that reported the crisis in Katanga was harassed by pro-government agents and their distribution networks disrupted. The state-owned media on its part reported that all was well with the country despite the ethnic cleansing that was going on in Katanga. *Telezaire*, the national television station, throughout the mayhem reported that "everywhere in the country is calm" (Frère and Marthoz 2007).

Though decrees that chained the media were repealed, media freedom remained far-fetched. Cases of repression and intimidation of the press continued, and the media remained an active tool in the hands of pro-government politicians on the one hand and the increasingly radical and violent opposition on the other. Media houses were bombed, journalists mobbed and newspaper editions burned. The printing presses of five press titles were bombed successively – *Terra Nova*, *Zaire Printing Service*, *La Voie de Dieu*, *Imprimeries du Zaire* and *Umoja*. There were several cases of journalists being kidnapped, imprisoned and in some cases assassinated. In 1991, the premises of *Elima*, a privately owned newspaper that had supported Mobutu during the one-party state era but later switched sides, were completely burned down. In 1994, Pierre Kabeya, an investigative journalist with *Kin-Martin*, was kidnapped, tortured and killed for his investigative reports about the commando squad that was involved in the massacre of Lubumbashi University students three years earlier. Another investigative journalist and editor of *Nsemo*, a local newspaper, Adolphe Kavula was also kidnapped, tortured and left for dead by commando units when he published an investigative report implicating the military after the seizure of 30 tonnes of bank notes at Kinshasa airport (Frère and Marthoz 2007). Aside from acts of direct violence against the media, the government used various other tactics to stifle opposition media. They were not only systematically starved of funds but also denied necessary communication equipment for their work. Internal means of communication including telephone and postal services that served the regions were made unreliable, and opposition-backed regional papers were systematically prevented from reaching the capital Kinshasa although pro-government Kinshasa newspapers still reached the regions. The cellular phone network that was meant to replace the obsolete landlines was priced out of reach, and Radio phones were being closely monitored by military intelligence, particularly in the Kasai region. To use a radio phone, a permit had to be obtained from the National Intelligence and Protection Service (NIPS) as well as from the Communications Ministry. An official of the Association of Zairian Journalists was quoted in a 1995 Reporters Sans Frontiere (RSF) report: "The central government has deliberately created and maintained this situation (the restriction of internal communication) to prevent people outside Kinshasa from knowing what is going on in the capital and other regions." This indeed was the case because the capital was literally disconnected from the regions. There was very poor road network linking the regions with the capital and people living in the regions knew nothing about what was going on in the capital and vice versa.

The Refugees Are Here, Oh Press Where Art Thou?

With the inflow of refugees and Hutu genocidaires from Rwanda in 1994, the level of instability increased particularly in the eastern region of the country. Regional War Lords emerged and the media was gradually pulled in not necessarily to report on the alarming influx of Hutu refugees from Rwanda, but to service the political objectives of the guerrilla entrepreneurs that emerged from the Hutu camps. What most aid agencies and indeed the international community did not know was that when the refugees arrived, the Hutu politicians and ex-FAR and Interahamwe militias among them came with a lot of cash (in dollars) as they had completely looted the Rwandan treasury on their way out. Money was used not only to buy weapons but to recruit Congolese politicians, the youth and the press to join the Hutu cause. It was a field day for the Press in the eastern region as they started acting as information mercenaries for the highest paying guerrilla entrepreneur. Under the heading of "political message", newspaper publications sold their columns to local politicians and guerrilla entrepreneurs so they could publish whatever they wanted. According to RSP (1995), it all happened with the connivance of journalists and their editors, "who often agree to write up the 'messages' in the form of fake interviews". News sourcing and presentation in this era fitted Richardson's position of news discourse as being "intimately linked with the actions and opinions of (usually powerful) social groups" (2007 1). With the economy of the country in tatters, the media houses in the other parts of the country were increasingly finding it difficult to pay their journalists and meet other financial commitments. Consequently, journalists developed self-survival strategies to survive the economic meltdown. It was indeed an era of *Débrouillez-vous or* "fend for yourself" as the media used every means to survive; poorly paid and most times unpaid journalists resorted to "coupage" from politicians for survival. Private media owners were eager to "sell" several pages of their papers to politicians and up-and-coming warlords for "political advertising".

The period between this phase and the Kabila era was particularly a difficult and dividing time for the media in the DRC. When Laurent Kabila's AFDL, supported by the Rwandan government, started the war in Kivu in 1996, Congolese media analyses of the conflict had strong ethnic undertones. Kinshasa press presented the conflict as being ignited by foreign forces from Rwanda and described it as a foreign invasion. However, with the increasing success of the AFDL's Laurent Kabila, it became apparent to the press that a serious challenger to Mobutu's 31-year dictatorship had emerged. At this point, there was fierce division between pro-Mobutu press and anti-Mobutu press. The pro-Mobutu press insisted that Kabila was a foreigner – due to his Banyamulenge origin. The media vehemently traced Banyamulenge ancestry to Rwanda. According to Frère and Marthoz (2007), the war in Kivu was presented by pro-Mobutu media as external aggression and "used to re-enforce Congolese nationalism in the service of a moribund government" (p. 49). However, when Kabila's military incursion into Kinshasa became unstoppable, government-owned media and other private pro-Mobutu press switched sides. *L'Avenir, Le Forum des As, La Cite Afri-caine* and *Le Palmares* among others, all previously pro-Mobutu media, declared their allegiance to the Kabila-led AFDL.

6.3 Era of Official Silence, Repression and *Coupage* (1997–2001)

This phase started when Laurent-Desire Kabila toppled the government of Mobutu Sese Seko in May 1997. The era was marked by repression of the media, arbitrary arrests and imprisonment of journalists, censorship and proscription of opposing media organizations. Kabila's regime was a particularly tough time for the media – both in terms of function and finance. The frenetic media boom that had character-ized the political party liberalization of the Mobutu II era was brought to an abrupt end when Laurent Kabila banned all political party activities. The press and Journal-ists were thus stripped of their main source of finance – the political class.

Between May 1997 when he came to power and January 2001, more than 160 jour-nalists were jailed without trial, for varying lengths of time and most times without any explanation (Frère and Marthoz 2007). Publications were seized, radio stations shut down and media premises firebombed and ransacked. Kabila also turned against international media by expelling foreign journalists and banning interna-tional radio broadcasts. Physical violence, including whipping, was used against journalists that opposed the government. President Kabila hired his predecessor's former information Czar and the brain behind Mobutu's *Authenticity* propaganda system, the reinvented Mr. Dominique Sakombi Inongo to head the Communications Ministry.

A key feature of the media landscape during Laurent Kabila's regime was the division within media. There were divisions along the lines of Journalists and media organizations that were pro-government and those that were anti-government. The pro-government Journalists goaded Kabila in his persecution of anti-government Journalists and even called for tougher stance against opposing media. In Novem-ber 1998, *Demian le Congo*, a Kinshasa daily, editorialized that the arrest and impris-onment of three reporters with *Le Soft* should be "the minimum sanction" for the opposition (RSF 1999). Another pro-government newspaper *Le Africain* commented concerning the arrest: "Elsewhere, traitors are shot" (RSF 1999).

But from the Beginning It Was Not So!

Kabila had not always been unfriendly with the media. When he came to power, he offered the private media a massive "coupage" of $1 million. The coupage was meant to be distributed among "co-operating" media groups. Editors of various media orga-nizations met to form *Caisse d'assistance et de solidarité pour les professionels des médias* (CASPROM) (Assistance and Solidarity Fund for Media Professionals) for the purpose of sharing the money. The "donation" caused divisions among the media community as editors of some newspaper groups saw the money as bribery and insisted it should be rejected. *Le Potentiel, Le Phare* and a few other titles rejected the "gift" while *Le Palmares, La Reference Plus, L'Avenir,* etc. accepted and shared the money among themselves. The Editors that accepted the money were mainly pro-Kabila, and they justified their acceptance by claiming that the money could be used to develop the journalism profession by training upcoming journalists. Doubtless, the major problem of journalism in the DRC has been lack of finance and inadequate equipment. But receiving such a huge donation from a President that came to power through a coup and was unapologetic about his disdain for free press, left a lot to be desired in terms of professionalism of the Kinshasa press. The very core of the Journalism profession and its practice was compromised at this appoint. The media organizations that received the money became fanatic about their support for Kabila and joined in attacking the anti-Kabila press. *Espirit de corps* was no longer existent, and according to JED (2000), there was no moral authority to assume the role of regulator within the profession as CASPROM was founded on a shaky foundation.

The Rise and Boom of *Radio Trottoir*

President Kabila's government was very secretive. The media were denied access to information regarding any government plans except plans that were deliberately released to the media to achieve specific objectives. The official government gazette ceased publication.

As a result, the media including the opposition media thrived on rumours. The media became an official "Radio Trottoir" or pavement radio (Congo's euphemism for roadside gossips). Gradually a system of *Radio Trottoir* was established as citizens, in the midst of the political uncertainties that clouded the country, depended on socially transmitted information and rumours. Socially transmitted information still remains a vital means of transmitting information particularly within networks in bars, markets, taxi parks and living rooms across the DRC. Also known as Radio Trottoir, socially transmitted information is ubiquitous, anonymous, endemic and most importantly uncensorable. A key characteristic for Radio Trottoir according to Ellis (1989) is that it is democratic in that a "story cannot be transmitted orally over any considerable distance or for any substantial period unless it is judged to be of interest by a significant number of people" (Ellis 1989, 322). Uncensored and drawing on an inherent African oral tradition (Reagan 2005; Furniss and Gunner 1995; Ellis 1989), rumours swirled across the government in the absence of official government information and the Press actively joined in reporting rumours as facts. *Radio Trottoir* gradually became institutionalized, and several times it found its way into mainstream media. In most cases, socially transmitted information is used as a political tool by politicians

(Whitman 2003). Whitman (2003) writes during the Inter Congolese Dialogue at Sun City, the head of the political negotiations, Sir Ketumile Masire, was a victim of DRC's politically motivated rumours. According to Whitman, it was rumoured all through Kinshasa that the Commissioners appointed by the Office of the Facilitator of the ICD were there for the money and that they were being paid $60,000 for their work. This false rumour, Whitman insists, was deliberately spread by the Kabila government in a bid to discredit the Commissioners and their work.

It was easy to use rumour as a political tactic during this era, because Government Ministers and Kabila himself for unexplained reasons refrained from addressing the media and chose to issue Press Releases instead. But the Releases could barely address the myriads of questions that the media had concerning the short and long-term plans of the new government, the restive east and several other issues.

Rumour Wars and State Persecution of the Press

With absence of information from government, media reports increasingly drew on the ever swirling rumour and speculation mills of Kinshasa. Some of the rumours and false speculations were deliberately modulated by both the government and opposition political actors. But with the non-publication of the new press law by the government, sanctions on journalists publishing "seditious" or "libellous" materials were arbitrary. Two journalists – Ngoy Kikungula, Managing Editor of the weekly *Le Lushois*, and the Editor Bela Mako – were arrested on 23 March 1999 and sentenced to eight months' imprisonment by a military tribunal for publishing false allegations against a regional Governor. In another case, *Le Phare*, a Kinshasa daily, published a story that Kabila was planning to establish an elite presidential guard like the one maintained by ex-dictator Mobutu Sese Seko. On 8 September 1997, the Editor Polydor Muboyayi Mubanga was arrested at his home by six armed men and kept in a solitary cell at Kinshasa's Gombé court before being moved to the notorious Makala Central Prison. Reporter Tshivis Tshivuadi, who wrote the story under the pen name Kaniema, fled to exile for fear of his life. The Editor Mubanga was charged on 17 September with "publishing false information" and "incitement to racial hatred" (RSF 1999). This sparked vehement protests among journalists across the country. Various journalist unions and press associations led the protest and the demand for the release of the editor. On 18 September, "a day without newspapers" was declared to demand his release. Mubanga was eventually released after three months of incarceration.

Several other journalists were arrested and imprisoned for "libel". On 12 January 1999, for instance, Thierry Kyalumba, Editor-in-Chief of the biweekly *Vision*, was arrested in Kinshasa and brought before a military tribunal for "revealing state secrets". Kyalumba had written a report under a pen name, suggesting that neighbouring Uganda had bought large quantities of missiles for rebel groups in the Kasai provinces (east of Kinshasa). He was held in solitary confinement at state security headquarters at the Kokolo military barracks. There he was tortured and beaten with a large metal buckle, and on 30 March 1999 a military tribunal sentenced him to four years imprisonment.

During this era, Laurent-Désiré Kabila used different methods; some brazen others downright ludicrous, to keep the media under tight-fisted control. According to RSF in its 1999 report, Journalists were held in custody for longer than the maximum period permitted by the law, and were rarely brought before a court. Those that were, were brought before a stage-managed military tribunal. Their lawyers and families were prevented from visiting them in detention. The dreaded Makala Kinshasa central prison was the main detention centre for arrested journalists. An unnamed journalist told Reporters Sans Frontières: "If I am arrested, I will beg them not to take me to Makala Kinshasa central prison". The solitary cells according to RSF (1999) were "in a disgusting state, with deplorable hygiene". This era was tough for journalism as a profession especially those of the "red press" as opposition newspaper were called in the DRC. There were several cases of arbitrary arrests and incarceration of journalists that dared to publish opinions that contradicted the government's side.

Roll-Call of Persecuted Journalists

The following is a roll call of some journalists that bore the hardest end of Kabila's fist as a form of tribute to them. While not exhaustive, the list represents the nature of repression during this era.

Albert Bonsange Yema

On 18 November 1997, Albert Bonsange Yema, publisher of a group of newspapers that included the titles *Mambega*, *L'Essor Africain* and *L'Alarme*, was arrested in Kisangani and incarcerated for days without trial. He was accused of working as an "agent" for a team of United Nations Investigators probing allegations of massacres in the former Zaire. He was re-arrested a few weeks later, this time along with his two wives and six children, three of whom worked for his press group and detained for weeks without trial.

This time he was accused of publishing an interview with an opposition party on the *L'Alarme*. The paper's front page ran the banner headline "Now or never, let's put an end to the Kabila dictatorship". After weeks of incarceration without trial, Mr. Yema was eventually charged before the state security court with endangering state security, and sentenced to a year in prison. After his release, he fled the country following further threats from the state security services.

Kidimbu Mpese and Awazi Karomon

Mpese was the Managing Editor of the triweekly *Le Soft*, while Kharomon worked as a reporter with the newspaper. They were both arrested on 25 May 1998 and held at the *Département Intérieur de la Détection Militaire des Activités* Anti-Parties (DEMI-AP-DI) (or Military Force for the Detection of Anti-Patriotic Activities). They were accused of "publishing reports that undermine the government's work". The "incriminating" report, in the 14 April issue of *Le Soft International*, had claimed that the country's central bank had been mismanaged. The journalists had nothing to do with the content of *Le Soft International* (the international edition of their paper) as it was published in Brussels. The two journalists were eventually released on 4 June 1998.

Jean-José Monzango

Monzango, a journalist with *L'Alarme*, arrested on 30 October 1998 and detained at the *Centre* de Détention et *Rééducation* de *Kinshasa* (CPRK) (or Kinshasa Penitentiary and Re-education Centre). His offence was reporting that the Interior Minister had fled to Belgium when fighting broke out between government forces and rebels militants from the Congolese Union for Democracy. He was released on bail after two months of incarceration.

Yvette Idi Lupantshia

Lupantshia's case was a bit special as she worked for the government controlled RTNC. She was arrested by police officers and taken to the Kinshasa Police Special Force Headquarters. She was accused of espionage-related offence for passing on videotapes of a press conference by President Kabila to the US embassy. Yvette was locked for three days in a tiny cell infested with mosquitoes and rats where she had to sleep on the bare floor. Her family members were prevented from visiting her and food brought for her by her mother was eaten up by the officers guarding her cell. One of the prison guards ordered 50 male prisoners to undress in front of her and forced her to watch. She was told to open her eyes wide "so you can tell the Americans who sent you all about it" (RSF 1999). She was released three days after her arrest and suspended without pay for a month.

Stephane Kitutu O'Leontwa

Stephane Kitutu O'Leontwa, Chairman of the Congo Press Union and former chairman of the state controlled RTNC, was arrested on 8 May 1999 and taken to "the criminal record" at Kinshasa-Gombé. This is a dungeon-like cell inside the buildings of the Prosecutor's Office Police (IPP) where most journalists were kept. He was arrested instead of the editor of a satirical newspaper *Pot-Pourri*, wanted in connection with publications that the authorities believed were "insulting". The only address given in *Pot-Pourri* was that of the Congo Press Union where O'Leontwa was the Chairman. For fear of arrests, most newspapers refrained from printing their business addresses, preferring to use the address of their professional union the Congo Press Union. Although O'Leontwa, (who had never written for *Pot-Pourri)* was publicly against the practice, he was held without charge by the IPP for four days.

Achille Kadima Mulamba

Journalists were oppressed not only by the Kabila government but also by people with connections within the political class and security agencies. Anyone with connections who was unhappy with the way they were portrayed by the media paid police officers, soldiers and other security agents to intimidate the journalist that wrote the article. For example, Achille Kadima Mulamba, Publishing Editor of the newspaper *Veritas*, was kidnapped on 24 August 1999 by thugs hired by the Chief Tax Officer in Kinshasa men. His newspaper had published a story alleging that the Chief Tax Officer was involved in a huge fraud. Mulamba was taken to the Kinshasa/Kintambo police division headquarters and held in a solitary cell for two days. During his incarceration, he was prevented from contacting his family, friends or colleagues.

The Ten Whipped Journalists of Kinshasa

On 25 November 1997, ten journalists in Kinshasa were whipped by the police for attending a press conference by an opposition leader. The journalists which included correspondents of *Deutsche Welle* and *Associated Press* were bundled from the venue of the press conference and taken to a police station. There, they were given a number of lashes proportional to their age and weight. Their work equipment were confiscated by the police.

Freddy Loseke Lisumbu

Publisher of triweekly *La Libre Afrique*, Lisumbu was arrested on 26 December 1998 and given 150 lashes by men of the president's special security force. His publication had accused the Chief of Staff in the President's office of embezzlement.

Patrice Kabemba

A journalist with Kasai Horison Radio Television (KHRT) was arrested on 6 January 1999 by the dreaded National Intelligence Agency (ANR) – one of the main instruments of repression used by the state against journalists. He was locked at Mbuji-Mayi in one of the notorious ANR dungeons. The following day he was undressed and given 100 lashes before being released.

Dodjo Kasadi

Editor of *La Palme d'Or* was arrested at his home in Kinshasa by armed men from ANR. His newsmagazine had published a story quoting inhabitants of Kivu saying they wanted to see Kabila face trial. He was held and tortured for two months.

Jean-Marie Kashila and Bienvenu Tshiela

On 26 July 1999, both journalists were arrested and whipped by policemen in Mbuji-Mayi in eastern Kasai Province. Kashila worked for the *Agence congolaise de presse* and Bienvenu Tshiela worked for *Kasaï Horizon Radio-Television*. The police, according to RSF (1999), were acting on the orders of Kalala Kaniki, the provincial deputy governor, who was upset about negative reports of him by the two journalists. Kalala Kaniki was actually a known figure among the press community in terms of his cruelty to journalists. He had earlier ordered another journalist, Robert Ndaye Tshisense, to be whipped.

Destruction of Press Assets

In addition to cruelty to journalists, the authorities also burned opposition newspapers and press offices. On 20 February 1998, copies of *Le Soft International*, a privately owned newspaper published in Brussels, were seized at Kinshasa/N'Djili airport and set on fire. The newspaper had carried a front-page story headlined "Tshisekedi, eternal victim of persecution" with a picture of opposition leader Étienne Tshisekedi wa Mulumba surrounded by a cheering crowd. On 23 March 1999, *Le Soft International* was again seized and burned, this time because of a front-page story with the headline "Can Kabila be saved?" The offices of the paper's local edition, *Le Soft*, were raided on 17 May 1997 by AFDL soldiers the day Kabila declared himself President.

The editorial department of *Elima* newspaper suffered the same fate on 22 December 1997 when soldiers looted its editorial and printing departments, carting away equipment worth several thousands of dollars.

Justifying its repression of the media, the Kabila government blamed its clampdown on the poor quality of the Kinshasa press, pointing to the insulting tone and libels of the *red press*.[7] The opposition press was very critical of the government and according to RSF (1999) sometimes completely ignored professional standards and ethics. In most cases, the media reported street rumours as facts without bothering to confirm the stories from authoritative sources. Asa Mudumbi, a freelance journalist and columnist with several papers during this era, told me the papers that defied Kabila needed to survive then. There were no adverts those days, he said, and "the few corporations that would have advertised were scared of being identified with the red press". The only means of income therefore was through circulation. And the sure way to boost circulation was by being sensational. He told me: "Did that mean, rumours were sometimes reported as facts? Absolutely Yes, it happened every time especially when the war started". In most cases, the journalists were not paid, and they had to depend on *coupage* for their livelihood. It was common practice for a journalist to receive some *coupage* from a politician and report his story. Times were tough and they needed to survive somehow.

Beyond what Mudumbi told me, the government, as earlier stated, operated a tight-lip policy. It was virtually impossible to obtain information from official sources in Kinshasa under Kabila.

In the midst of all the professional misconducts by journalists, the Kabila government was not even-handed in dealing with the media. RSF in its 1999 reported berated the "unequal treatment reserved for different media. For reporting similar facts, some titles escape any form of reprisals from the security forces, while others are harassed systematically". Furthermore, reporting about the army or the police was a "no-go-area" for the press except the government-controlled ones. During this era, media repression had become graver than during the Mobutu era (RSF 1999).

Hunting Down Foreign Media

Foreign journalists did not escape harassment from the Kabila regime. On 3 December 1997, **Mossi Mwasi**, the southern Africa correspondent of the *BBC* and *Deutsche Welle*, was arrested by the infamous Rapid Intervention Police Squad and held at *Centre* de DÈtention et *Rééducation* de *Kinshasa* (CPRK). He was accused of using false identification documents and espionage. Mwasi was released after four months of incarceration without trial.

Peter Böhm, a correspondent of the Berlin newspaper *Die Tages Zeitung*, was arrested by security operatives while taking pictures in the east near the border with Rwanda and Uganda. He was accused of "spying" and kept locked up at the Kinshasa security headquarters. He was freed after a month and deported.

---

7 Opposition media since the Mobutu era are called red press because of the red logo they used.

Aside from arresting and incarcerating foreign journalists, the Kabila government also took deliberate steps to curtail broadcasts from foreign media. On 30 November 1997, then Information Minister Raphael Ghenda banned indefinitely the broadcasts of three international broadcasters – the BBC World Service, Radio France International and the Voice of America for their role in spreading "disinformation and brainwashing". But Ghenda's main grouse was not with the international broadcasters but with the local stations that re-transmitted the news and information programmes of foreign media. International broadcasters such as the BBC Great Lakes Service, Radio France International, Deutch Welle, Voice of America, etc. transmit on shortwave bands. This reduces the number of listeners because most radio receivers owned by ordinary Congolese do not have antennae systems that are strong enough to receive clear shortwave signals. Also, in most parts of the country, reception of shortwave signals is extremely poor irrespective of how good the radio antennae are. To make up for this, the international broadcasters form partnerships with local radio stations to re-broadcast their news and information programmes on FM. Catholic-owned *Radio Elikya* in Kinshasa, for instance, retransmits programmes from *Radio Vatican*; *Raga FM* retransmits programmes from the Voice of America, the BBC World Service and Deutsche Welle; *Radio-Television Kin Malebo* re-broadcasts RFI; and *Tele Kin Malebo* re-broadcasts the newscasts of Canal France International. There are other local stations that "unofficially" re-transmit the programmes of international broadcasters without obtaining permission from the broadcasters. It was a major cause for concern for Kabila's government because of the uncensored criticism of the foreign media; moreover, locals tended to believe the international broadcasters more than the government-owned RTNC. The government was therefore determined to end the re-transmissions. When Didier Miming replaced Ghenda as Information Minister, he took extra steps to ensure that the re-broadcasts were brought to an end. On 22 July 1999, he ordered all privately owned TV and Radio Stations in the country to stop immediately the re-transmission of all foreign programmes or have their licenses revoked.

The order was unlawful considering that the broadcasts were guaranteed under the country's media laws. Article 50 and 51 of the June 1996 Press Law provides "the right to produce, transmit and receive any broadcasting material as long as it respects public order and morals and does not harm the rights of others". The government insisted that the rebroadcasts threatened public order and hence was unlawful and that the licenses of the stations prevented them from re-transmitting foreign programmes. The ban was however lifted in September 1999 after enormous internal and international pressure on the government.

It was not uncommon for the government to override the 1996 Press Law which by every standard was unusually liberal especially when compared with the previous press law – Decree 70/057 of October 1970 and Decree 81/011 of April 2 1981 (which modified the former). The previous law had specified that the journalists in the country were first and foremost militants of the national party MPR, responsible for spreading the party's ideals. But with the liberalization of the political space in

1990, the law had become obsolete. So in May 1995, the Etats Generaux de la Communication (Communications Convention) which brought together 320 journalists and observers from all parts of the country, revised the texts and its recommendations gave birth to Law 96-002 of 22 June 1996. The 1996 Press Law which still supposedly guided media practice in the country was liberal and spoke of the desire of the Convention to chart a new democratic course for the media – away from the state monopoly over the information sector of the Mobutu era.

The law also guaranteed the neutrality of the public media but to some extent did not guarantee the age-old journalism ethic of "confidentiality of source". The law obliged journalists to "reveal the sources of information in the cases prescribed by the law". But during this era, journalists were constantly harassed not only in the rebel-controlled territories but also under territories controlled by the Kabila government. In the rebel-controlled east in particular, opposition papers were completely put out of publication and radio stations that insisted on their independence were suspended. All stations were forced to broadcast only official news. Thus, the 1996 Press Law, despite its liberal underpinnings, was completely ignored.

Age of the War Lords: Attacks on the Media by the RCD

In the Kivus where the *Rassemblement Congolais pour la Democratie* (RCD) held sway, they censored or banned newspaper publications and radio stations. Journalists were constantly threatened, detained and harassed, and sometimes radio broadcast equipment and documents were confiscated. For instance, Radio Maendeleo in South Kivu, one of the mushrooming independent, non-profit radio stations, was incessantly harassed. Radio Maendeleo, an initiative of locally based NGOs, produced and aired news programmes on development, human rights and other information programmes created by NGOs. On 7 July 1999, officials from the RCD's Department of Information, Press and Cultural Affairs ordered the station to stop producing its own political news and magazine programmes and replace them with news programmes from the RCD-controlled RTNC. *Maendelo* ignored the order and continued broadcasting its own news stores. On 21 July 1999, armed men seized its equipment and Radio Maendeleo was forced to stop broadcasting. Nine days later, the Department of Information, Press and Cultural Affairs officially suspended the radio station (Amnesty May 2000). On 25 August 1999, the Director of the Radio Station, **Kizito Mushizi Nfundiko,** and its Head of Programme and Information, **Kamengele Oruba,** were arrested, accused of participating in a secret subversive meeting and listening to military secrets through their walkie-talkies (HRW May 2000). They and other NGO officials that supported the station were kept in detention for weeks without trial.

The RCD bared its fangs on its own RTNC to ensure a tight control over its programming. Staff that either deliberately or in error made any subversive broadcast were promptly disciplined. For example, two journalists working for the station, Primo

Rudakigwa and Delion Kimburumbu, were detained for several days in Goma following the broadcast of a programme they produced. Their "crime" was that their programme had speculated that Rwandan border may be extended into Congolese territory.

Harassment of Journalists by the RCD

The RCD routinely harassed journalists and forced them to report stories that favoured the movement's cause. Private news publications faced the brunt the most and were routinely clamped down. *La Croissance Plus*, an independent newspaper, was suspended in September 1991 when the paper's editorial wrote about the absence of democracy under the RCD. A photo journalist, **Raphael Kinyugi,** for *Junction,* a business journal, was arrested and detained for two days for taking pictures of street children. He was accused of trying to sneak out the pictures "to show the world that children of Congo were living in poverty and misery". International journalists were not sparred the harassment. In February 2000, for instance, **Delion Kimbolumpo,** a local stringer for the Voice of America, was threatened with punishment by RCD officials after a VOA report about a protest march in Goma by wives of soldiers who objected to their husband's involvement in the war. Kimbolimpo fearing for his life temporarily left Goma after the threats.

6.4 Era of Intervention and Governmentality (2001–)

During this era, the DRC managed to develop one of the freest and most liberal media – at least on paper. In 2006, for the first time in a long while the DRC had a single government, democratically elected and with constitutional authority over all parts of the country, although they lacked the instruments to exert full constitutional authority over the entire country. There is also one parliament and one Commander of the national army. Despite localized violence in various parts of the country, the DRC as a state has been relatively stable politically. Political stability during this era can undoubtedly be attributed to the active political and in some cases military engagement of MONUC. MONUC's Public Information Department's work during this era has to some extent been defining. But before going on to explore the intervention activities of MONUC's Public Information Department, I will first examine the new media policy architecture and the media regulatory mechanisms of the DRC during this era.

Media Policy Architecture & Instruments of Self-Regulation

Freedom of Expression, free press, broadcasting freedom and freedom of information is enshrined in the 2006 constitution. Also the Press Law of 1996 provides for free access to information. Although the Press Law which is still in force guarantees freedom of information and the press, defamation remains a criminal offence and is covered under the Criminal Code (Article 75).

By far the most defining revolution in this era was the establishment of *La Haute Autorite Des Media* or High Authority of the Media (HAM), during the Inter-Congolese Dialogue at Sun City. HAM is authorized to supervise and monitor adherence to the law and regulations by the media. It was one of the five institutions created at the Sun City dialogue to support the democratic process. Although HAM's responsibilities seemed to overlap with the oversight responsibilities of the Ministry of Press and Communications, HAM played a critical role during the transition and election process. Its core responsibilities during this era was to monitor and ensure media freedom; ensure public access to pluralist information and monitor and ensure that public media remained politically neutral. It was entrusted with both consultative powers in respect of the government and coercive powers in respect of the media. The following are some of the landmark rulings of HAM during the transition period:

– Suspended the broadcasting license of Horizon 33 TV for seven days after a presenter at the station used what was judged to be hate speech against people from another ethnic group.
– Banned a TV news programme broadcast that it deemed ethnically offensive.
– Banned the screening of films on television that it adjudged to be indecent.

Also, during the 2006 Presidential Election, HAM was involved in fighting against political hate speeches that got intensified during the run up to the elections (Frère and Marthoz 2007).

HAM also put pressure on public media to open up their programmes to opposition political voices. As a result, the state TV news also covered the campaigns of opposition candidates (Mweze 2006); in the DRC, this was unprecedented. HAM managed to operate independent government intervention due primarily to the external funding and technical expertise it received from external donors (including British, Belgian, French, German aid agencies and the UNDP). But it did not escape intimidation. In July 2006, its offices were ransacked by supporters of one of the candidates for the Presidential Election, Mr. Jean Bemba (Frère and Marthoz 2007).

Professional Media Organizations

There are so many professional associations that were set up to represent the disparate interests of the over 4,500 Congolese employed in the various arms of the media. But the associations fall under the *Federation des Organisations Professionelles des Medias* (FOPROMEDIA). To streamline the activities of the various associations and create better coherence, a National Press Congress was convened in March 2004 to set up a national structure – *Union Nationale de la Presse Congolaise* (UNPC) to defend freedom of the press and general interests of the media profession. A self-regulatory body that monitors the professional behaviour of journalists and their compliance with ethics of the profession, *Observatoire des Medias* (OMEC) was also established. Although OMEC is able to sanction media houses or journalists that "misbehave" the final say on sanctions lies with the UNPC.

To re-align the uneven relationship that characterized dealings between the media and the political class, a code of good behaviour was signed by the public and private media with political parties on 15 May 2004. According to Frère and Marthoz (2007), the aim of the agreement was to demonstrate a commitment by the media that they would grant even access to all political parties during the electioneering campaigns. On their part, the political parties made a commitment to respect and protect journalists covering election campaigns and desist from negative campaigning. This was a critical agreement because the media has always been used as a tool for propaganda and political ascendancy by politicians and powerful groups in the DRC; moreover, electoral campaigns here involves using sometimes ethnically charged rhetoric to mobilize ethnic and regional kindredship. So to a remarkable extent the self-regulation activities of the Congolese media were successful and in many ways helped to create an atmosphere of professionalism and ethical decorum among journalists during the election.

The Public Information Division of MONUC

MONUC's Public Information Department comprises the Publications Unit, the Video Unit and the Website Unit. The publication unit produces leaflets for MONUC's psyops, campaign posters, booklets, a weekly bulletin, monthly magazine and other materials. Most of the documents are translated in the national languages of the DRC.

The video unit produces media materials both for Congolese local media and the international media. At the moment, the Public Information Department's work is focused mainly on the DDRRR campaign. They were also heavily involved in creating awareness for the country's electoral process in 2006. To complement its mass media campaigns, the PID also makes use of popular theatre to transmit reconciliation messages.

The Humanitarian Need for Information Intervention

During the Inter-Congolese Dialogue (ICD) at Sun City, the country was divided into three parts, each part held by a different rebel group with its own administrative structure. The Rassemblement Congolais pour la démocratie or Congolese assembly for democracy (RCD) was in control of the North and South Kivu Provinces, Maniema Province, part of Eastern and Western Kasaï Provinces, the northern part of the

Katanga Province and the city of Kisangani. The *Mouvement de libération du Congo* or Congo liberation movement (MLC) controlled southern Katanga, Western Kasaï and part of Eastern Kasaï and strategic parts of Northern Equateur Province (while the south was held by the Kinshasa government). Consequently, there was no media of communication reaching all parts of the divided country. The Congolese were thus ignorant of what was going on at Sun City and what was going on in other parts of their country. In the regions held by rebel groups, there was no free and independent media to report events. The media groups were controlled by the different administrative groups who violently repressed any voice of dissent by the media. The media was used by the different regional administrations to accuse the other groups of ceasefire violations. Report of the Sun City negotiations by the various regional media was filled with incitements and campaign against other regional administrations. Given this situation, it became a humanitarian need to establish a radio station that would inform and unify the country. Moreover, objective knowledge of the Sun City negotiations and the contents of the peace agreements by all Congolese was necessary to put pressure on the antagonists to come to an agreement. UN actors believed that a flow of information across the various administrative parts of the country would push the actors to be more engaged with the Inter-Congolese Dialogue which was then going on in Sun City.

Disarmament, Demobilisation, Repatriation, Resettlement and Reintegration

DDRRR programme is a crucial element of MONUC's Public Information Operations. According to Peter Swarbrick, Director of MONUC's DDRRR programme, the presence of thousands of armed militia from Rwanda is at the core of the DRC conflict.

> *Unless and until this problem is resolved, lasting peace cannot be restored. The presence of foreign armed groups is not only damaging to internal security but also represents a standing obstacle to the improvement and normalisation of relations between DRC and its neighbours.* (Swarbrick 2004, 163)

The objective of the DDRRR programme is to solve this problem. The core of MONUC's Mission after the successful conduct of general elections in 2006 has been how to control the situation in the eastern DRC where most of the Rwandan Hutu FDLR elements are based. Other militant groups such as the Tutsi-dominated CNDP have insisted they will not disarm while the FDLR exists. The presence of these groups created a grave security situation particularly in the Kivus. As I will explain later, MONUC, due to its mandate and policy, restrained from fighting the FDLR, but provided logistic support to the Congolese army (FARDC) and the Rwandan army during a joint military operation (codenamed Kimia II) to root out FDLR elements in the Kivus. The operation has created huge humanitarian problems and controversies, and it has been less than successful. Indeed, the controversial joint operation has led to brutal killing of hundreds of civilians and raping of thousands including by the very FARDC soldiers the UN is backing (HRW 2009). Swarbrick (2004) who has headed MONUC's DDRRR operations since 2002 believes that the solution is not military but political. Drawing on Swarbrick's illumination on MONUC's mandate, the Lusaka Ceasefire Agreement and MONUC's policy regarding engaging with the FDLR, I will explain why a well-designed information intervention programme is essential in achieving MONUC's DDRRR objectives.

After the Lusaka ceasefire agreement was signed with belligerent forces in the DRC in 1999, MONUC was mandated by the Security Council under Chapter VII of the UN Charter to ensure the disengagement and withdrawal of all foreign forces in the DRC. While MONUC was envisaged to take care of the military-strategic part of the agreement, the Sir Ketumile Masire led Inter-Congolese Dialogue dealt with the political elements. By including both peacekeeping and peacemaking functions, the agreement had envisaged the UN to adopt the use of force in disarming armed groups, but the Security Council stated from the outset that any DDRRR programme would have to be voluntary. Paragraph 11(a) of Article III of the Agreement envisaged that the UN Security Council acting under Chapter VII of the UN Charter and in collaboration with the African Union constitute and deploy an appropriate peacekeeping force in the DRC to ensure implementation of the agreement: "and taking into account the peculiar situation of the DRC, mandate the peacekeeping force to track down all armed groups in the DRC" (Lusaka Ceasefire Agreement 1999, Article III, par. 11a). In Chapter 8 of the agreement, the signatories envisaged peacekeeping and peacemaking elements in any UN mandate. Paragraph 8.2.2 clearly outlines the peace enforcement expectations of a UN Force to include "tracking down and disarming armed groups ... working out such measures (persuasive or coercive) as are appropriate for the attainment of the objectives of disarming, assembling, repatriation and re-integration into society of members of the armed groups" (par. 8.2.2e). MONUC however has chosen to pursue the "persuasive" rather than the "coercive" element of the agreement, and as Swarbrick (2004) has noted, this was the point where MONUC differed significantly in its approach to DDRRR from what was envisaged by the Lusaka agreement. MONUC's approach to DDRRR is that it has to be voluntary based on persuasion and not coerced. It is essential I quote Swarbrick's reason at length:

> Not least because it would be difficult, if not impossible, to identify troop-contributing countries willing to contribute contingents to be deployed in eastern DRC for the forcible disarmament of groups accused of genocide and other serious crimes against humanity, at least in sufficient numbers and with a sufficiently robust mandate. It was believed that such an operation might last for years and could entail heavy casualties as well as an extremely heavy logistical and supply burden on local infrastructure with a very slender capacity. (2004, 166–167)

Even before deployment, the UN had foreseen how difficult it would be to execute any peace enforcement element of the agreement as it relates particularly to the FDLR. The 15 July 1999 Report of the Secretary General on the UN Preliminary Deployment in the DRC argued that the problem of armed groups is particularly difficult and sensitive. While acknowledging the huge threat such armed groups posed for the stability of the entire Great Lakes region, the Secretary General feared that "a purely military solution appears to be impossible, if only because the forces most able and willing to impose a military solution have clearly failed to do so" (par. 22). Instead of military engagement, the Secretary General noted the need for the establishment of a well-funded, well-planned and long-term programme of disarmament and demobilization, but emphasized the need for a robust public information component – "the benefits of such a programme will need to be widely publicized in order to attract the fighters now under arms" (par. 24). To this end, MONUC has embarked on a robust DDRRR programme, and so far, over 10,000 Rwandan combatants and their families have joined the programme. Considering the humanitarian situation in the Kivus, the enduring capability of the FDLR and other AGs to launch attacks and maintain its shadow transnational networks, MONUC's efforts have been less than successful. Compounding the problem for the UN is that it has very limited experience of dealing with a situation as complicated as the DRC's case. Although the UN has carried out several DDR operations in previous operations in Sierra Leone, Mozambique, Cambodia, Guatemala, Angola, etc., the present DDRRR project cannot be modelled on operations in those countries because according to Swarbrick the DRC situation is different in many important respects. The following are the main reasons:

1. The FDLR and other armed groups have not signed any agreement with MONUC or with any other party for that matter; hence, they still consider themselves at war.
2. Some of the FDLR leaders and members face serious criminal charges before an international tribunal; hence, the UN cannot contemplate making a political deal with leaders of the movement.
3. MONUC has a fixed policy of not considering the FDLR a party or partner of its DDRRR process and will thus not engage in any political discussions with them. (This is rather strange since FDLR members are the targets of MONUC's DDRRR programme.)
4. The DRC's uniquely difficult terrain, in addition to problems of infrastructure, security, transportation and communications.
5. Finally, since the combatants are foreign, they would need to be repatriated and not reinserted into the society. This element adds an international dimension that is unique to the DRC case.

In addition to Swirbrick's list, a high number of Rwandan Hutus, perhaps more than the UN would acknowledge, have actually settled in South Kivu and have intermarried and raised children.

All these factors create a very complicated situation as MONUC could neither launch a full-scale military operation against the FDLR nor engage in political negotiations with their leaders to achieve a comprehensive disarmament and demobilization.

The only option under the circumstance is for MONUC to by-pass the leaders of the FDLR and seek to convince their members to lay down their weapons and join the DDRRR. To achieve this, it is essential that FDLR elements be reached wherever they are. To this end, MONUC has adopted different strategies to reach them – including the use of mobile transmitters, leaflet drops, posters, stickers, satellite telephone calls, etc.

Gutahuka

Chief among MONUC's DDRRR toolkit is the radio programme *Gutahuka*, meaning "go back home" in Kinyarwanda. *Gutahuka* is produced by the Audio and Video Production Unit of MONUC's Public Information Department. The Unit travels regularly to Rwanda to meet and interview returned former rebels in transit or reintegration camps. MONUC provides *Gutahuka* not only to Radio Okapi for broadcast but also to several other radio stations across the DRC and directly through mobile transmitters in the equatorial forests of eastern DRC. But of all the broadcasters, Radio Okapi is the main medium of broadcasting the programme basically due to its wide reach. Radio Okapi broadcasts the programme daily. The purpose of *Gutahuka* is to speak to individual combatants of the FDLR in particular and Rwandan Hutus in the DRC in general to lay down their arms and return home. To achieve this, the programme takes different forms – first it explains the DDRRR programme and broadcasts interviews with returnees and families of the militants abroad. Returnees speak of the conditions at DDRRR camps and the entire programme while family members plead with loved ones still away to overcome their fear and return home.

Radio Okapi in the Service of MONUC

The responsibility of Radio Okapi, the UN-backed radio station in the DRC, is to contribute to the peace process through information. The next chapter will provide further detailed information about Radio Okapi. It broadcasts news, plays local music, points to the meaning of events and emphasizes on developmental and peace-building projects. It also covers the work of MONUC and other specialized agencies of the UN. In addition to daily news broadcasts, the station runs two important magazine programmes: *"Dialogue entre Congolais"* and *Gutahuka*.

Dialogue entre Congolais

Previously entitled *"Dialogue inter-Congolais"* (Inter-Congolese Dialogue), after the Sun City talks, the programme name was subtly changed to *"Dialogue entre Congolais"*

(Dialogue between Congolese) in April 2002. The reason for the change according to Jerome Ngongo Taunya, then Head of Radio Okapi's Political Desk, is because the ICD did not end with a comprehensive agreement between all the parties to the conflict. While the Kinshasa government led by Joseph Kabila and the MLC led by Jean Pierre Bemba had agreed with the conclusion of the ICD, the RCD and some other groups wanted the ICD to continue until a comprehensive agreement was reached. With the dispute and the various controversies concerning the ICD,

> It became embarrassing for Okapi to keep Dialogue intercongolais as the title of the broadcast. It would have been seen as backing those who thought the Inter-Congolese Dialogue was still ongoing. (Taunya 2004, 61)

MONUC has two slots to explain its activities to the Congolese population. The first slot, titled *"En direct avec le Porte-parole de la Monuc"* (Live on air with MONUC's Spokesman), is a question and answer slot where listeners have the chance of calling in to speak with MONUC's spokesman concerning issues of interest or simply to ask questions. Questions range from the political process to reports of humanitarian disasters or attacks by armed groups.

The second slot is broadcast weekly. It is titled *"Fenetre Ouverte sur la Monuc"* (Open Window on MONUC). It features an interview with the Special Representative of the Secretary General. Contents of the interview are made into news. In addition, the station also broadcasts the SRSG's weekly press conference.

Radio Okapi's Network

Radio Okapi's network has expanded massively within the last five years. In addition to the large network, Radio Okapi also collaborates with community radio stations across the country to rebroadcast their news and other programmes. Several factors drive Radio Okapi's deployment strategy. But the most crucial is the presence of an MONUC office in the town and the need for peace efforts therein. The most unstable parts of the country particularly in the east have benefited most from Radio Okapi's expansion efforts, and the deployment follows MONUC's deployment pattern. Radio Okapi's network of transmitting stations and partners across the DRC shows a higher concentration in the east where armed groups continue to operate. The UN also has robust presence in the areas.

7 Radio Okapi: The Making of a "Congolese Voice"

Radio is hugely popular in the Democratic Republic of Congo. It can doubtless, easily shape social and political discourses in the country. The UN-backed Radio Okapi is unique in many ways. It is structurally and operationally different from previous UN Mission radio projects. Radio Okapi is a partnership between the UN and the Swiss-based NGO – Hirondelle Foundation. While previous UN radio stations were directly operated by the UN, Radio Okapi is operated by Hirondelle Foundation but under the authority of the Special Representative of the Secretary General and Head of MONUC. Moreover, Radio Okapi sets its own news and information agenda. In its statement of values, Radio Okapi states its commitment to independence and autonomy. Its information programmes are "comprehensive, unbiased, independent and correct" (Radio Okapi 2006). Hirondelle Foundation's operation of Radio Okapi is driven by the philosophy that objective and impartial information should describe the realities of the conflict without any kind of embellishment. Hirondelle Foundation's leaders prefer not to frame Radio Okapi along any normative media regime such as development journalism or civic journalism. According to the Foundation's President, Jean-Marie Etter, Radio Okapi practices plain journalism, pure and simple – true, objective information and no embellishments (interview on 15 August 2007).

To have a clear and robust understanding of Radio Okapi – its ideology, ethical orientation, programme intentions and sustainability plans, in-depth interviews were conducted with the leadership of Hirondelle Foundation (HF). The interview followed an unstructured format. Three of the interviews were conducted personally at the headquarters of HF in Lausanne, Switzerland, while two were conducted on telephone with Caroline Vuillemin. The interviews were conducted at different periods in 2007. The following staff were interviewed: President of HF **Mr. Jean-Marie Etter**; Deputy Director **Mr. Dario Baroni**; Head of Sustainability **Mr. Jean-Pierre Husi**; and (then) Programme Officer of Radio Okapi **Ms. Caroline Vuillemin**.[8]

7.1 Creation of Radio Okapi: The IGO/NGO Mix

Radio Okapi was not borne out of a carefully planned UN policy; it was birthed out of necessity.

After the Lusaka Ceasefire Agreement was signed in 1999 by the six warring countries in Africa's Great Lakes region (Democratic Republic of Congo, Angola, Namibia, Zimbabwe, Rwanda and Uganda) and belligerent forces in the Democratic Republic of Congo, The UN Security Council deployed UN liaison personnel

---

8 Ms. Vuillemin now works as Operational Director of Fondation Hirondelle.

in August 1999 to support and monitor compliance with the ceasefire agreement. The liaison office became the UN Organization Mission in the Democratic Republic of Congo (MONUC). Acting under Chapter VII of the UN Charter, UN Resolution 1291 (2000) expanded the size and mandate of MONUC. But like most UN Mission mandates, the Resolution did not clearly articulate any public information responsibility to inform the Congolese on the peace process. Although the mandate authorized MONUC to support and cooperate closely with the Facilitator of the Congolese National Dialogue (par. 7 h), the mission was not empowered to provide information to the Congolese on the proceedings of the national dialogue. At this time, the DRC, the size of Western Europe, did not have any national radio or television station. So there was clearly a huge information gap between Kinshasa, tenuously held by government forces, and the other regions controlled then by different rebel groups and guerrilla entrepreneurs. Aware of the potential dangers such information gap posed to the peace process, and how long it would take the UN to authorize and set up a Radio Station, then Assistant Secretary General on Humanitarian Affairs, (late) Mr. Sergio Vieira de Mello asked Jean-Marie Etter and his associates at HF if they could set up a radio station in the DRC as quickly as possible – between 15 days and one month. HF had extensive experience of running radio projects in areas of conflicts including Liberia, Kosovo, Central African Republic (CAR) and in East Timor where they had worked with the UN Mission there to jointly produce a radio programme for Timor refugees. Jean-Marie Etter and his colleagues accepted the challenge, and in December 2001 a Memorandum of Understanding (renewed yearly ever since) was signed between the UN and HF to set up Radio Okapi in the DRC. The station was launched in February 2002. Radio Okapi therefore is a partnership of Hirondelle Foundation and the United Nations. While it functions as a Public Information arm of the UN Mission in the DRC, it is co-managed by MONUC and Hirondelle Foundation. Another unique element of Radio Okapi is that it is designed to outlive the UN Mission in the DRC.

The circumstance under which radio okapi was created suggests that collaboration between the UN and HF was based more on expediency than on a carefully researched IGO/NGO joint approach to information intervention.
If anything, it suggested a lack of policy than a carefully thought out policy. Although the partnership was created to get around UN bureaucracy, it seemed to depart from the UN's bureaucratic tradition because within the UN whenever expediency collided with principle or doctrine the former usually makes way. On the other hand, it can be argued that since the UN doctrine on Information Operations recommends the use of the most appropriate means of reaching specific target audience, it does give room for innovative approaches based on exigencies on ground. Moreover, this was the second time that HF would be invited by Special Representative Sergio de Mello to establish a radio station under a UN administration. The first was in 1999, when HF set up Radio Blue Sky in Pristina, Kosovo, under the UN Mission in Kosovo (UNMIK). Although

Radio Okapi was more of a child of expediency than a research-backed policy, it, like Blue Sky, fitted Monroe Price's (2000) prescription of an alliance between NGOs and IGOs to effect media transformation in post-conflict states.

Radio Okapi is run by HF but the programmes are under the general authority of the UN Secretary General's Special Representative in the DRC.

This collaboration offers a refreshing model for post-conflict information intervention because of its unique IGO/NGO collaboration. Hirondelle Foundation is an organization of journalists that specialize in setting up and operating media services in crisis areas. There are other international NGOs such as US-based Search For Common Ground and Holland-based LaBenevolencija that work in developing media in crises states. But Hirondelle Foundation is the only organization that has the specialization in creating and building radio stations in Africa from scratch. Most other NGOs such as SFCG and LaBenevolencija have specializations in developing specific radio programmes such as soaps, drama and spots.

Based in Lausanne, Switzerland, Hirondelle Foundation has created and managed several radio stations in crises states since its creation in 1995. Here is a list of their projects:

- Radio Agatashya in the Great Lakes region of Africa
- Star Radio in Liberia
- the Hirondelle News Agency at the International Criminal Tribunal for at Arusha in Tanzania
- Radio Blue Sky in Kosovo
- Radio Ndeke Luka in Bangui in the Central African Republic
- *Moris Hamutuk*, a radio programme for refugees in Timor
- Radio Okapi in the Democratic Republic of Congo
- Miraya FM in Sudan
- Cotton Tree News in Sierra Leone
- support to Nepal National Radio, Radio Nepal

The above projects have all had varying degrees of success. Radio Agatashya, for instance, was shut down in October 1996 when its station was attacked and equipment looted by armed groups. In Liberia, the organization's radio station frequently had political collisions with the government of President Charles Taylor, and it resulted in the ban of the station in 1999. The station was reopened after intervention by the US and other foreign Governments.

Hirondelle Foundation's information intervention programmes are driven on the principle that independent media has a fundamental role in societies where authoritarian and non-democratic regimes are in power. In such situations, where traditional media are intimidated and are forced to stay silent, Hirondelle Foundation believes that "independent radio can play a crucial role in furthering peace by dissipating rumours, avoiding propaganda and focusing attention on hard facts". Its main objective during intervention is to create a responsible and civic-minded exchange of opinions and dialogue so that justice and healing can take place.

7.2 Mandate and Funding

Radio Okapi's mandate is to promote the process of dialogue and peacebuilding.
It aims to provide unbiased information on its news contents. But the station does much more, it plays local music and this helps to draw youths. They also broadcast interactive programmes, service programmes and magazines. The crews at Radio Okapi are entirely locally staffed, except for the project leader. This lays a strong foundation for the continued existence of the radio after the UN Mission.

HF's funding is exclusively project-based.
Its projects are funded by governments of the following countries and international organizations: Switzerland, the United States, the Netherlands, Sweden, Britain, France and Canada; the European Union, United Nations High Commissioner for Refugees, UNESCO, the International Committee of the Red Cross, Organisation internationale de la Francophonie, the International Foundation for Electoral Systems (IFES) and the United Nations Development Programme. The extent to which HF's funding profile affects Radio Okapi's credibility on the ground and its editorial independence is subject to debates and further research. Since independence, the Congolese have been wary of foreign-backed intervention packages and overtures. But high listenership and audience participation rates suggest that Radio Okapi has indeed earned the confidence of a high number of citizens in the DRC. According to data from HF, Radio Okapi has a penetration index of 67% in the entire DRC. Its broadcasts can be received on the FM band and short-wave band. The short-wave band was launched on 1 March 2005 and broadcasts from a transmitting station in South Africa. It broadcasts in French and four national languages: Lingala, Tshiluba, Swahili and Kikongo.

7.3 Challenges

The major challenge of Radio Okapi at inception was to break the hegemony of powerful groups over information.
Breaking the hegemony of powerful groups over information called for a reconstruction of the Congolese public sphere so that ordinary citizens can have access to the media to tell their personal stories, their suppressed truths including difficult ones such as rape, abuse and personal loss. Integrating such personal stories of the

past, the present and hopes for the future within the framework of public narrative is never easy in the DRC. Already two of its journalists have been shot dead – Serge Maheshe in 2007 and Didace Namujimbo in 2008 while a few others have suffered intimidation.

7.4 Sustainability

Radio Okapi will be there long after the UN is gone.
Closing the station may result in a loss of democratic space for expression. Indeed, Jean-Pierre Husi told me that the United Nations is fully minded to ensure the station continues after its mission in the DRC. The plan is to register a Non-Governmental Organization in the DRC to take over the station at the termination of the UN Mission. Although the UN intends to donate Radio Okapi's infrastructure and equipment to the NGO that will eventually take over its operations, the major challenge would be the ability of the new owners to generate their own income or to attract the kind of funding that HF and the UN have achieved. Another challenge would be how to ensure that the new NGO has a strong enough status to avoid pressure from government and powerful social groups in the country. Already a Sustainability Unit has been created within Radio Okapi and a transitory organization has been set up to understudy the HF team and progressively take over responsibility.

Figure 7.1 illustrates the editorial focus of Radio Okapi over the different phases of the DRC conflict. The phases are derived from Lederach's (1997) *Time Dimension in Peacebuilding.* The locus at each phase demonstrates the editorial focus of Radio Okapi's information programmes. The four loci identify time-framed interventions. Multiple actions can be taken by information interveners in any conflict transformation cycle, but what is shown on each locus is Radio Okapi's editorial focus relevant to each transformation phase. The underlying current in this plan is that there is no quick-fix to conflict transformation (Lederach 1997).

Basically information intervention moves across four progressive timeframes of conflict: emergency disaster response and signing of peace agreements; political reforms; relational transformation; and economic/educational reconstruction and development. The plan harmonizes overlapping media interventions with the social and psychological semiotics of the conflict and long-term transformational goals. Information intervention is thus broken into operational units to create a coherent framework for media programming.

Radio Okapi broadcasts critical information programmes using different frames (including long-form profiles, town-hall style discussions with media consumers).

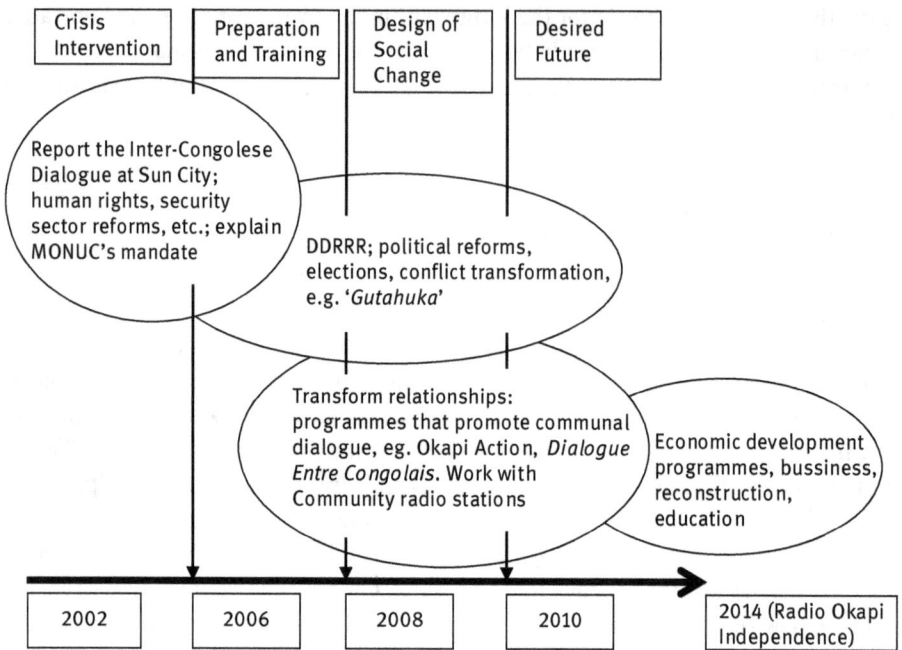

Figure 7.1: Radio Okapi's Editorial Focus across Conflict Phases – From Creation to 2010 (Post-Conflict Phase)

7.5 News and Information Programmes

News is broadcast in five languages.

There is also Daily Information on MONUC's activities and the peace process. During the programme, MONUC's spokesman answers live questions from listeners. There is also a weekly information programme titled *Fenetre Ouverte sur la MONUC* (Open Window on MONUC). The programme reports news events, rebel movements and their participation in DDRRR. There are also the following key Magazine Programmes:

– *Dialogue inter-Congolais* (Inter-Congolese Dialogue) now *Dialogue entre Congolaise* (Dialogue between Congolese): this is a political news magazine programme – the first of its kind in the DRC. It started as a platform for interaction between Congolese politicians and rebel groups participating in the UN-backed Inter-Congolese National Dialogue in Sun City, South Africa. For the first time, belligerents in the DRC were able to discuss their grievances openly.

– *Gutahuka:* A daily broadcast targeting Rwandan rebels in Congo. The objective of the programme is to persuade Rwandan Hutu combatants to leave the DRC.

– *Okapi Action:* Town-hall style talk show programme on human rights, social/ infrastructural developments, etc. Another first of its kind in the DRC, the programme affords listeners the window to phone and talk directly with NGO and development experts on issues of personal and communal interests.

Intervention programmes on Radio Okapi generally use different "frames" to cultivate social dialogue. In a country where the sourcing and construction of news by media outlets (both mainstream and clandestine) is intimately aligned with the opinions and aspirations of powerful social groups, such multiple news frames drawn from both libertarian and communitarian doctrines can play a critical role.

8 Information Operations: Contents and Metrics of Effectiveness

One of the most difficult challenges of the UN Mission in the DRC, in addition to its stability functions, was how to deal with deep inter-ethnic prejudices particularly in the eastern part of the country. As previously discussed, politics of ethnicity, citizenship and nationality has been part of the DRC's body politic since colonial rule. However, it was during the government of Mobutu Sese Seko that ethnicity, citizenship and nationality became sorely contested and rewarded, depending obviously on what side of the ethnic-citizenship divide your find yourself in. Even if all the rebel networks are diminished and all the guerrilla entrepreneurs in Eastern DRC are taken out, there can be no true conflict transformation or peace in the DRC if careful and deliberate effort is not made to build inter-group trust and cooperation. The greatest information operations challenge then for the UN in the DRC was not confined to persuading rebels to stop fighting. It included convincing the Congolese that it was in their own interest to lay aside their prejudices and build their society. In this chapter, attention is given to specific programs that can potentially achieve the two cardinal objectives of a successful mission in the DRC – convincing fighters to disarm and transforming inter-group prejudice. The chapter also explores methodological approaches to ascertaining effectiveness and impacts of interventions.

Contemporary understanding of the extent to which intervention media can change prejudiced perceptions of the Other and violent behaviour is vague. Also limited is our understanding of what really works in terms of the content of information intervention: the Information Approach that provides objective information without any embellishments or the psychological operations (or Psyops) approach broadly defined as planned operations to "convey selected information and indicators to foreign audiences to influence emotions, motives, objective reasoning" with the intention of inducing or reinforcing foreign attitudes and behaviour favourable to the originator's objectives (Joint Publications 3–13.2).

The intention of this chapter is firstly to highlight the different approaches to public information operations as adopted by MONUC on the one hand and Hirondelle Foundation on the other. The chapter also describes the innovative empirical approach used to evaluate the impacts of two typical intervention radio programmes on relations between two ethnic networks in South Kivu, Eastern DRC, in order to ascertain the nature of impacts in each information intervention approach.

The two intervention radio programmes are: *Dialogue entre Congolais* (Dialogue between Congolese) and *Gutahuka* ("go back home" in Kinyarwanda). Both programmes are broadcast on the UN-backed Radio Okapi. *Dialogue entre Congolaise* (*Dialogue* hereafter) is a political news-magazine programme broadcast twice daily, Monday to Friday, on Radio Okapi. It explains the peace process and gives opportunities to belligerents to discuss their grievances openly. *Gutahuka* on the other hand is produced directly by MONUC and aired daily, Monday to Saturday, on Radio Okapi and a network of partner radio stations to explain MONUC's Disarmament, Demobilization, Repatriation, Resettlement and Reintegration (DDRRR) programme. But *Gutahuka* does much more, and its specific targets are Rwandan Hutus in Eastern DRC; it seeks to convince them, particularly FDLR combatants, to return to Rwanda. It tells stories of reformed Hutu militants that have returned and were followed all the way to their villages in Rwanda by the programme's production team. It also consists of messages from families in Rwanda urging Rwandan Hutus in general and militants in particular still in the Eastern DRC not to be afraid to return home. The programme is not produced by Radio Okapi, but directly by MONUC's Audio/Video Production Unit and given not only to Radio Okapi to broadcast but also to other radio stations in Eastern DRC. This distinction is important as it will be later explained that the contents of the programme are at variance with "Informative Approach" espoused by Hirondelle Foundation in that it seeks "to induce or reinforce (Hutu militants') attitudes and behaviour favourable to the originator's objectives". International stations such as the BBC and the VOA in the Great Lakes region have previously turned down MONUC's requests to broadcast the programme because it contradicts their in-house policies.

8.1 Between Dialogue and Gutahuka: Streamlining the Debates

Within the UN itself, the preferred communications approach to public information operations remains contested. On his part, Hirondelle Foundation's Jean-Marie Etter believes that "in the long run, in areas of violent conflict, an Informative Approach – which may have fewer results in the short term, but will be more solid and will build confidence in the long term – will eventually be preferred" (quoted in Domeniconi 2004, 45). There has not been much empirical research on cases of this nature to find out what approach really works over time.

To have a more robust understanding of Radio Okapi and the ideological leanings of the two programmes – *Dialogue* and *Gutahuka* produced by Hirondelle Foundation's Radio Okapi and MONUC's audio production unit, respectively – in-depth personal interviews were conducted with the President of Hirondelle Foundation Mr. Jean-Marie Etter and other key actors at Hirondelle Foundation as well as with MONUC's Spokesman at the time and other key informants at MONUC.

Dialogue Represents Radio Okapi's Informative Approach

One of the unique features of Radio Okapi is that it has a policy of not editorializing. Hirondelle Foundation's methods are derived from the organization's experience working in crises states over two decades and from the expertise of their in-house staff. The Foundation's President, Jean-Marie Etter, believes that providing only frank and truthful information in conflict zones can help create stability and reduce panic and can be a tool for peace.

> Our experience now allows me to say that we know that just giving news is by itself a tool of peace and a very important one and it is in fact the basis on which you can build the other things. And everywhere, in Kosovo, in Liberia, in Rwanda, in Congo and everywhere, we realize that in conflict zones people have a tremendous need for accurate information and you can also experience that when you wake up in the morning and want to go anywhere, the question you ask yourself is what's happening today, can I get out of my house? What happened at night? Is everything calm? And you need to know these things. It is information you just need. And this is a basic, fundamental need because you are tired of staying at home and not moving at all. – Jean-Marie Etter[9]

This view was corroborated by Caroline Vuillemin, who was at the time Hirondelle Foundation's Programme Officer for Radio Okapi. She said Radio Okapi is purely an information radio. She said Radio Okapi sticks strictly to the information-only principle and would not broadcast dramas because such programmes tell people to take a particular form of action, hence conflicting with Radio Okapi's principles. When I asked her about *Gutahuka,* she said *Gutahuka* was an exception, although it is contrary to Hirondelle Foundation's ideology, it is broadcast daily principally because it was proposed and produced by MONUC. Ms. Vuillemin suggested that Hirondelle Foundation would not ordinarily include *Gutahuka* on its broadcast schedule because:

> If we want to talk about a specific rebel group or a community that is affected by the war or something, we will talk about it in our political show 'Dialogue entre Congolais' and do a debate on that but not prepare a 15 minute recording saying, you know, these rebels are bad and these things they do and you people should do that or this. This is not the way we work. – Caroline Vuillemin[10]

Essentially, Hirondelle Foundation would have preferred to use a different approach to achieve voluntary repatriation of foreign combatants in Eastern DRC. Left to Hirondelle Foundation, the task of persuading the FDLR to disarm would have been handled in the programme *Dialogue* because of their belief that at the long run an Informative Approach achieves more desirable objectives than *Gutahuka's* BCC approach. This position was corroborated by the Foundation's Deputy Director, Dario Baroni, in a separate interview with the author in Lausanne, Switzerland, on 22 November 2006. Mr. Baroni said Hirondelle Foundation's programmes are not intended to change or manipulate the state of mind of audiences as in *Gutahuka* but to purvey information on what is happening. "We bring what is behind the walls", he said. In distinguishing the approach of Radio Okapi from the approach of a "Peace Radio", Baroni said a Peace Radio may decide not to give information, or not to emphasize particular elements of the information that is judged to be capable of inciting the public to violence

---

9 Interview with author on 15 August 2007, Lausanne, Switzerland.
10 Telephone interview with author on 5 December 2006.

or hate. But Radio Okapi's informative approach on the other hand is to provide objective information by purveying all the views and interviewing all parties concerned in an "impartial and unbiased manner".[11] Objective information can achieve sustainable consensus building and common grounds by providing a platform for public debate on the common good. This approach can enable communities to know why a particular party to the conflict or the Other community feels aggrieved and what it would take to bring them to the reconciliation table.

8.2 Ethical Foundations of Hirondelle Foundation's Approach

Radio Okapi's Information Approach is derived from the organization's ethical standards honed over the years from its experience in conflict situations. Essentially, in conflict situations, fear is generated when communities are aware that there are differences between conflict parties without having any truthful knowledge of the nature of the problem and the intentions of the parties. A radio programme that creates a platform for conflicting parties to openly talk about and debate their positions with opponents can help to create confidence among the conflict parties and dissipate tension and fear among the population because people have better knowledge of their disagreement. Etter gave an example of two Generals in the Congolese Army that had bitter disagreements with each other. They were both invited to debate their differences on *Dialogue*. During the programme both Generals talked about their differences openly and frankly and answered questions from the Moderator and audiences. At the end, they resolved their disputes amicably on air. A key factor promoted in *Dialogue*, he said, is transparency, which, according to him, helps to reduce fear. To buttress his point fully, it is useful to quote him here at length:

> *We know that in conflict zones, people want and need accurate information, complete information. We also know that people want political debates and in conflict zones very often when people have an argument either it is hidden or secret, ... they try to settle, but they do that behind closed doors. It is a secret procedure and nobody knows what they do and why they do not agree – what is the problem and so on. This is what makes fear, it is the source of fear – people don't know, they don't even know what they should be afraid of. But when you bring those disputes, those arguments into the public scene and ok, this general and that general do not agree and they say it publicly and all the country knows they do not agree, why they do not agree, what it is all about, and then it becomes much more human, it becomes understandable. I mean it does not necessarily solve the problem, sometimes it does, but at least it becomes understandable. Because people know what it is about. ... Just by understanding, and just by knowing what it is about (people) can engage. –* Etter[12]

---

11 Dario Baroni – interview with author on 22 November 2006, Lausanne.
12 Interview with author on 15 August 2007, Lausanne.

Hirondelle Foundation's information intervention programmes are therefore driven on the primary objectives of providing information and creating a platform for responsible and civic-minded exchange of opinions and dialogue aimed at achieving greater citizen engagement with new democratic values and institutions. Their position essentially is that objective information eliminates or reduces fear and creates a platform for citizens to be engaged with transformational or conflict resolution processes. Hence, as a policy Radio Okapi does not editorialize or purvey its own comments.

> *We don't have commentaries, we do not give opinions we give the different views, debates and we have interviews, so all the political parties responsible for the people that are in charge can say what their opinion is. They are welcome. But we as Radio Okapi we do not comment. – Etter, Ibid.*

It is prudent to question the nature of opinion by *the political parties responsible for the people* that are allowed access on Radio Okapi particularly when considering the fragile nature of the society it operates in. The social and political problems associated with such "Truth-Telling" activities have been genealogically debated by Michel Foucault in his lecture on *Parrhesia* (the ancient Greek culture of "Truth-Telling"). One of the main problems of Parrhesia in the emerging democratic Greek society was the nature of opinions accorded *Parrhesiastic* access (Foucault 2001). *Parrhesia* could be dangerous when it is used in a pejorative sense – dissidents using the freedom of opinion and open access to make incendiary comments which, Foucault notes, could pose danger to a city (Foucault 2001). This was the case during the 2006 Presidential Election in the DRC when defeated candidate of the Movement for the Liberation of Congo (MLC) Mr. Jean-Pierre Bemba was interviewed for a news programme in Radio Okapi. Mr. Bemba had earlier rejected the outcome of the election and called on party members to make their voices heard. The UN considered that granting Bemba air-time on Radio Okapi was capable of inciting violence and asked editors of Radio Okapi to call off or at least delay broadcast of the interview until tensions dissipate. Although the broadcast was delayed for two weeks, there were still clashes between Bemba's supporters and supporters of the winner, President Joseph Kabila, after the interview. Again, this suggests the potential impact of negative or pejorative *Parrhesia*. For Radio Okapi editors, it was their responsibility to also purvey Mr. Bemba's side of the story by granting him access.

8.3 Conceptualizing Hirondelle Foundation's "Informative Approach" in Conflict Zones

During conflicts, there are fundamental information needs that are as important even as food and health care. In crises societies, objective and reliable information may be all that people need. The public would normally gravitate towards whoever satisfies that need. In developing an information campaign in conflict or post-conflict societies, there is a fundamental need for information support for critical elements of the intervention.

Information Support for Humanitarian Relief

In situations of conflict or complex emergencies, there is usually a shortage of credible information – sometimes such information deprivation is a deliberate strategy by the warring factions. Media intervention to provide objective information can immensely help reduce fear. It can also prevent combatants from taking pre-emptive action based on suspicion of the intentions of enemy parties. Objective information can also enable citizens to know where to go for help or whether to relocate, stay indoors, etc. Information on the conflict, human rights issues, health, education, etc. can prepare citizens for a post-conflict reconstruction phase and redefine their view of the conflict from objective lenses.

Information, particularly through radio, can reach isolated populations in cut-off areas affected by war or disasters and enable them to know what is going on in other parts of the country. Knowledge of causes of the conflict, peace agreements signed, parties that have surrendered, etc. can help in reducing tensions and countering the propaganda of armed groups who would otherwise want to keep the populace uninformed or misinformed.

Information Support for Peacebuilding and DDR/RR

Information can support the process and basis for DDR and in the case of foreign combatants in the DRC, repatriation and reintegration in their homeland. Objective information on opportunities for training, skill development or integration in the national army and the rewards therein is capable of making current or ex-combatants and commanders to make informed choices about their future and that of their community and their roles there in. Objective information about democratic reforms, new institutions to support peace and democracy, emerging economic opportunities as well as long-term opportunities for reintegration can help combatants to understand new economic, social and political opportunities available to them if they choose to renounce violence and participate in ongoing reconstruction processes. Unembellished information can then form the basis for combatants or armed groups to decide for themselves whether to join the peace process or not.

Furthermore, an objective media can play a critical role in the peace process by objectively explaining complex peace negotiations and the incentives or opportunities there-in for all parties involved. Peace agreements can be explained within the context of immediate and remote causes of the conflict, hence creating a well-informed citizenry that is able to provide feedback. Objective information can neutralize the sensational reports of the regional or factional media which often take one side or the other when reporting peace agreements or negotiations. The role of objective information thus is to truthfully report ongoing peace processes, agreements, concessions, etc. This is important in conflict situations particularly in divided societies where agreements or concessions are viewed with suspicion or even seen as capitulation. Oftentimes, expectations are skewed by vested interests in the conflicts. Objective information devoid of sensationalism can therefore contribute to long-term stability or conflict transformation by managing expectations, providing details and implications of peace agreements, providing information about the other parties thus allaying fears or suspicions about them.

Objective reports about procedural and retributive justice systems and procedures including truth and reconciliation commissions, war crime trials, etc. can enable citizens to connect with the events in a positive way and reduce or eliminate fear of victimization. Furthermore, reports of events in other parts of the country can create a common sense of nationalism particularly in cases where the country was divided not only politically but also geographically by war.

Information Support for Credible Elections

Objective media is an essential element in the organization of peaceful, free and fair elections in crises states. Objective Information campaigns can mobilize the electorate to register to vote and participate peacefully in the electioneering process. Furthermore, information about voting centres, procedures, policies of candidates or political parties can enhance civic participation. With adequate information, citizens can become more aware of their civic responsibilities and the imperatives of casting their votes for transformational candidates and not just candidates that pursue ethnic, regional or religious agenda.

But beyond providing information, objective media can also play a watch-dog role by publicizing results promptly, monitoring votes and reporting irregularities. For instance, during the July 2006 Presidential Elections in the DRC, Radio Okapi began broadcasting special programmes dedicated to the election. These special information programmes were needful because it was the first general election in the country since independence from Belgium in 1960, and the Congolese needed to be informed about the processes, the political parties and the policies of candidates. The broadcasts, the first of its kind in the DRC, included live reports featuring journalists at polling stations, an hour long news bulletin, and a special two-hour edition of *Dialogue entre Congolais* featuring three experts who analysed the elections.

As a run-up to the election, Radio Okapi developed a self-regulatory document detailing its responsibilities and values during the electioneering campaigns. New information programmes were added to the broadcast schedule. One of the programmes, *"Le Débat"* (The Debate), aired in the five national languages, featured discussions between party representatives and candidates on national and regional issues. Another programme, *"Le Journal de Campagne"* (The Campaign Log) reported the campaigns and activities of the various political parties. It had two segments: the first, titled "Info Services Elections", provided detailed information on the political and electoral schedule; the second segment, titled *"Profession de Foi"* ("What I Believe"), gave various candidates, political parties and Civil Society groups the opportunity to express their views on a range of national and regional topics. When the presidential election results were published, Radio Okapi broadcast live the speech of the Chairman of the Electoral Commission. The station also broadcast the post-election violence in Kinshasa, from 20–22 August 2006, between bodyguards and supporters of President Joseph Kabila and the opposition Presidential candidate, former Vice-President Jean-Pierre Bemba of the MLC.

Radio Okapi's role of providing robust information during the election was critical to the success of the election which ushered in a post-conflict phase in the DRC. Radio Okapi worked with the electoral commission to pass their message to the population. Indeed, Radio Okapi was the only channel on the election day and after to be able to go out to polling stations reporting that the election was going on as planned without any problems and that people are voting. It really contributed to reassuring the population as a whole.

Information Support for Accountable Governance

By reporting events objectively and creating a platform for civic participation in national debates, intervention media can support the development of a responsible and transparent government that sees itself as accountable to the people. Moreover, when citizens are well informed of government's programmes, they tend to be better engaged with them. This can thus prevent corruption which if left unchecked can threaten peace. Also, intervention media can provide objective information on the activities and responsibilities of government institutions. Such information can help strengthen new democratic institutions and thus support the new government.

Information Support for Humanitarianism

Hirondelle Foundation's position is that Radio Okapi's "humanitarian mandate" is different from the behaviour/attitudinal change objectives in Radio Missions that have *Stabilization* mandates. The objective of the media during stabilization missions, appropriately named CfS or Communication for Stabilization, is to provide "conflict sensitive news" and create programmes to achieve behavioural and attitudinal change.

In different interviews with leaders and programme staff of Hirondelle Foundation, Radio Okapi's mandate is consistently portrayed as humanitarian and its objective as providing factual and objective information in the DRC. Lack of information in situations of war and political emergencies is indeed a humanitarian need worthy of intervention.

Deliberate information deprivation or negative uses of the tools of information by politicians or guerrilla entrepreneurs ought to be seen at the same par as natural disasters or grave humanitarian violations worthy of some form of international intervention. Where groups are uninformed, misinformed or disinformed as a deliberate strategy or for the purpose of committing atrocities against humanity, it is needful for the international community as in other cases of humanitarian crises to intervene by countering the incendiary media through the provision of accurate and objective information. Jamming the broadcasts of incendiary media is a rather simplistic reaction to a much deeper form of relationship that exists between the listener and the "speaker" or the incendiary media source. When a broadcast signal is jammed or a transmitter bombed, it is only one side of the relationship that is dealt with while the other side remains and could even become disgruntled. Radio must be fought with radio. Wrong or false information fought with right or correct information. The way to fight hate radio is to convince people that listen to this radio that it is hate, false and harmful radio. This can be done through the provision of truthful and objective information – using another radio.

Objective and accurate information is required to win over listeners of hate radio. Essentially, this approach demands of itself more than merely silencing the incendiary voice or using persuasive tools to convince listeners to adopt a desired form of behaviour. Its totem is objective information – a rigorous treatment of facts – which, at the long run, can transform negative discourses, create a more engaged population and promote dialogue across political or ethnic divides in crises states.

The Informative Approach of Dialogue

Hirondelle Foundation's Informative approach is evident in its flagship programme *Dialogue entre Congolais*. During the period of listenership monitoring (4 December 2008–6 January 2010), a total of 335 topics were discussed in 284 fresh *Dialogue* episodes broadcast on Radio Okapi. Each episode lasted 45 minutes and was broadcast twice daily during weekdays – from 7.15 pm to 8 pm and from 4.15 am to 5 am. The scheduling of this programme is instructive. Mano (2005), Hendy (2000) and Ellis (2000) have all written eloquently on the implications of broadcast programme scheduling. They affirm that scheduling suggests a deliberate positioning and sequencing of programmes to attract specific audiences at specific times. Indeed as Mano has noted, broadcasters "consciously seek to find appropriate programme for particular and relevant moments in an already existing schedule" (2005, 95). The intention is to fit in particular programmes on programme schedules for the best times its intended audience would tune in to listen. In South Kivu, sundown (between 6 pm and 9 pm) is a critical programming moment because it is the time that families, friends, age-grade associations, etc. sit together at the end of the day to banter and listen to radio. It is a prime time for achieving group listenership. The repeat slot at 4.15 am follows *Gutahuka* which is broadcast from 3.45 am to 4.15 am. This sequence is meant to get *Gutahuka* listeners to also listen to *Dialogue* and to reach early-risers and lone listeners. In South Kivu, it is not uncommon for people to tune to radio late at night or very early in the morning. This is because early morning is when the broadcast signals are clearest. Those that tune to radio at this time do so for the main purpose of listening to news or to music. The two slots of *Dialogue* therefore is intended to reach as many listeners as possible – both group and lone listeners.

The programme draws on a model of dialogue, or information sharing that seeks, not necessarily to achieve behaviour change but to achieve mutual understanding, agreement and/or collective action. Jean-Marie Etter attempts to distinguish the Informative Approach of *Dialogue* and the approach in *Gutahuka* in a comment quoted in Domeniconi (2004):

> *The DDRRR awareness-raising message (Gutahuka) falls within the field of Communication. The aim of Communication is to get the audience to take action or make a gesture. The aim of the DDRRR message (Gutahuka) is to encourage foreign rebel combatants still based in the Democratic Republic of the Congo to go home. This does not prevent Communication from providing news that is accurate, of course, but the intention is different. The intention of (Hirondelle Foundation's Informative approach) is to reflect the true facts without seeking to elicit a specific form of behavior. I believe that in the long run, in areas of violent conflict, an "informative" approach – which may have fewer results in the short term, but will be more solid and will build confidence in the long term – will eventually be preferred (p. 4).*

Conceptually, *Dialogue's* Informative Approach is supported by Rogers and Kincaid's (1981) Convergence/network model of communication. Essential to the Convergence model is Rogers and Kincaid's argument that communication is a dynamic process of knowledge or information sharing through an ongoing process of dialogue or mutual interaction between or among active *participants*. Rogers and Kincaid's Convergence model addresses the intersection between shared information, mutual understanding and (collective) action. Information may originate from a participant, the actions of a group, radio news discourse or an organization such as church, mosque or an NGO. A key element in the model as shown in Figure 8.1 is that dialogue or information sharing occurs horizontally among participants. The outcome at the individual level is perception, interpretation and understanding which can lead to belief and subsequently mutual agreement. Another critical element in the model is that it implies an ongoing dialogue between participants until a mutual agreement is arrived at to enable (collective) action. It is important to note that within the model, individuals do not always converge – they can diverge. There could be misperceptions, misinterpretations, misunderstandings and disbeliefs which can ultimately lead to disagreements and conflicts. But the model envisages a cyclical process of dialogue between two psychological realities where the feedback gleaned can lead to more dialogues and potentially lead to mutual understanding, mutual agreement and collective action. Convergence does not necessarily imply perfect agreement but beliefs becoming more similar and more common and more in the same direction (Figueroa et al. 2002; Rogers and Kincaid 1981).

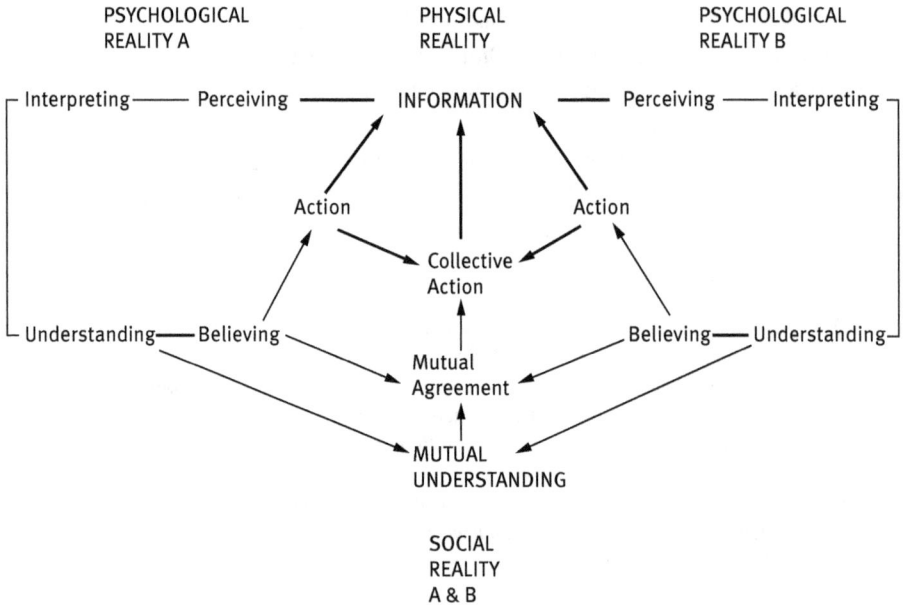

Figure 8.1: Components of Rogers and Kincaid's Convergence Model. (Source: Kincaid 1979; Rogers and Kincaid 1981; Figueroa et al. 2002)

8.4 MONUC's Approach to DDRRR

The UN's PIO approach to DDRRR in the DRC is novel. This is not unconnected with the unique nature of the DRC conflict. In previous cases, the UN's Disarmament, Demobilisation and Reintegration (DDR) activities involved troops within the countries of operation. In the DRC however, in addition to DDR, it involved additional components of Repatriation and Resettlement of foreign combatants to home or third countries. Further complicating this task is that the foreign armed groups, notably the FDLR, had not signed any peace agreements, and the UN is politically and militarily constrained when dealing with armed groups that do not have any peace agreements to honour. Although the UN partnered with the Congolese armed forces (by providing logistic support – such as food rations, helicopters, etc.) to engage the FDLR militarily, success was very minimal compared with the civilian casualties and the political ramifications thereof. The FDLR did not have any well-defined location or territory of control or communications installations that could be targeted. They either operated in the dense forests in Eastern DRC or lived among civilian Hutu populations. Military attempts (such as Operations *Umoja Wetu*, *Kimia II* and *Amani Leo*) to neutralize the FDLR resulted in disproportionate civilian casualties. Terrain posed another difficulty to the UN peacekeepers. The DRC is a vast country with dense forests and several parts that are completely inaccessible by road, hence providing an ideal terrain for an armed group to successfully operate and evade capture. With these unique challenges, it would have been inappropriate for the UN to model the DRC's DDRRR programme with any previous operations such as ONUC, UNMIL, UNAMSIL, UNMIBH, etc. To achieve a "voluntary" or non-military DDRRR of foreign combatants, the UN needed to firstly reach the combatants where they were and secondly try to convince them to come out of hiding and disarm, and thirdly repatriate them to Rwanda, rehabilitate them and reintegrate them in their communities. And this is where *Gutahuka* came in – a media intervention mechanism to reach combatants through radio and persuade them to come out of hiding and return "home" to Rwanda.

As previously noted, unlike other programmes which are produced by Radio Okapi's production unit, *Gutahuka* is produced by the Audio and Video Production Unit of MONUC's Public Information Department. The MONUC production team travels regularly to the reintegration camp in Motubo, Western Rwanda, and other parts of Rwanda to meet and interview repatriated ex-combatants in reintegration camps and family members. *Gutahuka* is broadcast not only by Radio Okapi but also by other radio stations across Eastern DRC and directly through mobile transmitters in the dense forests of the region. But of all the broadcasters, Radio Okapi is the main medium of broadcasting the programme basically due to its wide reach and partnership with the UN. The programme, which is broadcast daily, consists of three segments. The first explains the DDRRR process and the second segment features "true stories" of ex-combatants who have returned to Rwanda. Families of ex-combatants as well as former FDLR Commanders that have returned are also interviewed in the second segment, and usually they talk of conditions at the homeland and urge fighters to set aside their fear and return. The third segment is the call by the narrator on combatants to take up MONUC's offer of repatriation while it is still possible. International broadcasters with high credibility in the region have been approached by the UN to air the programme, albeit without success. The VOA, for instance, has declined to air the programme but have left the door open for broadcasting select interviews from the programme in future. The BBC World Service also declined to broadcast the programme for ethical reasons. Ironically, the British government had been the main sponsor of *Gutahuka* and various other "Soft Power" strategies in support of DDRRR in 2009–10 fiscal year. Through the African Conflict Prevention Pool (jointly funded by the DfID, MOD and FCO), the UK government provided $391,000 in 2009 mainly for the purpose of enhancing targeted sensitization to repatriate FDLR commanders, provision of communications support and capacity building for local radio stations involved in the broadcast of the programme.

MONUC officials[13] interviewed said that the purpose of *Gutahuka* is to speak to "individual combatants" of the FDLR in particular and Rwandan Hutus in the DRC in general to lay down their arms and return home. According to MONUC's Spokesman, Madnodje Mounoubai, *Gutahuka* is an "alternative to military pressure" and was designed to fulfil the DDRRR mandate of the mission. He described *Gutahuka* as:

> *a response to the difficulties to reach the FDLR combatants and an attempt to get information to non combatants ... to provide them with information on how they can go back to their country on a voluntary basis.*– Madnodje Mounoubai (then MONUC's Spokesman)[14]

On Radio Okapi, *Gutahuka* is broadcast daily on weekdays and on Saturdays between 3.45 am and 4.15 pm. Various other radio stations and mobile broadcast units in South Kivu broadcast the programme at different periods but mostly early mornings and late evenings. The scheduling of *Gutahuka* at this seemingly odd hour can be attributed to two primary reasons. First, the prime targets of the programme (FDLR combatants) usually listened to the programme secretly because their commanders see listening to *Gutahuka* as an early sign of treachery. Secondly, most of the combatants would normally not have the time to listen to radio during the day because of their kind of routines.

Conceptualizing MONUC's Psyop Approach

For the UN, an information intervention approach that uses communication creatively can achieve immediate results and also help fulfil overall Mission stabilization objectives. The organization, structure and contents of *Gutahuka* can be seen as Psyop. Generally, the purpose of Psyops is to *induce* or *reinforce* the attitudes and behaviours of usually an opposing or foreign audience to favour the originator's objectives. Although Psyops has been rebranded and given different names to avoid an association with lies and deception, the central purpose remains the same – using tools of communication to influence perceptions, attitudes and behaviours of opponents. Psyops is one of the forms of Strategic Communications (...). MONUC's approach to Psyops is demonstrated in the three main elements of the programme *Gutahuka*:

---

13 During the course of the research, a number of MONUC staff were interviewed 'informally', but they preferred not to be quoted since they were not authorized to make official statements. Only MONUC's Official Spokesman, Madnodje Mounoubai, accepted to be quoted.
14 Interview with author on 9 March 2010.

1. Descriptive Information: The first part of the programme gives information about DDRRR processes, as well as other related events. This includes reports of ongoing military efforts and the successes achieved in rooting out foreign armed groups particularly the FDLR.
2. Normative Appeals: The second segment of the programme involves interviews with repatriated ex-combatants and commanders in Rwanda. Interviewers usually talk about the current situation in Rwanda and urge combatants to disarm and return home. This segment also features family members' appeals to their loved ones to stop fighting and return home.
3. The Call or Appeal to Injunctive Norms: The narrator calls on combatants and Hutus to give up and return home before it becomes "too late". The narrator usually talks about any ongoing military offensive against foreign armed groups and then urges combatants to disarm and save their lives.

The three segments of *Gutahuka* are intended to achieve a form of normative influence. There have been a number of researches that support the *Communicative* approach of appeal to perceived norms (Aarts and Dijksterhuis 2003; Aarts et al. 2003; Goldstein et al. 2008; Teddy et al. 1999; Darley and Latane 1970; Kincaid 2004; Lapinski and Rimal 2005; Cialdini et al. 1990; Rimal and Real 2003, among others). In the past two decades, there has a been a surge in communication influence programmes aimed at changing, among others, health behaviours using appeals to social norms. BCC or Behavior Change Communication Projects have ranged from anti-smoking to recycling campaigns. A number of works, including Donaldson et al. (1994); Larimer and Neighbors (2003), Neighbors et al. (2004), as well as Schultz and Neighbors (2007), have explored the use of normative influence as a tool for changing or transforming social behaviours. What has not been found in the research literature however is how normative appeals can be used as a tool for persuading combatants to disarm and voluntarily repatriate. The major assumption of descriptive normative appeal is that individuals use their perception of peer norms as a standard for their behaviours (Schultz et al. 2007; Baer et al. 1991; Perkins and Berkowitz 1986). The task of social norms campaigners therefore is to adopt communications strategies that transform or "correct" targets' "misperceptions" about the prevalence of the behaviour (Schultz et al. 2007; Cialdini et al.'s 1991; Cialdini and Goldstein 2004). This is the first level or descriptive appeal to social norms. Descriptive norms present the message that contrary to what target audiences think, more of their peers are involved in the prescribed "correct" or desired behaviour. *Gutahuka* constantly broadcasts testimonials from repatriated ex-FDLR elements and their family members in Rwanda. For example, Daseroni Zayton, a former FDLR fighter, has been interviewed on *Gutahuka* several times. He had been in the FDLR for 14 years – since he was eight years old. According to his testimony, he was desperate to leave, so after listening to *Gutahuka* he lost the will to fight for the FDLR. In one of the interviews, he describes how he fled:

While we were marching I told my commanders I was going to pick up some firewood. Then when they were not looking, I ran away. MONUC soldiers picked me up and took care of me and returned me to Rwanda. I am safe now. (Gutahuka, monitored in Bukavu 4 February 2008)

Another example is Sebahinzi Fulgence interviewed on 10 April 2010. In the interview he said:

I am freed at last because I am in the hands of MONUC now, and they will repatriate me to Rwanda shortly ... (My family in Rwanda) is in the state of disbelief that I am still alive and will be rejoining them. (Gutahuka, quoted on MONUC's Press Release on 10 April 2010)

By interviewing ex-combatants and extended family members, perceived norms are tied to the group identity of not only the FDLR network but also the Hutu ethnic group, to appeal as it were, to their sense of oneness, not only as a rebel network but also as a family – an ethnic group. In every edition of *Gutahuka*, MONUC fulfils Rimal and Real's definition of descriptive norms in seeking to influence perception about "individuals' beliefs about how widespread a particular behaviour are among their referent others" (2003, 185).

While many Behaviour Change Communications (BCC) specialists have adopted strategies of social norm transformation in their campaigns, success levels as evidenced from researches have been mixed. Whereas some studies confirm its effectiveness (Lapinski and Rimal 2005; Neighbors et al. 2004; Rimal and Real 2003; Agostinelli et al. 1995; Haines and Spear 1996), some other studies have failed to show any significant changes in behaviour of targets (Granfield 2005; Russell et al. 2005; Clap et al. 2003; Peeler et al. 2000; Werch et al. 2000). A few but equally significant studies have even evidenced that rather than change behaviours, peer norms campaigns actually reinforce the undesirable behaviours along with the "misperceptions" they sought to transform (Perkins et al. 2005; Wechsler et al. 2003; Werch et al. 2000).

Schultz and his colleagues (2007) have tried to explain the inconsistencies in results and the boomerang effects evident in some studies. They argue that the problem is inherent in the nature of descriptive norms. Descriptive norms provide specific descriptive normative information that serve as a baseline or standard by which individuals can compare and accordingly adjust their behaviour. Deviance from descriptive norms could be either above or below the norms. Schultz et al. (2007) therefore argue that although descriptive normative information may decrease an undesirable behaviour among individuals in cases where they performed "above the norm", the same message may increase the undesirable behaviour in other cases where individuals performed the behaviour at a rate "below the norm" (p. 430). Cialdini, et al.'s (1991) Focus Theory of normative conduct recommends a second social norm to fix the boomerang effect of descriptive norms – the Injunctive Norm. Whereas descriptive norms convey perceptions of what is prevalently done by most or "wise" members of one's social group or network, Injunctive Norms express the sanctions (social, political, judicial or cultural)" that are applicable if individuals do not comply with prescribed behaviours (Kallgren et al. 2000; Cialdini et al.'s 1991). Focus Theory therefore envisages that in cases where descriptive normative information is ineffective or elicits a boomerang effect, adding a message that conveys injunctive norms may achieve desired outcomes (Schultz et al. 2007; Cialdini and Goldstein 2004; Kallgren et al. 2000).

A salient example of the use of Injunctive Norms in *Gutahuka* is when the Supreme Commander and President of the FDLR Mr. Ignace Murwanashaka was arrested in Germany on 17 November 2009 along with his first Vice-President Stratton Musoni on charges of war crimes and crimes against humanity committed in the DRC. Major General Paul Rwarakabije, a Commissioner in RDRC, himself an ex-FDLR combatant and Commander, emphasized in a number of interviews broadcast on *Gutahuka* that the German government arrested the FDLR leaders "because of the unacceptable actions of the FDLR in the DR Congo" (*Gutahuka,* monitored in Bukavu on 26 November 2009). Across all *Gutahuka* units including the mobile transmitting stations, specially prepared messages were recorded and presented on the arrest of the two FDLR leaders. In addition, various key DRC government officials were interviewed, and they emphasized that the two leaders were arrested because the international community knew that they deserved to be punished for war crimes. They were also frequent talks about the unwelcome status of FDLR members in the DRC after the arrest of the two leaders.

In addition to descriptive and injunctive norms, a third frequently used normative appeal in *Gutahuka* is what Ajzen and Fishbein (1980) have termed Subjective Norms. Though related to injunctive norms, it is functionally different. Essentially, it conveys normative information of what personalities deemed important by the targets think and/or say ought to be done. Subjective norms define a target's perception of whether a Referent important to him/her thinks the behaviour should be performed. The critical element of subjective norms is that Referent X's opinion is weighted by what motivation Target A has to comply with the wishes of Referent X. This will be explored in more detail later in this chapter where I will express subjective norm as the sum of Target A's Perception X motivation assessments for Referents in *Gutahuka* and relevant Referents in the lives of targets, including spouses, family heads and other relevant *influentials* (Eagly and Chaiken 1993; Fishbein and Ajzen 1975; Ajzen and Fishbein 1973). *Gutahuka* frequently broadcasts interviews of repatriated FDLR ex-Commanders who speak about the futility of continuing the fight and advise that the right thing to do is to give up and return to Rwanda and live a better life. For example, on 26 November 2009, an interview was broadcast on *Gutahuka* with Major General Paul Rwarakabije, a former FDLR commander who surrendered and voluntarily repatriated to Rwanda in November 2003. In the interview, he appealed to his former compatriots to do the same, because "fighting is not the way to right any grievance" (MONUC Press Release, 26 November 2009). The interview was also broadcast on other programmes and was featured in a Press Release issued by MONUC. During the interview, General Rwarakabije also made a personal appeal to one of the key FDLR commanders to join the DDRRR process:

> *I am advising Commander Iyamuremye Gaston and others to open a discussion with MONUC, the DR Congo army, the FARDC, and the International Community to allow FDLR combatants return home peacefully.* (Ibid)

General Rwarakabije was a highly respected FDLR military commander and strategist. He is currently a Commissioner of the Rwandan Demobilisation and Reintegration Commission (RDRC). In addition to being the subject in *Gutahuka's* appeal to subjective norms, it is emphasized in the programme that General Rwarakabije's current position is a testament that ex-combatants can be appointed to senior positions in Rwanda if they repatriate.

    Gutahuka therefore conveys three levels of normative appeals: Descriptive Norms, Injunctive Norms and Subjective Norms. As shown in Figure 8.2, the programme also explains the DDRRR processes and the financial benefits involved for returnees depending on their status.

    Various other sensitization activities including direct phone calls and one-to-one contacts in addition to military and political pressures combine to buttress *Gutahuka's* message. There are other pressures – political and military, that are exerted on FDLR elements to impel them to perform the desired behaviour of repatriation. The next section will examine other MONUC's *Soft* activities in pursuit of its DDRRR efforts.

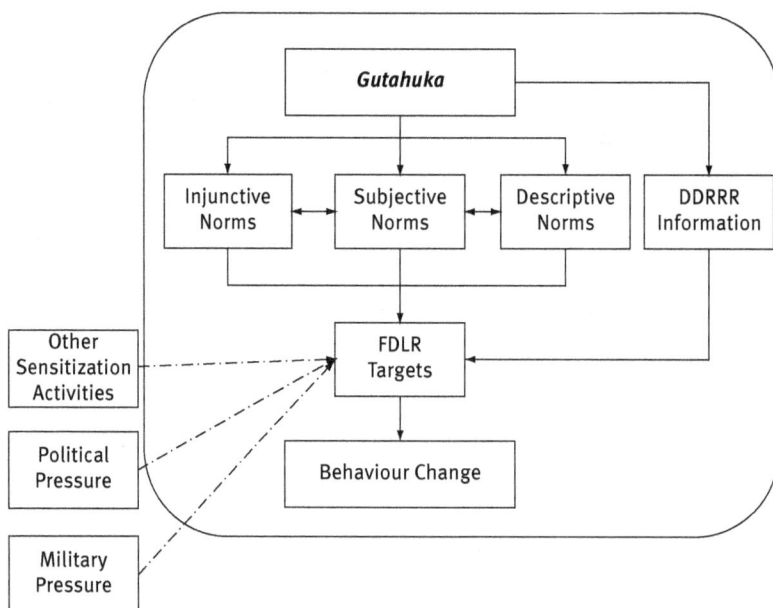

Figure 8.2: Appeal to the Norms: *Gutahuka* BCC strategy

8.5 *Gutahuka* Soft Follow-up Actions

There are various other follow-up activities in support of DDR/RR in addition to *Gutahuka*. These include sensitization and information with leaflet air drops inviting combatants to join the DDRRR programme and spelling out how to do so and the benefits thereof. There are also attempts of direct contacts through telephone calls with FDLR commanders and direct community contacts through Joint Protection Teams and Quick Impact Projects to win over local hearts and minds in order to alienate the FDLR.

Leaflet Air Drop Missions

MONUC has dropped several thousands of leaflets on known FDLR positions. Messages on the leaflets urge combatants to "come out of the bush and go home". The messages also inform FDLR combatants and their dependents of the option of voluntary repatriation and seek to "persuade them to abandon hard-line leaders and a hopeless future in the bush" (MONUC, 28 September 2009). In addition, the leaflets contain phone numbers of MONUC's DDRRR staff for those that wish to call and information on how to listen to *Gutahuka*.

Phone Sensitization

A key element in MONUC's recent DDRRR push is the Mobile Phone Sensitization Service. As already noted, MONUC airdrops leaflets containing phone numbers in rebel areas so that combatants can call to surrender. The phone sensitization programme also involves rehabilitated combatants either calling former FDLR colleagues still active in the forests and attempting to persuade them to disarm and surrender or sharing the phone numbers with DDRRR staff who would then contact the fighters and/or commanders directly. This has been a key strategy in the *Amani Leo* military operation. A celebrated example of the success of this strategy is the surrender in March 2010 of a commander with the rebel group *Raliement Pour Unité et la Democratie* or Rally for Unity and Democracy (RUD) Colonel Ngoboka Rachid in the remote village of Mashuta in Luofu, (167 kilometres from Butembo town) in the southern Lubero territory of North Kivu. From dropped leaflets (containing the DDRRR Sensitization phone numbers), Colonel Rachid made a phone call to DDRRR staff who then arranged for Peacekeepers to meet and extract him and six other armed combatants at a secret location. They were eventually repatriated to Rwanda. Successes such as these are applauded because they are few and far between. Generally, repatriation successes have been modest compared with the number of current FDLR combatants including those that have on their own stopped fighting and integrated in Hutu civilian communities either on a permanent basis or temporarily. From 1 January to 21 May 2010, MONUC's DDR/RR Unit demobilized/received a total of 664 FDLR combatants. In the whole of 2009, 1564 FDLR foreign combatants were repatriated along with 2187 dependents. As shown in Figure 8.3, repatriation has been modest in 2010 up to 21 May when the last data was obtained.

There is no reliable information on the actual number of FDLR fighters currently in combat or the number of ex-combatants that have integrated into civilian life in Eastern DRC. But estimates of current FDLR fighters range between 3000 and 15,000 fighters.[15] In any case, the above repatriation figures illustrate that MONUC still has a long way to go in its DDRRR operations.

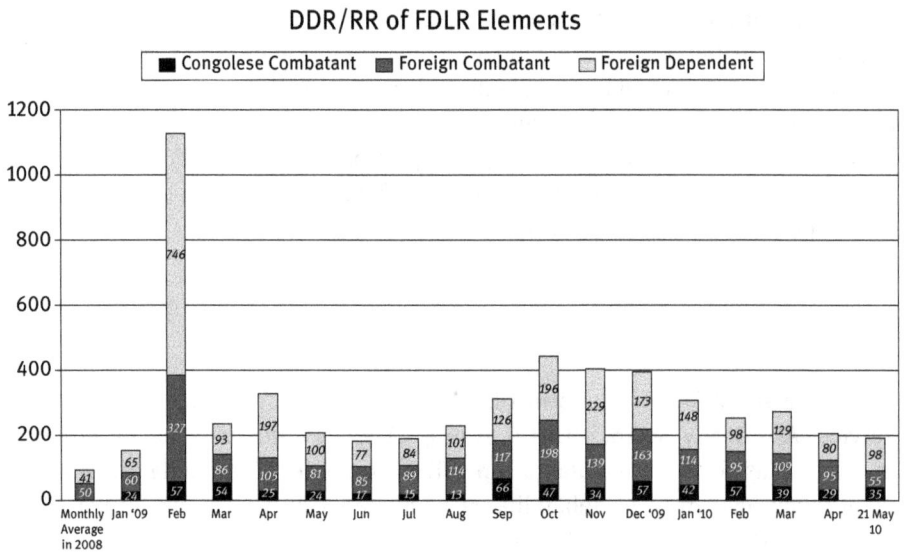

DDR/RR of FDLR Elements

Legend: ■ Congolese Combatant ■ Foreign Combatant ▢ Foreign Dependent

Values (Congolese Combatant / Foreign Combatant / Foreign Dependent):
- Monthly Average in 2008: 50 / 60 / 41
- Jan '09: 24 / 65 / 327
- Feb: 57 / 54 / 746
- Mar: 25 / 86 / 93
- Apr: 105 / 197
- May: 81 / 100
- Jun: 85 / 77
- Jul: 17 / 89 / 84
- Aug: 13 / 114 / 101
- Sep: 66 / 117 / 126
- Oct: 47 / 198 / 196
- Nov: 34 / 139 / 229
- Dec '09: 57 / 163 / 173
- Jan '10: 42 / 114 / 148
- Feb: 57 / 95 / 98
- Mar: 39 / 109 / 129
- Apr: 29 / 95 / 80
- 21 May 10: 35 / 55 / 98

Figure 8.3: Repatriation Figures of FDLR elements up to 21 May 2010. (Source: MONUC Public Information Unit)

Joint Protection Teams

Part of MONUC's DDRRR and overall stabilization strategy is the synergization of humanitarian and military components of the mission in a way that is unprecedented

---

15 The number depends on who you ask. UN and other GoDRC sources estimate that the number of FDLR fighters (as at December 2009) is between 2000 and 4000 fighters, whereas FDLR sources put the number at between 10,000 and 15,000.

in UN PKO history. Three new peacekeeping concepts have been developed to deal with the unique terrain and nature of conflict in the DRC. These are the Joint Protection Teams (JPTs), the Company Operational Bases (COBs) and Temporary Operational Bases (TOBs). While COBs and TOBs are quick response military operational bases brought closer to vulnerable communities in the Kivus, the JPTs represent a novel addition to MONUC's civil-military approach. It is aimed at improving community relations in order to enhance information flows within operational environments. The JPT is part of the Civil Affairs Unit of MONUC and comprise Civil Affairs, Human Rights, Information and Child Protection experts deployed in vulnerable communities.

A critical DDRRR function of JPTs is to identify and assess threat levels and patterns of the FDLR as well as vulnerabilities of specific villages/towns to FDLR attacks. In addition to carrying out sensitization activities, JPTs also create networks to enhance communication between MONUC and local communities. Their deployment to areas which had previously not been accessed helps MONUC gather useful contextual information, establish a form of presence and build confidence among local communities so that they are encouraged to share information with the UN about activities of FDLR guerrilla elements. JPTs and TOBs as can be seen in Figure 8.5 have not been deployed in Fizi. This can be attributed to the relative calm and cohesion between the ethnic groups in the town.

Winning Hearts and Minds for QIPs

A unique *Soft Power* approach by MONUC to win hearts and minds in communities in the DRC is through an extensive and strategic use of Quick Impact Projects (QIPs). QIPs are small-scale and rapidly implementable projects that provide direct benefits to communities. By building bridges and roads, rehabilitating basic infrastructures, providing benches in schools, or building markets, among others, MONUC hopes to enhance its peacebuilding mission efforts and support enhanced relations with Congolese communities. In 2007–2008 fiscal year, MONUC implemented 37 QIPs amounting to $344,257. An example of a QIP project is the construction of bridge linking Bokengia and Ibonzi communities in Equateur Province which had been cut off from each other due to heavy rains thus undermining trade and communication between the two communities. The QIP bridge, constructed by workers recruited from the local area, is now an important asset to the community as it has stimulated not only easy transportation across communities but also mutual relations and trade exchange. Locally named "Pont MONUC", the bridge cost the UN $8182.

By providing QIPs in local communities, MONUC hopes to change the negative impressions of Peacekeepers in most of the local communities particularly in the Kivus, build confidence and encourage communities to "side" with the UN, thus undermining FDLR influence.

QIPs in addition to JPTs and Phone Sensitization activities were key components of MONUC's non-military strategy to put additional pressure on FDLR to disarm and join the DDR/RR process.

8.6 Research Impacts of Communication Interventions

In assessing impacts and effectiveness of Information Operations activities, the big challenge usually centres around how to map clear causal pathways to link effects on audiences with specific IO products and programmes while isolating other variables.

Different research methods have been proposed in researches of information or media content/effect linkages. The choice usually has been between laboratory controlled experiment and field-based studies. Both methodological traditions do have their inherent drawbacks. Experiment would involve testing particular elements of the information intervention on the subject group within a controlled setting. Their responses are then noted and conclusions drawn. The problem with experiment however has always been with interpretation and contextualization. Concerning the DRC, no matter how sensitively prepared, laboratory experiment methods cannot adequately reproduce the complex cultural, socio-political and historical environment within which individuals engage with mediated messages. Moreover, in the DRC socially transmitted information (or what is called in Kinshasa *Radio Trottoir* or "Pavement Radio") plays a critical role in how individuals and networks engage with media messages. A laboratory experiment will not be able to compensate for this critical variable and its potential influence on media engagement outcomes. Furthermore, the factor of audience intimacy with broadcaster (which develops over time) is also a variable that is most times ignored in experiment methods.

Field-based research, on the other hand, has its own limitations, particularly when mapping causal pathways. Field-based methods have the problem of sampling particularly as it relates to selective exposure biases. When selecting respondents who report they meet the desired audience selection criteria, it is difficult to clearly decipher why they meet the selection criteria and how it could affect the research outcome. For instance, personal attitudes can determine media preferences – people with egalitarian disposition tend to consume egalitarian-themed media products (Paluck 2009; Ball-Rokeach et al. 2001; Hur and Robinson 1978; Sears and Whitney 1973). Hence, measuring the intervention's impacts on transforming prejudice on such audiences may not be reliable.

Another problem with field-based study usually is length of exposure. The length of time audiences are exposed to specific media intervention treatments can be critical. In most field studies, researchers rely on the self-reported exposure of respondents which usually cannot be verified.

The third option would be to organize exposure groups where participants are invited to listen to a radio programme over a set period of time with outcomes measured after a time-framed exposure. Again the problem with this method is appropriate contextualization. Such exposure groups – away from the naturalistic setting of listenership, with the usual interruptions, banters, explanations and comments by group members – can make the listening experience too formal and potentially restrict normal group engagement with the programme.

Faced with this methodological "trilemma" and the overwhelming consciousness of the potential methodological shortcomings of these approaches, it can be prudent to depart from the norm by combining the virtues of experimental and field-based methodological approaches while limiting or eliminating the drawbacks in both approaches. The two methodological traditions do not have to be mutually exclusive. Experimental methods can be blended with field evidence.

A combination of the two empirical traditions can enrich contemporary debates on media content effects particularly regarding conflict transformation, development and change. A combination of both approaches is needed to marry larger variables such as networks, contexts, historical narratives and relational fears to the precision of experimental research. Findings from research using this approach can stimulate further theoretical work on media impacts across the broader spectrum of cognitive and/or behavioural outcomes not only at individual level but also at the level of networks.

For radio contents, it is important to monitor listenership over a long period – not by creating artificially modulated listening workshops, but by allowing for an uncontrolled and naturalistic listening environment complete with the usual psychodynamic variables such as affinity with announcer and contextual variables such as group listenership, interruptions and debates while listening, etc. Using locally based peer researchers or facilitators to informally monitor listenership and maintain contacts with participants can immensely enrich the research and remove any outsider or intrusive monitoring mechanism that can potentially alter the natural listening experience desirable in researches of this nature.

Since they live locally, peer researchers can informally meet with research subjects or participants within their clusters daily or weekly during their normal day-to-day activities, monitor listenership and ensure that each listener maintains a log book of programs listened to. Each peer researcher or facilitator can have 10–17 participants in a listening cell, meeting formally once a month with each participant to collect the listenership logbooks.

This approach was used in researching the impact of two programmes on the UN's Radio Okapi on select participants. Participants were able to listen to *Dialogue entre Congolais* on Radio Okapi and to *Gutahuka* on Radio Okapi and on any of the other radio stations that broadcast the programme. Participants committed to listening to a minimum of one edition a week of their assigned programmes and not to listen to the other programme. The listening lasted for a period of 13 months.

8.7 Ontological Foundations of Public Information Research Design

Post-modern thoughts rooted predominantly in the works of Foucault, Deleuze and Guattarri among others as well as works in Complexity theories such as those of James Moffatt and Henrik Jeldloft Jensen can help provide the conceptual or even philosophical foundations for the design not only of intervention contents but also the research procedure. For example, Foucault's conceptualization of "Parrhesia" or "unadorned truth" can be used as the analytical framework for the media philosophy of Radio Okapi. The theoretical section of this work has explored the Foucauldian concepts of biopolitics and disciplinarity and situates them within the larger architecture of Information Intervention. Deleuze and Guattari's (1987) work on Rhizomatism and Normadology provides the basis for a more participatory methodological and analytical approach to researching deterritorialized networks operating within the eastern region of the DRC and transnationally. The non-hierarchical social structure of the networks studied required a study technique that is web-like in structure – connected but unstriated. As found in Deleuze and Guattari's Rhizome, the Hutu networks operated autonomously from the larger structure within each context but the "nodes" (networks in context) work together within the larger network to achieve specific ends. Interestingly, across the various nodes studied, the networks were not static, but constantly evolving, moving and adapting to new information and complexities at the national and transnational levels. Drawing on James Moffatt's (2003) complexity theory, it is interesting to explore how the "nodes" deal with information within a complex and constantly evolving conflict system that is intimately linked and co-evolving with the local socio-economic and political contexts. Harnessing the principles in complexity theory and rhizomatism for contents impact research leads to the self-consistent necessity of studying not only larger contexts of information but also the "nodal" contexts thereof and the various other social or informal means of information transmission within the ethnic networks.

In locating the contexts for the research, a stratified sample of communities and groups made up of Rwandan Hutus and autochthons in four towns in South Kivu (Mwenga, Walungu, Fizi and Uvira) were selected to listen to either of two radio programmes on Radio Okapi for a period of 13 months. Participants were pre-selected based on the levels of social embeddedness within their communities. I adapted Eric Nisbet's (2005) refinement of Kelly and Berry's (2003) engagement model of opinion leadership for the pre-selection. Using matched randomization techniques, select participants were assigned to listen to either *Gutahuka* or *Dialogue*. The information intervention treatment lasted for a total of 13 months and was within the normal community setting of participants. Participants committed to not listening to the other programme for the duration of the entire treatment period.

At the end of the treatment, participants met in focus groups, arranged according to networks in contexts or nodes, to talk about issues that disclose their attitudes towards the Other, perceptions and knowledge of the DDRRR programme as well as engagement and understanding of conflict transformation activities and nascent democratic changes in the DRC. Perceptions and attitudes of *Gutahuka* listeners were compared with perceptions of *Dialogue* listeners across the four contexts studied. The purpose was to find out if there were patterns of significant differences in measured perceptions and attitudes between the two nodes in all contexts.

In the research, two structural elements were critical and need early explanation:
1. ***Networks*** within which and through which individuals operate. It could be trans-regional and/or transnational in nature. The networks, defined in terms of ethnic identity, also operate as informational networks within which members send, receive and process information beyond the contexts they reside. It describes an individual's affiliation or embeddedness in either a Hutu or an autochthonous community within the four geographically bound contexts. Responses to Pre-test Questions were used in categorizing participants into networks.
2. The specific ***Context*** of location where a cluster of individuals or network members reside. Context was measured as a town or neighbourhood unit. Four contexts were randomly selected in South Kivu for the research – Uvira, Walungu, Mwenga and Fizi. These contexts are defined socio-politically along the geographic lines of these four towns.

Another critical concept in the DRC that needs explanation is ***Autochtonie.*** *Autochthonie* (Fr.) and *Allochthonie* or *allogene* (Fr.) are used frequently in the DRC to differentiate authentic or "true" Congolese citizens from "fake" ones and/or immigrants or "new-comers". It connotes a claim not only to citizenship and all its rewards but also to ethnic identity and belonging, territory, land and its resources (for a detailed analyses of the politics of Autochthony/Allocthony and citizenship in the DRC please, see Jackson 2006, 2007; Geschiere and Jackson 2006; Vlassenroot 2002, 2000). While acknowledging that the notion of *autochthonie* and/or *allocthonie* is highly contested and in no way a given, it is operationally used throughout here to designate members of Congolese Bantu tribes with ethnographic presence in their Congolese homeland prior to the proclamation of the Congo Free State in 1885. For the purpose of the research only, autochthons exclude the Banyamulenges of South Kivu (ethnic Tutsis). Although they arrived in the DRC in the early 19 century, they are still seen as *allogenes* or *allochthons* by most Congolese.

8.8 Sampling Design

In the study, a multi-stage sampling design was used. Geographically bound territories or contexts in South Kivu were selected at the first stage as primary units. Within each context, two ethnic networks were selected as secondary units. The ultimate units or "Influentials" were selected from within each network in each of the contexts using a refinement of Eric Nisbet's (2005) engagement model. *Influentials* or opinion leaders are important because personal influence at community and interpersonal levels have been widely recognized as capable of shaping political behaviour, perception, idea diffusion and ultimately public opinion (see Lazarsfeld et al. 1944; Katz 1957; Weimann 1994; Keller and Berry 2003; Rogers 2003). "Influentials", a term used by Keller and Berry (2003), for opinion leaders, are selected based on their information seeking and giving behaviour at personal and community levels. In selecting participants, the interest is not only in their information seeking behaviour but also in their information giving behaviours. These elements of opinion leadership and its consequences for public opinion formation and/or political participation have been well articulated by Burt (1999) and Rogers (2003). According to them, social embeddedness is a key element in sorting Influentials. In this case, Weinman's (1994) three dimensions of opinion leadership were used in selecting participants:

1. information seeking behaviour
2. information giving behaviour
3. social embeddedness

Information seeking behaviour was defined in terms of participants' level of exposure not only to the local media but also to other informal or social information transmitters. Information giving behaviour was defined in terms of *Influentials'* ability to inform members of their network. Social embeddedness was defined in terms of the density of ties that participants have within and/or outside their networks and/or groups and the level of their social relations and community participation (Weimann 1994; Knoke 1990a, 1990b).

Based on the above three dimensions, Eric Nisbet's (2005) refinement of Kelly and Berry's (2003) engagement model of opinion leadership was adapted for the purpose of selecting *Influentials*. The model can be adequately adapted to cover the above three dimensions across divided communities. Originally developed by Roper ASW, the model identifies opinion leaders based on a number of indicators ranging from civic engagement or political activism to social embeddedness. Activities used in Keller and Berry's (2003) engagement model to ask respondents if they had engaged in any of 12 activities within the previous 12 months were adapted for this purpose. To make up for some contextual drawbacks in the model, an indicator for information seeking behaviour was included in the activities. Any respondent within a selected network that answered "yes" to activity 1 and to at least 3 of the other 11 activities below was selected into the "participants pool" within their networks at the first instance.

List of Engagement Activities: *(Adapted from* Keller and Berry 2003, 19–20):

- Listened to radio once a week
- Written or called any politician at the state, local, or national level
- Attended a political rally, speech, or organized protest of any kind
- Worked for a political party or a militant group or as a journalist, a teacher or a public servant

- Been an active member of any group that tries to influence public policy or government
- Held or ran for political office
- Attended a public meeting on community peace-building or reconciliation matters
- Served on a committee for some local organization
- Served as an officer for a local socio-cultural or age-grade club or organization
- Made a speech at a community or extended family meeting, or to a group of soldiers or fighters
- Commanded or been an armed fighter for any group
- Met secretly or overtly with other members of their network to seek the interests of the network

The decision to adapt the engagement model in selecting participants was informed by the need to gather participants that were not only embedded but also engaged in their socio-cultural contexts. This is because engagement and embeddedness opens access to giving and receiving information. Political information is circulated not only through organized media but also through informal social interactions or *Radio Trottoir* (rumour mill) within both structured and unstructured patterns of the society. Although this model was originally tested in the US (Keller and Berry 2003) and in Europe (Eric Nisbert 2005), it is reproducible and can be suitably adapted across various socio-cultural contexts to sort opinion leaders or Influentials. Marshall and Gitsordarmo (1995) argue that some characteristics of opinion leaders are consistent across contexts though with some variability within each characteristic. After testing a scale of opinion leadership across eight different countries to examine commonality of characteristics across cultures, Marshall and Gitsordarmo (1995) observed that opinion leaders indeed shared common characteristics across cultures. Such characteristics include higher media exposure, interest and sociability. Marshal and Gitsordarmo therefore concluded that a general conception of opinion leadership is valid and may therefore be adopted across cultures. Using factor analysis and reliability tests in a previous study, Weimann (1991) also demonstrated the stability of the opinion leadership construct across social and cultural settings.

8.9 Sampling Groups

The study sample used in the study represents the critical parties to the DRC conflict in South Kivu and primary targets of MONUC's *Gutahuka* and Radio Okapi's *Dialogue*. These are Rwandan Hutus (including current and former members of the FDLR in Eastern DRC) and autochthonous communities in the Eastern DRC, respectively. The purpose was firstly to have a deeper awareness of how they engaged with the programmes within their naturalistic contexts; secondly to assess the causal impacts of each programme on each ethnic network across different contexts in terms of beliefs and perceptions of interventions, democratic reforms and civic engagement; thirdly to assess the causal impacts of exposure to the other group's intervention programmes in terms of attitudes towards the other group and understanding of the other group's problems; and fourthly within the naturalistic context of a representative of the target audience of the programmes. Two networks were selected across four contexts in South Kivu:

1. Rwandan Hutus
2. autochthonous communities

The following towns were the selected contexts for the research: Goma, Idjwi, Kalehe, Kabare, Bukavu, Walungu, Mwenga, Uvira, Fizi, Shabunda and Kindu.

In each context, the engagement questionnaires were administered randomly by peer researchers in their communities. In each community, a total of 50 questionnaires were distributed. The peer researchers explained the research project and the questions to respondents and where necessary ticked the appropriate answers on behalf of the respondents. In some cases, the peer researchers asked the questions instead of giving out the questionnaires. This method was useful particularly in areas such as Mwenga and Walungu where literacy was comparatively low. Responses were received after two weeks of simultaneously administering the questionnaires in four texts. Table 8.1 shows the number of Positive Engagement Returns received across the four contexts.

Table 8.1: Table Showing Number of Positive Engagement Returns

Context	Fizi		Uvira		Mwenga		Walungu	
Network	H	A	H	A	H	A	H	A
Number of Engagement Questionnaires administered	50	50	50	50	50	50	50	50
Number of Positive Engagement Returns (PERs)	31	28	32	34	23	28	21	26

H= Hutus; A= autochthons. Positive Engagement Returns indicate the number of respondents that answered Yes to Question 1 and three other questions.

The Positive Engagement Returns (PERs) or respondents that qualified were inducted into listenership. Participants that meet the minimum listenership requirements would eventually be selected from each network and context for the focus group discussions.

8.10 Summary of Procedure

This qualitative study involved in-depth personal interviews of principal actors at Hirondelle Foundation and MONUC's Public Information Department as well as

various other key informants in the DRC. The principal targets of MONUC's PIO programme *Gutahuka* are Rwandan Hutus – most of who make up the FDLR. In South
Kivu, several of the fighters have settled and integrated into the Congolese society –
marrying and raising children with Congolese women, although such relationships
have been mostly exploitative and abusive (Refugees International Field Report,
September 15, 2009).[16]

The research procedure was designed to examine the impacts of the two radio
programmes among Hutu and autochthon listening groups. Figure 8.4 summarizes
the four key strands of the research.

	Hutus	**Autochthons**
Gutahuka	Impacts of *Gutahuka* on Hutus in South Kivu: •Within unmitigated social patterns of day-to-day life in South Kivu •Within 'settled' Hutu networks opertaing within the same contexts with autochthon communities	Impacts of Gutahuka on autochthones in South Kivu: •Within unmitigated social patterns of day-to-day life in South Kivu •Within autochthonous networks opertaing within the same context as Hutu networks
Dialogue	Impacts of *Dialogue* on Hutus in South Kivu: •Within unmitigated social patterns of day-to-day life in South Kivu •Within 'settled' Hutu networks opertaing within the same context as autochthonous networks	Impacts of Dialogue on autochthones in South Kivu: •Within unmitigated social patterns of day-to-day life in South Kivu •Within indigenous autochthonous networks operating within the same context as Hutu networks

Figure 8.4: Four key strands of the research on the Impacts of the Two Radio Programmes Among
Hutu and Autochthon Listening Groups

The purpose of all strands of research were three-fold: firstly, to map patterns (if any)
of significant differences in perception and attitudes between nodes that listened
to *Gutahuka* and nodes that listened to *Dialogue* across the two ethnic groups. Secondly, to map patterns (if any) of significant differences in levels of knowledge and
engagement with nascent democratic reforms and values between nodes that listened
to *Gutahuka* and nodes that listened to *Dialogue* across the two ethnic groups. And
thirdly to measure attitudes of each ethnic group towards the other ethnic group after
exposure to information contents meant for the other.

---

16 'Settled' status is used in this report to mean foreign combatants in foreign soil that have taken
up residency within a civilian or refugees community, and either built a home or planted long-term
crops, such as cassava, yam, palm fruit trees, etc., or inter-married, or told me that they have now
settled in the DRC.

To achieve these, two networks were selected across four contexts. It is essential to point out the theoretical difference between networks and contexts as used in this study. The study adopts Huckfeldt and Sprague's (1987) concept of networks as being individually constructed and contexts as being structurally imposed. Contexts are defined in terms of factors that are external to the individuals researched such as the prevailing political climate in the area, history of mutual suspicion, presence of internally displaced persons (IDPs), poverty, etc. Networks on the other hand represent the outcomes of personal choices of associations made by individuals within the opportunities and limitations of their contexts. Consequently, two structurally related elements are germane to the research:

1. The politico-cultural and socio-informational networks within and through which individuals process the radio programmes.
2. The larger and local socio-political and geographic space or context within which individuals reside.

For this study, both networks and contexts representing specific villages in South Kivu were contacted for the purpose of developing a relationship. This was achieved through the use of Peer Researchers. Context was defined at the level of selected communities and how the conflict had affected the dynamics of the community since 1994 (after the Rwandan genocide) in terms of:

(a) population mix,
(b) displacement and relocation,
(c) inter-marriages among autochthonous and Hutu communities, and
(d) conflict affectation.

These mixes constitute the Context of Political Behaviour in this study and are defined not only socio-culturally but also geographically. Networks on the other hand are observed in terms of sphere of political discussion and more importantly ethnic affinity. It is noteworthy that networks and contexts do not necessarily overlap geographically, culturally or even politically. Hutu networks, for example, cut across boundaries of contexts researched, and the network of FDLR fighters in South Kivu extended regionally to North Kivu and transnationally to Rwanda, France, Belgium, Germany and Burundi. The study therefore was designed to be sensitive to how meanings are negotiated within networks and how networks and contexts create congruence and/or dissonance for MONUC's information intervention programmes in South Kivu.

Contexts of Research

The following four towns were selected in South Kivu as contexts for the research:
-   Uvira
-   Walungu

- Mwenga
- Fizi

Networks Researched

Hutus in South Kivu were the selected sample because they, according to several reports, represent the most challenging impediment to the return of peace and reconciliation in Eastern DRC (Crises Group 2009; Prunier 2009; Feelay and Thomas-Jensen 2008; Turner 2007; Nest et al. 2006; Swarbrick 2004). Also MONUC's *Gutahuka* is targeted at FDLR elements in particular and Hutus in general. Some of them have been accused of participating in the 1994 Rwandan genocide. The second group is autochthonous community in South Kivu. The purpose with this group was to see how Congolese autochthons engage with MONUC's information intervention programme *Dialogue* and how it has in turn enhanced their knowledge and affected their attitudes towards conflict transformation processes in their country and also the extent to which the "go back home" messages of *Gutahuka* have affected their relationship and imagination of future relationships with Rwandan Hutus living currently in their communities.

On both fronts, the purpose of the research is to track the nature of influence of information intervention over transformations in individual and network perception of interdependence between Hutus and autochthones, imagination of future relationships, possibilities for cross cultural and inter-communal dialogue, issues such as relational fears, hopes and collective goals in terms of affectivity and interdependence.

The two networks were selected from within the same contexts in Uvira, Walungu, Mwenga and Fizi all in South Kivu. South Kivu was selected because it has been one of the worst affected by the conflict since 1995. The area has been home to various rebel networks including FDLR, CNDP, Mai Mai, PARECO, etc. At the same time, it has the highest number of ex-Hutu combatants and refugees who have attempted to settle into as close a normal way of life as possible.

Listenership

The two networks in each of the four towns or contexts were selected in South Kivu and assigned to listen to either of two radio programmes on Radio Okapi – *Dialogue* or *Gutahuka*.

Hutu Network Listenership

A total of four Hutu groups (one group from each of the four contexts) were selected to listen to *Gutahuka*. A total of four Hutu groups (one from each context) were selected to listen to *Dialogue*.

Autochthonous Community Listenership

A total of four autochthonous groups (one from each context) were selected to listen to *Gutahuka*. Four autochthonous groups from each context were selected to listen to *Dialogue*.

Listening and Control Groups

Using random assignment technique, participants in all contexts were split into main treatment and control groups for listenership purposes. For Rwandan Hutu Network, the control group listened to *Dialogue* while the treatment group listened to *Gutahuka*. For Autochthons, the control group listened to *Gutahuka* while the treatment group listened to *Dialogue*. This method was for three main reasons designed to make the control groups listen to "the other's" programme. Firstly, it enabled me to isolate the impact of the contents of each programme on specific networks within the same contexts of media consumption as control listeners.

Secondly, listening to the other's programme created another level of analysis for the research. The unusual element about this approach is that the control group is also critical to the research because in addition to providing a point of analytical departure for Hutu/*Gutahuka* listeners and Autochthon/*Dialogue* listeners it also provided a resource for understanding the impacts of exposure of conflict groups to the other's messages – another critical element of the study.

And thirdly, for budgetary reasons, it would have been impracticable to have different treatment and control groups for assessing the impacts of listening to the other's intervention programmes. It would have been far beyond an already over-stretched budget of this study to monitor listenership of extra groups and engage the services of more Peer Researchers. For budgetary considerations, there was alternative of using a non-listening control groups on all cases. But on careful consideration, this would have increased the inter-group error variance because the contexts of non-listening control subjects would have been different in terms of a sense of participation and the feeling of empowerment listenership brings – both of which were critical to this research. A sense of empowerment drawn from involvement in the over one year of monitored listenership and end-game focus group discussion had the potential of enabling participants (some of whom are previously unheard and/or marginalized) to feel a sense of worth and thus be more assertive in their comments.

Method of Assigning Listenership

Using a matched randomization technique, I assigned the PERs or pre-selected Hutus and Autochthon Influentials to listen to one of the two radio programmes. Each cellule, representing participants from a specific ethnic network within a given context, was split into two groups for listenership to either *Dialogue* or *Gutahuka*. Each group was then matched with the most similar demographic characteristic in the other group. The observable characteristics used were: gender ratio (female), age, previous armed group involvement (ex-combatants) and Civil Status (married or co-habiting). In all networks and contexts, the number of men exceeded the number of women, so to balance for sex I evenly split pre-selected women in each cluster to assign them to each programme. For age, I matched age at a ratio of 50%/50% for under 25s and over 25s. In terms of Civic Status, I evenly distributed married/cohabiting participants between both groups. For Combat Status, I evenly distributed ex-combatants across the groups. Where there were odd numbers for any characteristic, the one remaining person was randomly assigned to any group. This technique ensured a near-identical participant grouping, please see Table 8.2.

One of the two groups was then randomly assigned to listen to *Gutahuka*, the other to dialogue. This stratification procedure helped to provide demographic balance while minimizing observable differences among the groups.

Although a maximum of 10 participants in each cellule were invited for the focus groups, all pre-selected PERs were involved in the listening treatment. This was due to the need to maintain a back up list of pooled participants in order to make up for any volunteers that discontinued the treatment.

Table 8.2: Demographic Characteristics of Pooled Participants

							Contexts									
	Fizi				Walungu				Mwenga				Uvira			
Networks	Hutu		Autoch-thon		Hutu		Autoch-thon		Hutu		Autoch-thon		Hutu		Autoch-thon	
Programme	G	D	G	D	G	D	G	D	G	D	G	D	G	D	G	D
Sex (women)	3	4	3	4	3	3	3	4	4	4	4	4	4	3	3	3
Combat Status (ex-combatants)	5	6	2	2	3	2	3	3	3	3	1	1	4	4	0	0
Civic Status (married/ co-habiting)	3	3	7	7	2	2	6	6	3	4	9	9	4	4	15	14
n	15	16	14	14	11	10	13	13	11	12	14	14	16	16	17	17

G = *Gutahuka*, D = *Dialogue*.
Information on combat status was voluntarily contributed. Some participants preferred not to provide any information about their combat status. The figures here are those of participants that volunteered that information, but actual number of ex-combatants may have been more.

In order to ensure a full understanding of the objectives and procedures of the listenership programme, Peer Researchers were involved in follow-up explanation to provide additional details and answer questions on the programme and the responsibilities involved to each participant in their cellules. So they personally contacted each participant and explained the programme assigned and broadcast schedule. The participants were also given a log book with which they would make a mark against the date and programme they listened to. The participants felt comfortable knowing that they were working in a project that one of "their own" was directly involved in and wanted to do their part. Participants were offered a monthly supply of two pairs of D-size batteries to help power their radio sets during the entire length of the listenership programme and a small stipend. When supplying the batteries, the Peer Researchers also collected participants' log book for the month. The Péer Researchers, like most Congolese, enjoyed being trusted with responsibilities and they discharged their assignments excellently well.

During the listenership treatment, participants were not told the kind of questions they would be asked at the end of the treatment but were told that those that complete the listenership treatment would be invited to participate in Group Discussions on the way forward for their communities. I deliberately refrained from explaining to Peer Researchers the full purpose of the research in order not to influence their engagement with their group members.

8.11 Ethical Considerations

It is very important to give thought to the ethical foundations of research – particularly in violently divided societies, emerging from violent conflicts. During the planning stage of the research project, ethical issues were given serious considerations. Participants were informed to listen to the radio programmes within their homes or wherever they felt safe to do so.

Informed Consent was an important consideration. Participants were fully briefed by their Peer Researchers of what the research entailed. It was not necessary to give them full details about the research questions and the objectives thereof. They were informed that the purpose of the research was to increase knowledge of how the Congolese and Rwandan Hutus listened to radio in their localities, and how people felt about peace, conflict and new democratic reforms in their societies in particular and in their country in general and how they were affected by their radio-listening practices. All participants voluntarily accepted to be part of the research after understanding what it entailed and what would be required of them throughout the course of the research. Confidentiality was another key ethical issue. There was commitment to the confidentiality and anonymity of all research participants as they requested. Anonymity was important to most of the participants for security reasons. This was achieved by assigning codes to comments rather than names.

After the entire focus group sessions, all participants were fully debriefed by their Peer Researchers. Peer Researchers explained in detail to all participants what the research sought to achieve and gave assurances that their comments have been anonymized. Participants were also given the correct information about MONUC's repatriation offer.

8.12 Networks and Contexts of Research: Defining the Mixes

As previously explained, *Networks* are the spheres within which and through which individuals operate. It could be transregional and/or transnational in nature. The networks, defined in terms of ethnic identity, also operate as informational networks within which members send, receive and process information beyond the contexts they reside. It was calibrated in terms of individual's embeddedness in either a Hutu or autochthonous community within the four geographically bound contexts. Responses to Pre-test Questions were used in categorizing participants into either of the two networks studied.

Secondly, *Context* is the location where a cluster of individuals or network members reside. Context is measured as a town or neighbourhood unit. Four geographically-bound contexts were selected in South Kivu for the research – Uvira, Walungu, Fizi and Mwenga. Selection as earlier noted was based on two cardinal criteria – the number or density of Hutus resident as a community or groups in the towns and the relative stability of the towns. Both criteria were important because of the need to conduct the research, particularly the listenership elements within a relatively peaceful and stable socio-political context. The four towns, compared with other towns in the Kivus or Eastern DRC, in general were among the most stable at the time the research was initiated. Also, the four towns had a high number of Rwandan Hutus, most of who have settled and inter-married with Congolese autochthons. Also, they spoke Swahili (the main language of interaction) and their autochthon neighbours also spoke and understood Kinyarwanda – the language of Rwandan Hutus and the radio programme *Gutahuka*.

Interaction between Networks and Contexts of Study

Context is used here as a village or location of social structure made up of individuals drawn from various backgrounds (ethnic, political and economic), sharing a common physical experience and subject to the same external issues ranging from infrastructural or political (under)development to environmental scarcity. Contexts are made up of individuals but they are external to the individual – the individual willy-nilly finds himself within a context with all its inherent social structures, politics and culture.

Networks on the other hand represent the associations forged by individuals within a given context either for self preservation or for hegemonic ascendancy.

Networks are created by individuals banding together either based on their shared history, ethnic origin, socio-economic class or constraints. They are created based on expediencies of opportunities and constraints within the context. To present an example from this study, Uvira (one of the contexts of this research) is a small town that has Hutu and autochthonous networks living side by side with each other. Both networks since 1994 (when Hutus arrived fleeing from Rwanda) have had a shared experience of war but with varying levels of impacts and are vulnerable to the same weak controls of the central governmental in Kinshasa. Although everyone lives within the same externally controlled context, it was envisaged that information flowed better within the networks than between them. This implies that information flows better among Hutus living in different contexts than with autochthons living within a homogenous spatial context and vice versa. In the contexts studied, it was observed that social patterns of daily live were distinctly marked by network affinity. Although both networks interacted at everyday social levels of buying and selling, political or strategic information flew better and faster among network members. Both networks use what Burton (1978) describes as "telling" to "tell" what network someone belongs. The "telling" mechanism used by Burton (1978) and Harris (1986) supposes extreme sensitivity to signs and other explicit factors such as name, physical appearance, shibboleths, etc. to enable a correct categorization of an individual to a particular group even at first meeting. Likewise, in South Kivu, the same factors and other more physical elements such as height, style of dressing and sometimes walking style are used to "tell who is who". The distinction between both networks in certain contexts is so pervasive that inter-cultural communication is problematic and dialogue particularly on political issues is distorted.

As stated earlier, although the two constructs seem to overlap territorially, for the purpose of this study, networks have been restricted to their specific contexts of residence. For example, though the Hutu network is transnational – networked around Burundi, Rwanda, Germany and France and maintains a close-knit information complex – in the study, participants had to be members of the network within the context studied.

Rwandan Hutus in the east of the DRC were selected at the first instance because they are the target audience of *Gutahuka*. *Dialogue* is a general interest programme targeted at all Congolese, and the intention of the programme as shown earlier is to inform and mobilize audience engagement with ongoing democratic reforms in the country. However, as it is with most targeted programmes, all networks and contexts in the country are also exposed to the same intervention programmes. Media Audiences choose information consumption based on their personal preferences, but they also consume and engage with what is not meant for them but are available (Huckfeldt and Sprague 1987); it was envisaged that their biases in turn have the potentials of affecting how they process "the other's" media message as reported in Jones (1986). It was envisaged that in the contexts studied it had the potential of generating feelings of affinity or understanding with "the other" and, at the same time, the potential of generating hostility and bias against the other. Hence, the two different networks were treated with the same information intervention programme (meant for the other). The intention was to create a deeper awareness of how networks operating within the same contexts engaged with information intervention treatments meant for "the other" which they are also exposed to and how it in turn affects their relationship and perception of "the other".

Although participants from the two ethnic networks were drawn from homogenous contexts in each case, it was envisaged that interpretation of information intervention contents would be distinct and shaped by their heterogeneous history, discursive formations, disparate metaphors, ethnic origin, political affiliation and social interactions which could in turn influence how they relate with "the other".

It was also envisaged that the sample procedure used in the study to select participants across the two networks in each context would counteract the homogeneity in audience engagement with media intervention programmes so often reported in researches of contextually associated individuals (Jones 1986; Huckfeldt and Sprague 1987; Eulau 1986). Selecting samples from the same contexts but different networks ensured that respondents were not too dispersed or disconnected from the other's socio-political experience. Irrespective of how divided the societies are, information is processed, not by socially alienated individuals, but by culturally, historically and socially inter-dependent beings within a common network and contextual experience albeit with different expectations. In some communities, mediated information is consumed in groups of age grades and social affinities. This can be attributed to culture or could be because radio is not owned by everyone, hence the need to share. In other cases, individuals may work in groups either in farms or markets. A single radio is listened to during such moments and the contents debated. Such debates do not end when the programme ends. Information engagement within these contexts are not limited to the nature of contents alone, but susceptible to influence by leaders of opinion within listening cellules. Moreover, negotiation and (de)construction of meaning is further subject to influence during the process of repetitive social interactions within networks even after the end of the information programme.

Listenership Monitoring

A substantial part of the follow-ups, monitoring of listenership and mobilizing participants was done by Peer Researchers. They were trained to be sensitive and to avoid giving participants the impression they were under pressure to listen to the programmes. It was important that listenership occurred under an atmosphere as close to real life as possible. Peer Researchers were encouraged to discuss the contents of the programmes with their volunteers during their monthly visits to keep the interest going. Since the Peer Researchers lived locally and were previously known to the participants they would usually meet during their day-to-day social interactions, so meeting between Peer Researchers and participants were in all cases more than once a month. In some contexts such as Mwenga and Walungu particularly among Hutu networks, it was daily. During such informal meetings, Peer Researchers were encouraged to inquire about the listenership. The monitoring was thus built on intimacy and personal relationships. In most cases particularly among the Hutu network, participants listened to the programmes in groups either with other participants or family members. Roasted yam, *foufou* meal, kola nut and local gin were usually shared during the group listenership.

Focus Group Discussions

At the end of the treatment, each Peer Researcher was trained to moderate and record the focus groups in his cellule. All participants informally interviewed by the researcher preferred their Peer to an outsider as the moderator. It has been recognized that there are advantages in having a moderator with characteristics similar to the participants (Krueger and Casey 2000). The moderators shared the same ethnic characteristic, language and a common field of experience with the participants in their cellules, and the sessions provided an uninhibited forum for participants to express their opinions without any reservations which may be created with the presence of an outsider. The eight peers were thus invited to join the researcher and the research assistant in Bukavu (used as the control point for the research) for two full days' training (which included role plays) on conducting focus group discussions. I trained them on how to use the recorder and how to ensure that it was recording. This was essential because it was imperative to have all the discussions fully recorded and thereafter transcribed verbatim.

Using Peer Researchers had several advantages. Among others, it guaranteed cultural sensitivity. It was particularly essential among the Hutus especially in Uvira, Fizi and Walungu because since the start of the Kimia II military operation by the FARDC to purge out Hutu militants, most Hutus resident in the areas became reluctant to come out openly. In some cases, they even denied they were Hutus in order to avoid persecution or attack by FARDC forces and by extremist FDLR elements who prefer to have dense civilian Hutu populations where they can retreat to when attacked by FARDC and/or MONUC forces.[17] Furthermore, the ex-combatant participants would only disclose their statuses based on assurances that it would remain strictly confidential with their peer researcher, who already knew about their combat status.

---

17 Interview with Paul Wakenge (ex-commander AFDL, South Kivu).

Focus Group Invitation and Attendance

At the end of the listenership treatment, 10 participants from each cellule were selected and invited for focus group discussions. Only participants that had over 70% listenership (based on information on collated figures from listenership log books) were invited. Selection was biased in favour of women in the groups. All women in the listenership pool were invited as they all achieved the 70% listenership threshold. Focus group membership was restricted to a maximum of 10 participants to avoid overcrowding. The men that achieved the required listenership threshold were randomly selected to participate in the focus group discussions. This technique helped to reduce inter-cellule heterogeneity, thereby controlling the error variance when assessing the information intervention effects. Tables 8.3 and 8.4 show the demographic characteristics of participants at the focus groups in the two networks.

Table 8.3: Demography of Hutu Ethnic Network Focus Group Discussants – Sample Demonstrating Balance between Listening Groups in Hutu Groups

Contexts	Uvira		Walungu		Fizi		Mwenga	
Programme	**G**	**D**	**G**	**D**	**G**	**D**	**G**	**D**
Mean Age	32	33	38	36	32	31	32	33
Sex (% women)	30	30	30	30	30	30	40	30
Combat Status (% ex-combatants)	40	40	20	20	50	50	30	30
Civic Status (% married/co-habiting	30	30	20	20	20	20	30	30
Cellule Listenership Compliance (%)*	100	98	98	97	98	96	95	94
n	10	10	10	10	10	10	10	10

G=*Gutahuka* listening cellule; D=*Dialogue* listening cellule.
CLC percentages were derived from participants' recordings of listenership in their monthly log book returns in each cellule.

In all sites, Focus Group attendance was 100%. This is wholly attributed to the hard work of Peer Researchers who used their personal contacts to follow up on participants in their clusters. They arranged dates that were convenient for all participants in each case. With few exceptions, the Focus Groups were held in the homes of one of the participants. Since participants all lived around the same vicinity, it was as easy as walking across the road to bring over any participant that was late in showing up. A total of 16 focus groups were conducted across the four contexts of study – eight for each ethnic network. This involved eight focus groups for each listening group and four focus groups in each context, representing two for each network.

Table 8.4: Demography of Autochthon Network Focus Group Discussants – Sample Demonstrating Balance between Listening Groups in Autochthon Groups

Contexts	Uvira		Walungu		Fizi		Mwenga	
Programme	G	D	G	D	G	D	G	D
Mean Age	43	42	33	33	33	34	32	31
Sex (% women)	30	30	30	40	30	40	40	40
Combat Status (% ex-combatants)	0	0	30	30	20	20	10	10
Civic Status (% married/co-habiting)	80	80	50	50	60	60	70	70
Cellule Listenership Compliance (%)*	91	97	80	87	86	90	76	78
n	10	10	10	10	10	10	10	10

G=*Gutahuka* listening cellule; D=*Dialogue* listening cellule.
CLC percentages were derived from participants' recordings of listenership in their monthly log book returns in each cellule.

8.13 Order of Focus Group Discussion and Moderator Guide

Moderators were given an order of discussion and sufficiently trained on the contents. The order of discussion covered knowledge themes and impact themes and varied slightly across networks and listening groups. Moderators were trained to tailor discussions around the knowledge and impact themes. Impact themes were important in all discussion groups, but knowledge theme on DDRRR processes was to be given utmost importance in Hutu *Gutahuka* listening groups. The following is the order of discussion for the focus groups.

Knowledge Themes

The following knowledge themes were explored:
1. DDRRR
2. UN peacekeepers
3. The peace process/democratic reforms
4. The DRC's central government

DDRRR: Guided discussions to reflect what participants knew and thought about the Disarmament, Demobilization, Repatriation, Resettlement and Reintegration

(DDRRR) programme, rehabilitation and reinsertion processes in Rwanda. Discussions should also reflect knowledge about intervention activities by the UN and other agencies to promote positive inter-social/ethnic relationships and reintegration in their communities. Focus group questions and discussions were designed to purvey a combination of the following elements:
- participants' perceptions of interdependence with the Other;
- Attitudes towards Other groups in everyday social interactions;
- DDRRR processes – what it is about.

UN Peacekeepers: Discussions about UN peacekeepers should reflect participants' knowledge of the reasons for their presence and their responsibilities to the civilian population.

The Peace Process, Peacebuilding and Democratic Reforms: Discussions about the peace process and post-conflict reconstruction should reflect participants' knowledge of a combination of the following elements:
- social integration processes and programmes as well as activities by any agency involved in the mobilization of peace constituents both in Rwanda and locally;
- activities by civil society groups (including Church organizations and self-help groups) to build local cultures of peace;
- community peacebuilding practices;
- new democratic reforms (including new institutions);
- causes of violence in the Eastern Region and how MONUC is dealing with it;
- structural and regional causes of the conflict;
- mechanisms and institutions/systems of procedural and retributive justice both in the DRC and in Rwanda;
- opportunities for personal development and civic engagement.

DRC's Central Government: Activities of the President Joseph Kabila government to create peace with regional neighbours – mainly Rwanda – as well as recent or current development projects carried out by the central government that have direct bearing with their personal lives.

Impact Themes

Concerning Impact Themes, moderators were trained to control discussions to reflect a combination of specifically identified themes. Please see Table 8.5.

Table 8.5: Impact Themes

Hutu Groups	Autochthon Groups
– How participants engaged with the radio programmes	– How participants engaged with the radio programmes
– What participants thought of Radio Okapi's credibility	– What participants thought of Radio Okapi's credibility
– What participants thought about Hutus returning to Rwanda	– What participants thought about Hutus returning to Rwanda
– What participants thought about the credibility of the personal stories of soldiers in *Gutahuka* programme	– What participants thought about the credibility of the personal stories of soldiers in *Gutahuka* programme
– If participants thought it was needful for Hutus to return to Rwanda	– If participants thought it was needful for Hutus to return to Rwanda
– What participants thought of the condition awaiting returnees in Rwanda	– What participants thought of the condition awaiting returnees in Rwanda
– What participants felt about they themselves returning to Rwanda	– What participants felt about FDLR elements disarming and returning to Rwanda
– What participants felt about FDLR elements disarming and returning to Rwanda	– Talk about any feelings of alienation
– Talk about any feelings of alienation	– What "autochthones" think of Hutus in general, and FDLR in particular remaining in the DRC
– Past memories of war and imagination of future relationships	– Past memories of war and imagination of future relationships
– Relational fears and hopes in terms of affectivity and interdependence	– Relational fears and hopes in terms of affectivity and interdependence

8.14 Specific Topics for Discussion

In narrowing the above general order of discussion, each focus group session had the objectives of stimulating dialogues on specific topics related to the purpose of the research. Discussions therefore focused on the following specific topics (modified across networks and listening groups):

1) DDRRR (Hutu Groups)
   i) Understanding and perception of MONUC's DDRRR processes and barriers
   ii) Understanding and perception of opportunities for reintegration in their communities in Rwanda
   iii) Understanding and perception of political and social conditions in Rwanda that enables personal development and restoration
   iv) Understanding and perception of the restorative and retributive justice system in Rwanda (primarily the Gacaca Court system)
   v) Perceptions of descriptive and prescriptive levels of interventions in the DRC

2) Attitude towards the Other (Hutu and Autochthons)
   i)   Perception of victims and villains of conflict
   ii) Imagination of future relationships with autochthons
   iii) Perception of inter-dependence, inter-marriage and community
   iv) Perception of barriers to relationships
3) Democratic Culture and Local Peacebuilding Processes (Autochthons)
   i)   Beliefs regarding democratic values and non-violent processes of social and political change at community, territorial and national levels
   ii) Perception of barriers to peace at territorial and national levels
   iii) Perception of opportunities for self development, healing and reconciliation
   iv) Perception of structures and institutions that support democracy and peace at local and national levels (including GoDRC and MONUC)
   v)   Level of engagement (including participation) with nascent democratic reforms within their communities or territories

9 Local Meanings and Perceptions of UN Information Interventions Programmes

In Uvira, a group of listeners sat round a table with a bush lantern at the centre, there was palm wine for everyone and the highly intoxicating locally brewed gin, *Kavujini*, for the strong-hearted. They were listening to the programme *Isange Mu Banyu* on Rwandan Radio. The programme explained the demobilization and repatriation exercise, the number of returnees and interviews with those that had just returned, their families and people from the villages describing the situation of things in the village and their day-to-day lives. Up till the time the interview started, listeners were bantering and talking about issues of concern. But as soon as the interviews started, there was a sudden silence. Everyone actively listened to the interviews. Normal conversation only started when women in one of the villages where people were interviewed started singing and calling on their husbands, children and friends of their sons in far off lands to return home. Discussions, after the interviews, turned to the veracity of the claims by the returnees interviewed that things are far better than what they had expected. Soon, conversation moved to the policies of the Tutsi-led government in Rwanda and some of the anti-Hutu policies of the regime. Two of the men talked about interviews on *Gutahuka* they had listened the previous night. Different members who either had or had not listened to the programme debated the underlying meaning of contents of interviews and its implications as it relates to the collective interests of the community. Then a few banters, a few jokes and the night came to an end. It lasted for about an hour but it was interesting to observe actual radio listenership and how meaning was shared and negotiated – collectively, communally and transactionally.

Many studies and handbooks on radio have emphasized the "personal" and "intimate" elements of radio as a medium (Schulberg 1996; O'Regan et al. 2002; Mcleish 1994; Wilby and Conroy 1994). The result has been what Hendy (2000) has described as a gulf "between a concept of the audience as a community" on the one hand and the "highly personal nature of the listening process" on the other (p. 115). In South Kivu, radio listening occurs within group settings. The groups are usually made up of people that share a common cultural affiliation, age, locality and in several cases a common sphere of experience ranging from occupation (such as farming or herding) to memories of a shared past.

9.1 Radio Listening in South Kivu

Radio is a key medium of mass communication in South Kivu for a number of reasons. Access to the towns and villages is very difficult. In Shabunda and several other adjoining *collectivities*, for instance, there are no telephones and no postal services and access to the territory is very difficult except through an airstrip in Shabunda locale. Thus, newspapers are almost non-existent. In addition to low literacy levels, a rich oral tradition (Belcher 1999; Gondola 2002; Philips 2005) makes radio the natural medium of choice for most people here. Television has not yet made a strong entry. Price (2003) has argued that in the absence of television, radio listenership is unusually high. There is also a strong sense of community in the villages which results in a collective engagement with radio messages.

Taking account of the unique contexts of the study, the technique used in the research sought to provide an understanding of the everyday ways that groups listened to and made sense of radio messages in South Kivu. An early understanding of how communities and individuals engaged with media messages in the contexts researched was important. Focus group was intended to provide a more robust understanding of how ethnically defined social groups within the context of violently divided societies construct meaning. The objective of each session therefore was to re-create an informal communicative context where individuals freely and informally exchanged views on issues that concerned them.

Focus groups moderated by a peer researcher were preferred to other methods such as ethnography or participant observation because of the closed-up nature of the socio-ethnic networks researched and the sensitivity of the topics discussed. Moreover, participants, out of fear of reprisal attacks, were wary of opening up to "outsiders". That would have created complications for a "non-member" researcher while also restricting freedom of discussions. Peer researchers enabled the re-creation of a real-life discussion which was essential to the research. To all intents and purposes, the focus group design was aimed at achieving Lunt and Livingstone's description of an ideal focus group discussion as "simulations of social relations, or rather, as social occasions in themselves which bear sufficient resemblance to the social occasions under study" (1996, 9). The work studied socio-ethnic networks, not as aggregates of individuals but as social entities bound together by a shared history, strong ties, culture, language, common aspiration and a commonly negotiated construction of social realities. As in Burgess et al. (1991), my key objective in using focus group was to "replicate in so far as possible ... the domestic and other social settings which people live" (p. 502).

9.2 Re-Stating Purpose of Research

The purpose of the study was to have a deeper awareness of how ethnic networks across different contexts engaged with intervention media contents in order to assess impacts on (1) their attitude towards the Other, (2) perceptions of descriptive levels of transformation (beliefs about post-conflict democratic reforms and values), (3) perceptions of prescriptive levels of transformation (beliefs about what conflict interveners prescribe as appropriate action to take) and (4) knowledge of and engagement with new democratic and conflict transformation reforms and values.

The focus group discussions were therefore designed to provide a deeper awareness of how vital aspects of perception of descriptive and prescriptive levels of transformation and attitude towards the Other do or do not transform after sustained exposure to Information Operations contents. To this end, questions asked during the discussions centred on three of the research questions:

1. Can *Gutahuka* influence perception of Rwandan Hutus concerning the "right action" of "returning to Rwanda" as prescribed in the programme? On a broader level, can intervention media influence groups to voluntarily lay down their arms and participate in a demobilization and repatriation and reintegration programme?

2. Can *Dialogue* influence the perception of Congolese autochthons concerning descriptive levels of transformation and their attitude towards Rwandan Hutus? More broadly, can media interventions that provide "objective information only" positively influence an audience's engagement with new democratic values and culture in a post-conflict setting?

3. What kind of impacts can media intervention contents meant for autochthons have on Hutus' attitudes towards them when they are exposed to such messages and what impacts can media intervention contents meant for Hutus have on autochthones' attitudes towards Hutus when they are exposed to such contents. On a broader level, what impacts can Group A's exposure to intervention media designed for Group B have on perceptions and attitudes of Group A towards Group B?

9.3 Purpose as per Ethnic and Listening Groups

The purpose of the study was broken down to each listening group within each ethnic network.

Hutu Network

Hutu networks across the four contexts of the study were divided into two groups: *Gutahuka* group and *Dialogue entre Congolais* group for the purpose of listening to the two programmes and for the focus group discussions. Each group as pointed out previously had committed to not listening to the Other's programme.

Gutahuka **Group:** The purpose of focus group discussions for the *Gutahuka* group was to understand the impacts of MONUC's *Gutahuka* on Hutu networks across four contexts in South Kivu.

This group also served as a control group for understanding the impacts of Ethnic Network A listening to programmes meant for Ethnic Network B within the context of a violently divided society.

Dialogue **Group:** The purpose of focus group discussions for the Hutu *Dialogue* group was to understand the impacts of *Dialogue* on the attitude of Hutu networks towards Autochthons (the chief targets of the programme).

This group also served as a control group for understanding the impacts of *Gutahuka* on perceptions of Hutus towards the DDRRR programme and voluntary return to Rwanda.

Congolese Autochthons

Autochthons across the four contexts of the study were also divided into two groups: *Gutahuka* Group and *Dialogue* Group for the purpose of listening to the two programmes and for the focus group discussions. As in the Hutu network, each group committed to not listening to the other programme for the period.

Dialogue **Group:** The purpose of focus group discussions for the autochthon *Dialogue* group was to understand the impacts of Radio Okapi's *Dialogue* on their perceptions of democratic reforms, values and beliefs across the four contexts of study.

This group also served as a control group for autochthon *Gutahuka* listening group in terms of understanding the impacts of exposure to the other's intervention programme on relationships with the other group.

Gutahuka **Group:** The purpose for this group was to serve as a control for understanding the impact of *Dialogue* on perceptions of autochthons. Discussions from this group will also provide an understanding of the nature of impacts of this exposure to attitudes towards Hutus.

Central to all discussions therefore were participants' attitudes towards the other ethnic group, perception of descriptive levels of transformation and perception of prescriptive levels of transformation. Descriptive transformation is used here to refer to general changes stimulated by interveners in response to conflict. It involves knowledge of the social conditions that can create conflict including structural patterns within the society (Lederach 1997). Prescriptive level of transformation on the other hand describes knowledge of intervention programmes or processes that are able to promote non-violent changes, conditions that foster structures that meet human development needs including issues of substantive and procedural justice and local participation in decision making. Prescriptive level of transformation prescribes appropriate actions that should be taken to end conflict or deliberate interventions aimed at minimizing destructive effects of conflict in the society (Lederach 1997). Perception of prescriptive levels of transformation therefore seeks to understand how subjects perceive goals set by interveners in their intervention communications. In the case of *Gutahuka*, for example, the goal is for Rwandan Hutus to return to Rwanda and participate in the DDRRR programme while *Dialogue* seeks to engage in dialogue with citizens on ongoing democratic changes to achieve civic engagement.

9.4 Focus Group Participants

There was synergy of group participants as prescribed by Green et al. (2003) and Casey and Krueger (2000). This was easy to achieve because members of each focus group knew each other on a personal level. Also they all knew the moderator personally and regarded their moderators as one of their own. All moderators belonged to the same ethnic group and spoke the same language as participants; hence, it was easy to achieve trust between the participants and the moderator. Morrison has emphasized the need for a minimum of trust to be established so that participants can "feel comfortable in exposing feelings and giving opinions" (2003, 120). With a cultural insider moderating the discussions, self-disclosure was enhanced, trust was secured and participants were encouraged to speak. Aside from ethnic origin, participants shared several other characteristics – they lived around the same area, had a common sphere of experience and most were involved in the same profession; they belonged to the same age bracket (with few exceptions in Fizi and Uvira); and participants met regularly (prior to the focus group session). Views were thus expressed spontaneously. Also, participants knew each other's personal story, positions and views prior to the sessions; it was thus easy to reach a consensus. There were cases where participants nodded when another participant related a personal story because they had been aware of the incident prior to the session.

9.5 Focus Group Design

A double-layer design was used for the focus group study. It was derived from the categories of listenership involving four geographically defined contexts in the first layer and Hutu and autochthon participants at the second layer. As earlier stated, participants from each ethnic network in each context were categorised into two groups based on programme listened. Please see Table 9.1.

Table 9.1: Focus Group Design

Layer 1 (Context)	Layer 2 (Network)	Programme Listened
Mwenga	Hutus	*Gutahuka*
	Audience 1	*Dialogue*
	Audience 2	
	Autochthones	*Dialogue*
	Audience 1	*Gutahuka*
	Audience 2	
Walungu	Hutus	*Gutahuka*
	Audience 1	*Dialogue*
	Audience 2	
	Autochthones	*Dialogue*
	Audience 1	*Gutahuka*
	Audience 2	
Uvira	Hutus	*Gutahuka*
	Audience 1	*Dialogue*
	Audience 2	
	Autochthones	*Dialogue*
	Audience 1	*Gutahuka*
	Audience 2	
Fizi	Hutus	*Gutahuka*
	Audience 1	*Dialogue*
	Audience 2	
	Autochthones	*Dialogue*
	Audience 1	*Gutahuka*
	Audience 2	

9.6 Focus Group Plan and Organization

Peer researchers from each listening group contacted participants within their cellules individually to inform them and remind them of the dates and venues for the focus group discussion. Except for the sessions in Fizi, all the focus groups were either held at the home of one of the participants or in a "kibanda" (a shed where people usually meet at night to listen to radio together or discuss). In Fizi due to limited space, the two Hutu sessions were held in a "bwalo" or palm wine café usually frequented by the participants. The settings for the focus groups were deliberately designed to be familiar to the participants so that an informal communicative context can be re-created. It was important to the research that participants engaged with topics discussed within the context of everyday talk.

There were a total of 16 focus groups with 10 members in each group. The 10 members were chosen from a list of 14 to 16 pre-selected listeners in each listening group. Selection was based on the highest listening rates based on participants' logging. In cases where there were equal listening rates, selection was based on sex (female) first and then social embeddedness.

In each context or town, four focus group discussions were conducted – two in each ethnic network. Each session was moderated by the Peer Researcher in charge of the cellule with questions prepared by the researcher.

Each FGD session followed the same pattern and structure and lasted approximately one hour. At the start of each of the sessions, participants were encouraged to talk freely about how they found the listening project. This was intended to put participants in a talking mood preparatory to the questions. Although there was the tendency for participants to wander off the topic and banter with other participants, the moderators diligently brought them back to the issues under discussion.

At the end of each session, the proceedings were transcribed verbatim by the moderators working alongside the research assistant for this project and then translated from Kinyarwanda (in the Hutu groups) and Swahili (in the autochthon groups) into French by the research assistant and two students from Lubumbashi University in the DRC. The French version was eventually translated into English on a free translation internet portal: www.freetranslation.com – powered by Google Translation and SDL (a popular language translation software developer). The translation was reviewed by the researcher and a school French language teacher – Ms. Grace Kwabeng. Care was taken to ensure that meaning was not lost during the "multi-tier" translations. This was ensured by discussing individual comments again with the Peer Researchers. After all the language checks, the English version of the transcripts were then examined by the researcher to identify and categorize consistent themes.

9.7 Question Design

Following Krueger and Casey's (2000) recommendations, the questions were phrased and sequenced so that participants could easily understand them and were in the participants' native languages. They all followed a natural logical sequence progressing from general to specific topics. As previously stated, the questions in the FGDs were not intended to measure the knowledge of participants regarding the radio programmes they listened to. Rather, they were generally about conditions in the DRC; participants' knowledge of democratic values; participants' perceptions of conflict transformation efforts of the GoDRC and MONUC (descriptive); beliefs regarding transformation, peaceful change in terms of what should be done at individual, relational, cultural and structural levels to achieve peace (Prescriptive); and relations with other ethnic groups including the Banyamulenges (ethnic Tutsis in South Kivu). The intention was to find out how participants' views concerning the above indices varied based on programme listened to across contexts and networks after 13 months of exposure.

List of Questions

What or who do you consider to be the main barrier to peace in South Kivu in particular and eastern DRC in general?

Purpose of question: This question was intended to understand the pattern of participant's beliefs and perceptions regarding conflict multipliers across contexts and programme listened.

What have the GoDRC and MONUC done and/or not done to overcome or reduce these barriers?

Purpose of question: This question was intended to measure participants' perception of descriptive norms in terms of efforts by MONUC and GoDRC to build peace particularly in local areas. The "not done" aspect of the question sought to understand participants' perception of prescriptive norms in terms of personal/group perceptions of what should be done to achieve peace. The question afforded the researcher knowledge of patterns of perception of descriptive and prescriptive norms across the four contexts and two networks in terms of beliefs regarding conflict transformers. It also afforded an opportunity to assess the extent to which Okapi's and MONUC's expression of their peacebuilding efforts have resonated with participants.

Who are the worst affected victims of the DRC conflict and who has benefited most from it?

Purpose of question: The intention was to understand how participants saw themselves and others – whether they perceived themselves as victims and how such perception figured in their attitude towards the other. The question also provided an understanding of how listening to the other's programme affected perceptions or understanding of the other's issues. In this regard, the question afforded the researcher the opportunity to look out for feelings of empathy, resentment or aloofness.

Are there any opportunities for your personal development – career, capacity building, or civic engagement: what are they and how positive are you about their availability or accessibility?

Purpose of questions: To understand participants' construction of available options to enhance their livelihoods. This was also intended to provide an understanding of participants' perception of opportunities for civic engagement in their communities.

What is the situation in Rwanda, what arrangements are in place to help repatriate Hutus and what is available there to assist returnees to be reintegrated into the society?

Purpose of question: Targeted at Hutus, this question sought to find knowledge factors that could enhance or affect repatriation.

What is the appropriate action for Rwandan Hutus settled in South Kivu to take in order to help achieve peace and what are the main barriers for them returning and reintegrating in Rwanda?

Purpose of question: To understand Hutu participants' beliefs regarding the political situation in Rwanda particularly restorative and retributive justice systems; to understand factors interfering with *Gutahuka*'s message to them to return to Rwanda.

9.8 Framework for Data Analysis

There is a lot in common between Yin's (1984), Bogdan and Biklen's (1982) and Kruegger and Casey's (2000) frameworks for analysing qualitative focus group data. The three authors emphasize searching for patterns from comments. Ritchie and Spencer's (1994) Framework Analysis approach is more methodical involving five well-defined steps: transcript familiarization, developing categories from transcripts to identify a thematic framework, finding emerging themes, charting or marrying quotes with appropriate thematic category and finally developing conceptual maps based on data generated. Other authors notably Bobdan and Biklin (1982), Morrison (2003), Morgan and Spanish (1984) and Strauss and Corbin (1999) have written on flexibility as being "one of the great benefits of focus group research" (Morrison 2003, 125). Methodological flexibility can be used advantageously to juggle different approaches in order to meet specific or contextual requirements. In my analysis, I combined the approaches in Bobdan and Biklin (1982), Straus and Corbin (1999) and Kruegger and Casey (2000) to design an analytical framework that was flexible and fit to purpose. I drew on Bobdan and Biklin's (1982) approach of organizing data and breaking them down to manageable units, searching for patterns, and isolating what is important to address the propositions of the study. In breaking down what was a huge mass of data into manageable units, I first used Strauss and Corbin's (1999) open coding to identify and name conceptual categories to group observed phenomena.

Open Coding

The categories were descriptive and functioned mainly as preliminary framework for analysis. The next level involved an axial categorization of observed patterns of phenomena (including direct quotes) to establish themes and linkages to build a framework for interpretation. The opening coding was carried out one group at a time across all contexts. To this end, I first read through transcripts from *Gutahuka* listening groups across all networks and contexts followed by transcripts from *Dialogue* listeners. I then split the transcripts from each network in each context into units of quotes and the quotes matched with categories drawn from questions asked. Quotes that did not relate to any of the categories were discarded. Within each category, quotes across all networks and contexts that followed a similar pattern were grouped together, while those that differed were labelled accordingly. The next stage was selecting emerging themes from all the quotes. Consideration for coding a quote or selecting a quote as a theme was derived from Krueger and Casey's (2000) work and was defined based on the following factors:

1. Frequency – how frequently it was said.
2. Specificity – specific comments with details and examples including personal stories or real-life stories.
3. Emotion – more weight were given to comments made emotionally, passionately or enthusiastically as noted by transcribers.
4. Extensiveness: the number of different people saying the same thing was coded.
5. Agreement/congruence: level of general consensus concerning what is said.
6. Contention: how contentious what is said was in terms of how heavily it was debated.
7. Relevance: selection was also based on its relevance to the topic researched.

Emerging Themes

The following themes were derived from narratives from transcripts. The themes were derived from patterns of discussions from each of the ethnic networks. For analytical clarity, the themes were grouped into three broad categories representing the ethnic groups from which the quotes emerged. In themes relating to relationships (including integration), there were quotes that matched this category from both networks. Afterwards, the quotes were split into categories of listening groups for analysis.

Emerging Themes from Hutu Ethnic Group
- Perception of barriers to peace
- Perception of interventions
- Perception of structures and institutions that support transformation at personal and relational level
- Access to information/knowledge
- Perception of DDRRR
- Perception of socio-political reforms and justice systems in Rwanda
- Perception of possibilities of (re)integration in Rwanda or Congo and imagination of future relationships with other ethnic groups.
- Perception of availability of opportunities for civic engagement and personal development
- Perceptions of villains and victims of the conflict

Emerging Themes from Autochthons
- Perception of barriers to peace
- Perception of interventions
- Perception of structures and institutions that support transformation at personal and relational level
- Perception of democratic values, institutions
- Perception of channels or means of achieving non-violent change
- Perception of possibilities of (re)integration
- Access to information/knowledge
- Perception of availability of opportunities for personal development
- Perceptions of villains and victims of the conflict
- Perception of possibilities of (re)integration and imagination of future relationships with other ethnic groups.

9.9 Analysis of Focus Group Discussions

This section of the chapter reports participants' comments across the various groups based on pre-defined themes. It is divided into two parts. The first part explores patterns and variations in comments from Rwandan Hutus across the listening groups and contexts, while the second part covers Congolese Autochthons. In all groups, participants were encouraged to reach a consensus on answers and where a consensus could not be reached, they were encouraged to present their different positions. In most cases, there was generally a consensus among participants.

PART 1: RWANDAN HUTU FOCUS GROUPS

This part analyses comments from eight focus groups made up of Rwandan Hutu ethnic networks in Mwenga, Uvira, Fizi and Walungu contexts. In each context, there were two focus groups representing the two listening groups.

Gutahuka Listeners' Perception of Barriers to Peace
Participants across all contexts were asked to discuss among themselves and decide the greatest barrier to peace in South Kivu.

Government of Rwanda (GoR) – the Greatest Barrier to Peace
There was a consensus among participants across all contexts that the government of Paul Kagame in Rwanda was the greatest barrier to peace in the DRC. Participants talked passionately about their opposition to the Tutsi-led Rwandan government

which they said was "oppressive" and "illegitimate". In all contexts, participants believed the Government of Rwanda (GoR) was carrying out genocide against Hutus in the Kivus.

They believed that the GoR has been responsible for all the suffering that Hutus have passed through in Congo. They also believed that the GoR was deliberately causing crises in the DRC in order to keep the country unstable for their own gains. For these reasons, they identified the GoR as the main barrier to peace. Most participants' anger was against the policies of the Rwandan government in Kigali which they believed were anti-Hutu. Participants were surprisingly familiar with goings-on in Rwanda in terms of politics and expressed frustration at the way Hutus were being sidelined and said those that dared to challenge the regime were being persecuted

> *Rwanda is intent on breaking up Congo. A big, peaceful and prosperous Congo will be a threat to Rwanda so they don't want that happening.*
> *(Fizi Group)*

> *The Rwandan government is paying CNDP and now FARDC to fight Hutus. So because of that FDLR has not disarmed and Mai Mai has not disarmed because of that as well because no man wants to sit down and cross his hands while a stranger comes in to plunder his home.*
> *(Walungu Group)*

> *As long as the Rwanda government continues its policy of persecuting Hutus both inside Rwanda and in the Congo, there won't be peace. They want to establish a Tutsi country in the Kivus and eventually join it with Rwanda and Burundi to create a Tutsi empire. That is the major problem here, that is what all the fight is about.*
> *(Mwenga Group)*

> *When we were refugees in Chimanga the Rwandan government used Laurent Kabila's AFDL to kill several thousands and no one did anything about it, Hutu people are being killed today everyday and the Rwandan government is responsible. The Congo war had ended a long time ago, what is happening now is Rwanda's war against Hutus. That is the truth you won't hear in the news.*
> *(Uvira Group)*

MONUC – The Second Greatest Barrier to Peace

Although participants agreed that it was not in the best interest of the FDLR or Hutus in general to engage MONUC militarily for any reason, there was a consensus across contexts that MONUC's peacekeepers were among the main barriers to peace in the east and a part of the conflict. Reasons for their opinion ranged from lack of trust for peacekeepers because of claims of double dealing and illicit sale of arms to the Tutsi-dominated *Conseil National pour la Défense de la Démocratie* (CNDP), lack of commitment by MONUC to protecting Hutu civilians against attacks by CNDP and integrated battalions in the Congolese army – *Forces Armées de la République Démocratique du Congo* (FARDC).

MONUC can't be trusted. They look the other way while Nkunda and now Ntaganda walk free to kill. FDLR is there because MONUC has allowed Ntaganda to continue to kill Hutu people.
(Walungu Group)

MONUC is siding with CNDP to kill Hutus. They have done brassage (integration) for CNDP commanders and fighters just so that they can have the official power to go after Hutus in the Kivus.
(Fizi Group)

MONUC soldiers want the war to continue so they can make money I'm talking mainly about those of them from Pakistan and Bangladesh. I know all of them because I worked with them in Ituri about four years ago to translate. As long as they are here there won't be peace. Also, if you have a problem or are attacked today and call them they won't come to help. So what are they here for if they can't defend civilians without any weapons in trouble?
(Uvira Group)

MONUC has been secretly supporting FDLR for years now both in weapons and in knowledge. The last thing they want to see happen here is peace.
(Mwenga Group)

Dialogue Listeners' Perception of Barriers to Peace

Listeners of *Dialogue* were also asked to discuss among themselves and choose the greatest and second greatest barrier to peace in South Kivu.

Weak GoDRC – The Greatest Barrier to Peace

Across all contexts, *Dialogue* listeners asserted that the greatest barrier to peace in South Kivu was the Government of DRC (GoDRC). Participants used expressions such as "weak", "lacking in honesty" and "childish" to describe both the provincial and national governments. The participants believed that the inability of the GoDRC to take a definitive stand against the Rwandan government's aggressive use of armed groups, particularly the CNDP to fight a proxy war in eastern DRC, showed weakness. They said they were disappointed that the GoDRC could not protect them even as refugees. They also said the weakness of the government had enabled guerrilla entrepreneurs to hold sway in parts of the east to deal on raw materials.

There is no government here. It is a situation of free for all. Any entrepreneur that has men and guns can set up an enclave ... take little boys and women hostage, mount road blocks, collect taxes, dig up some ores for sale and run his own state. That is how it is in this place.
(Uvira Group)

MONUC and the radio people keep talking about FDLR, Mayi Mayi, and all Rwandan speakers as the problem, but it is not true. There are several other small groups that do not even have names that oppress people here. That is because the government has ceased to exist in these places. When nothing happens, dust settles.
(Mwenga Group)

The government and the president is too weak. He even went to Rwanda and agreed for RPF to come to Congo to fight for them (makes gestures of abominable shame).
(Walungu Group)

If Kabila had insisted from the beginning that he would never do business with Nkunda there is no way that Kagame would have pushed him to do it. But they made overtures to Nkunda and that is where they showed their weakness. Rwanda knew they could make more cracks in the Congo.
(Fizi Group)

FARDC – The Second Greatest Barrier to Peace

Participants in all four contexts repeatedly said that although the FARDC was not to blame for the conflict, they have in recent times become accessories in the hands of the GoR. The problem with FARDC, they believe, started with the *mixage* of two of belligerent General Laurent Nkunda's CNDP (81st and 83rd) brigades with three brigades of FARDC (110th, 116th and 1st Reserve Brigades) in North Kivu in 2007. The *mixage* which they believed was brokered by the GoR and Congo's General John Numbi without the approval of MONUC did not involve the usual rigorous process obtained in the MONUC-backed *brassage* system but only involved mixing of command structures between the Congolese army and General Nkunda's dissident group made up mostly of Kinyarwandas and Banyamulenges or ethnic Tutsis in North and South Kivu, respectively. They expressed the belief that the infiltration of the command structure of the FARDC in the Kivus by the Tutsi belligerents and the Rwandan government started with the mixage process. With that, they perceived that the army has become a mechanism for hunting down Hutus. They said although historically there have been good relationships between FARDC and Hutus, the FARDC has in the past four years been infiltrated by the Rwandan government and used as an instrument for targeting Hutus in the Kivus.

The FARDC keep attacking Hutus because they are members of CNDP that have been dressed in army (FARDC).
(Mwenga Group)

The national army in the Kivus is now CNDP. They only call themselves FARDC, but it is CNDP. Everyone knows that and their job is to hunt Hutus wheresoever they may be found. You ask yourself, why didn't they go through the normal brassage? And why did they hide it from the UN first time?
(Walungu Group)

What are people like Ntaganda doing in the FARDC? He and other Tutsi ... (derogatory term used has been removed) are there because they are paid to look for and kill Hutus everywhere. That started in 2007 with the mixage campaign.
(Uvira Group)

At the beginning Hutus fought side by side with FARDC because we are brothers, we have more in common with the Congolese than they do with the Banyamulenges. But the FARDC was pressured to mix with Nkunda's army. When that happened, FARDC started hunting Hutus. That's been the cause of war in the past two years. Normally FARDC and FDLR should not fight each other. Brothers don't fight.
(Fizi Group)

Perception of Barriers to Peace that Cut Across Listenership Groups
General Bosco Ntaganda[18] **– a Barrier to peace:** Participants across listening groups in three of the contexts (Walungu, Uvira and Mwenga) spoke very passionately about General Ntaganda being in the FARDC and said they believed he had a personal agenda of exterminating Hutus. Although Bosco Ntaganda has been indicted by the ICC, he is a general in the FARDC. He was formally a commander with the CNDP but after the *mixage* programme of CNDP and FARDC, he was brought into the FARDC. Participants specifically identified General Ntaganda as one of the main barriers to peace. Despite appeals by a number of human rights organizations and several other international partners to the GoDRC to arrest Bosco Ntaganda, to answer charges of crimes against humanity at the ICC, the government has refused to carry out the arrest. In sum, participants felt that it if FDLR disarmed there would be no one to protect Hutu civilians from Ntaganda's agenda.

> *The government is claiming Kimia II had nothing to do with Ntaganda but that is the worst lie ever. He was actively involved, his soldiers are still actively involved in exterminating Hutus in Shabunda, in Rutshuru even in this place and, everywhere there are Hutus.*
> *(Walungu Group DIALOGUE)*

> *Ntaganda was taken an oath on behalf of Kagame to exterminate Hutus in Congo and set up a Rwandan state in the Kivus and I can tell you that Kabila and MONUC are too scared of Kagame to do anything about it.*
> *(Uvira Group GUTAHUKA)*

> *Why is the FDLR still fighting? Because people like Terminator (Ntaganda) walk about free even after the world court (ICC) has ordered his arrest. And he is part of the FARDC determined to hunt down all Hutus. That is why the Abacunguzi is still bearing arms.*
> *(Uvira Group DIALOGUE)*

> *A big problem is Tutsi Commanders in the army like Ntaganda. His men have caused a lot of bloodshed and rape on women in the Kivus. They are also involved in mining.*
> *(Mwenga Group DIALOGUE)*

> *That man is evil, his hands are dripping with the blood of Hutu children. The Abacunguzi says they will keep fighting until Ntaganda and people like him are brought to justice and I don't blame them.*
> *(Mwenga Group GUTAHUKA)*

> *As long as Ntaganda is part of FARDC, and the UN go on to back the FARDC, there can't be peace. As far as I am concerned I think Ntaganda is the worst enemy of Hutus in Kivu and as long as he continues to wear Congolese army uniform I believe there won't be peace in the Kivus.*
> *(Walungu Group GUTAHUKA)*

---

18 General Bosco Ntaganda is currently facing trial at the International Criminal Court for War Crimes.

Perception of Interventions
Perception of two levels of transformation was assessed – descriptive and prescriptive transformation. As earlier stated, descriptive transformation refers to general changes in response to conflict and actions taken to transform conflict and/or alleviate its impacts (Lederach 1997). Prescriptive level of transformation on the other hand describes knowledge of appropriate actions that should be taken to end conflict or deliberate interventions aimed at minimizing destructive effects of conflict (Lederach 1997).

Gutahuka Listeners' Perception of Descriptive Interventions
Participants were asked what have been done by either the government or MONUC to create peace and end the conflicts in South Kivu and what they thought of such intervention efforts.

MONUC's Interventions Are Weak and Biased
Participants believed MONUC did not have their priorities right and were reluctant to militarily engage with armed groups even ones that attacked civilians. Although they expressed some knowledge of MONUC's efforts at negotiating a ceasefire with armed groups, they believed such negotiations were not from a position of strength but out of weakness. Participants across the four contexts of study had a surprisingly negative attitude and perception of MONUC peacekeepers and the UN in general. They said MONUC could not achieve much because they were there to fulfil the bid of the USA, Britain, France and Rwanda.

> *MONUC has put some pressure on Kabila to negotiate with some armed groups but that is because they don't want to fight the armed groups themselves.*
> ***(Walungu Group)***

> *I know they helped bring everybody to sign the agreement in South Africa back in 2003 to end all the war that time. After that it is as if they went to sleep, nothing much has been achieved since then. By now you would have thought peace would be everywhere.*
> ***(Fizi Group)***

> *The UN is here preaching everyday that we should return to Rwanda, they promise they would take us and our family back there and give us some pocket money to survive there, teach us a trade and so on, but the truth is that as soon as you get back there, they take their hands off you. You are left in the mercy of the Tutsis and their Gacaca system. No one fights on your side anymore because the UN has no mandate in Rwanda. It's all a trick to deceive those that don't think properly.*
> ***(Uvira Group)***

> *The only good thing I can say that the peacekeepers have done is when they escorted the women to markets in Bukavu and to the fields. Other than that, it is talk talk and talk on radio.*
> ***(Mwenga Group)***

Gutahuka Listeners' Perception of Prescriptive Transformations

Participants were asked what they thought about the return home messages of *Gutahuka* and if they were willing to return to Rwanda.

Gutahuka's *Message Has to Change*

Participants thought the UN was too partial to achieve any meaningful intervention. In all contexts, participants told stories of how UN peacekeepers have been involved in various illicit activities including mining, rape and selling weapons to combatants. Their main disaffection with the UN was that they do not distinguish between civilian Hutus and Hutu combatants. Although there have been sensitization activities about FDLR and calls on them to return home, there has not been a similar sensitization to encourage Hutu ex-combatants and civilians who have integrated and inter-married in the communities and wished to remain where they are. They said the UN should help them more and defend them from attacks from Tutsi militants and extremist FDLR commanders. An interestingly recurring theme in all contexts was that the UN should change its "Return Home to Rwanda" message and encourage all Hutus that want to settle in Congo to do so and help protect them from attacks. They believed that the "go back home" messages further alienated Hutus because "home" for them is now Congo. Because of the rich texts from some of the participants, I have quoted them and the conversations at length.

> WG 4[19]: *The UN should try to encourage Hutu civilians that want to settle peacefully in Congo to do so. Even in Europe and America you have Hutu people that live there peacefully on refuge so why can't we live here peacefully and do our own business?*

> WG 7: *I know there are people that are going back but if they had their way, they would have preferred to remain here and build their lives here. See, the men are tired of fighting, we have been fighting for a good part of 15 years in the rainy season and in the dry season. People are tired and want to live a normal life before they become too old, so instead of continuing to fight forever, they have taken on the only choice of going back to Rwanda, not because they love it, but because it is the only way out of the life of fighting. No one, not even the commanders enjoy this life of fighting and constantly running. The UN should take this into consideration.*
> **(Walungu Group)**

> *Instead of preaching that Hutu fighters should go back to Rwanda, they should start preaching that Hutu fighters should remain and integrate in their communities. There are many thousands of Hutus including the militants that have intermarried here, assimilated the culture and speak the language, they know there is nothing for them in Rwanda.*
> **(Mwenga Group)**

---

19 Codes were used to represent each speaker, (rather than real names) due to confidentiality agreements.

FG 1: The UN should start seeing us as human beings that are capable of contributing to life here. Some of the most hardworking farmers, herders, teachers and healers here are Hutus from Rwanda. Go to Changugu and Kibua and see the schools that Hutus built, go to Nindja, Luchungo and Kagembe, Hutus built hospitals there without any help or money from anywhere ... and you will see what I am talking about. But unfortunately, the UN makes it look as if we are all combatants and should return to Rwanda.

FG 4: I sometimes think the UN does not understand some things here. Most of the FDLR fighters are young men that left Rwanda when they were only little boys. Their fathers are dead and they do not have any known relatives in Rwanda. Most of them are married to Congolese women and have in-laws here. MONUC need to change their message and involve them in the brassage and rehabilitation process here. It is offensive telling these young men to return to Rwanda. They don't have anything to return to there. As far as they are concerned this is home.
(Fizi Group)

UG 9: They need to change their way of asking all Hutu fighters to go back. That cannot work. Rather they should be given the chance of joining the army here if they want to or starting their own businesses here if they want to. If MONUC does that you will see the number of fighters that would come out to join the process. ... I agree the recognition of service money could be attractive to some people that qualify for it but most of the FDLR fighters are young men that would not qualify for the reinsertion and would be happier to be integrated here.

UG 2: Personally I do not know any of my relatives in Rwanda. I cannot remember any of them. I know I have a brother to my father and two sisters and one brother of my mother. But I am not sure they would even want to have anything to do with me or want me in their family. But here I have people around me, my wife, my sons, my wife's parents and brothers. They care about us and I see myself as part of the family. I have been involved in the FDLR fighting because I had to protect my family, but now I own a small kiosk where I sell divers[20] that my father-in-law helped to set up for me. Going back to Rwanda is out of the question because I do not know where I would start from. The UN can help because there are several young men like me that are in the fighting ranks and going back won't work for us.
(Uvira Group)

Dialogue Listeners' Perception of Descriptive Interventions
GoDRC's Interventions Are Feeble and Ineffective
Participants talked mainly about the intervention efforts of the GoDRC. They said they were dissatisfied with the intervention efforts of the GoDRC. They believed that the intervention efforts of the government were "half-hearted" and "feeble". There was a consensus among *Dialogue* listening participants in all contexts that the government's efforts particularly regarding working with armed groups to resolve the crises in the Kivus was ineffective. Although participants showed good knowledge of current intervention efforts of the government relating to resolving the crises by

---

20 All sorts of merchandise – soaps, salt, cigarettes, second hand shoes, fruits, etc.

negotiating with armed groups, creating peace constituents, expanding democratic space by encouraging people to engage more in politics at local levels, etc., it was generally seen from the perspective that any government's action was doomed to fail. In all contexts, participants expressed a lack of faith in the ability of the government to transform the conflict, create development, fulfil personal development yearnings of people and build peace. In the Fizi context, participants were particularly critical of the government and felt the government was non-existent. Participants expressed more faith in traditional systems of authority, Hutu self-help groups and religious authorities than in the Congolese central or provincial government. The distance or weakness of the government they believed was responsible for most of the atrocities committed against civilians by armed groups who have taken over administration of several towns and villages and were collecting taxes.

> The government has co-operated with CNDP to remove FDLR, but that as you can see is not working.
> **(Walungu Group)**

> The government has co-operated with Rwanda to arrest Laurent Nkunda, but I think it is all deceit. Why has he not been tried or handed over to the court (ICC) like they have done with Bemba for prosecution?
> **(Uvira Group)**

> The government has co-operated with Rwanda to bring in their army to fight FDLR. But you see you cannot shake hands with a person who is suffering from leprosy and expect that your hands would remain the same.
> **(Mwenga Group)**

> The only government here are the Chiefs (Hutu Tribal Leaders) and the Church. Well you can see the few things they are doing like schools for children and medical care for the sick and for women that are giving birth. That is what a government is supposed to do, but since they are not doing it, we see those that are doing it as the real government.
> **(Fizi Group)**

Dialogue Listeners' Perception of Prescriptive Transformations
GoDRC Should Negotiate with FDLR; Stop All Military Collaboration with the GoR and Tutsi Armed Groups

When asked what they perceived as the appropriate intervention activity needed to achieve peaceful change and stability, participants were unanimous in prescribing the cessation of all military alliances with Rwanda and the CNDP and for the government to open direct talks with FDLR leadership. Though they were highly critical of the government, participants were surprisingly adamant in their belief that the government is capable of taking appropriate action to end the conflict if it spurns the influence of the Rwandan government. Of all prescriptions, the most consistent across contexts and most emphasized was that the GoDRC should sit down with FDLR and talk about a way forward, cease military alliances with Rwanda, followed by provision of security for civilians, primarily pregnant women.

In all contexts of the study, participants' perception of prescriptive level of intervention centred mainly on the Congolese government's interaction with the Rwandan government.

> *The way forward is to sit down with FDLR commanders and talk out a solution. FDLR and the Kabila family have never been enemies. I am sure if the government can do that a lot of unresolved security issues can be sorted out even before daybreak.*
> ***(Mwenga Group)***

> *I know very well that if Joseph Kabila wants to stop all the nonsense he can do it. But he is afraid of what killed his father. When he is man enough to stop all alliances with Rwanda, remove them from his army and take charge of the country, things will be alright here. All the talk about Hutu people being the problem in the Congo is just a lie to remove attention from the main problem on ground which is that Rwanda is fighting to annex Kivu.*
> ***(Walungu Group)***

> *Kabila should ... first remove all CNDP soldiers that joined the army from Nkunda's group, two, monitor the boundary with Rwanda to prevent them bringing weapons in here and three take full control of all the mining places here and use the money to build roads and maternity hospitals.*
> ***(Uvira Group)***

> *Congo should discontinue their co-operation with Rwanda. Kagame only comes close to you when he wants something from you. As soon as he gets it, he turns against you. He has to learn from what happened to his father. All the Tutsi soldiers should either be removed or sent to any other area to work and not the Kivus because if they are here they would keep killing our people and trading in ores.*
> ***(Fizi Group)***

Gutahuka Listeners' Knowledge/Perception of MONUC's DDRRR Programme

Questions under this category were meant to assess knowledge factors among Hutus in terms of MONUC's arrangements for repatriation and reintegration of Hutu ex-combatants in Rwanda. Participants were asked to talk about what they knew about the DDRRR programme, particularly the resettlement and reintegration elements of the programme in Rwanda.

Poor Knowledge of DDRRR Processes

Participants' comments in three of the four contexts showed lack of basic knowledge of specific resettlement packages that await them if they returned to Rwanda. The case was significantly different in Uvira where participants' comments suggested a better grasp particularly of recent political reforms in Rwanda and knowledge of remuneration packages and demobilization, repatriation and reinsertion processes that await returnees. As a follow on, three participants together with the Peer Researcher from the group were further interviewed. They attributed the higher knowledge in Uvira locale (which is the most urban of all four contexts studied) to other follow-up activities in the territory such as distribution of DDRRR brochures by MONUC and interaction with MONUC's DDRRR field sensitization officers and with people travelling to and from Rwanda on business who have first-hand information. Also, one of MONUC's repatriation transit camps is located in a nearby town. Another possible reason for greater knowledge is that some participants in Uvira frequently listened to *Isange Mu Banyu* – a programme on Rwandan Government Radio on the repatriation programme. Participants interviewed said they found *Isange Mu Banyu* more credible and more informative. This was surprising because the programme is broadcast on Rwandan government radio station and participants had a negative attitude towards the Rwandan government. But participants said *Isange Mu Banyu* reported the activities of the Rwandan Demobilisation and Reintegration Commission (RDRC) in much greater detail than *Gutahuka*. The programme also interviews ordinary people in Rwanda about life there, whereas *Gutahuka* was seen as *"propagande"* because of its constant appeal to them to go home. Sometimes, they said, the announcer makes threats and would say they should return before it is too late.

Aside from the Uvira context, participants displayed lack of knowledge about exact resettlement packages and the entire process of re-insertion. They also felt the information they received were not up-to-date and felt they needed a more trusted and personal source about the kind of treatment and benefit they would receive and guarantees that they would not be persecuted particularly in the Rwandan *Gacaca* traditional courts. Participants said most of the interviews on *Gutahuka* are with former commanders and the few ones they conducted with local villagers did not seem real. Rather than being told to return, participants said they would appreciate frank information on specific repatriation packages in terms of exact money they would be paid; how long they would be paid for; how long they would remain in the camp before being allowed to return to their villages; the kind of treatment they would receive in their villages; and whether they would have access to farmland in their villages so they can farm and raise livestock or engage in other small-scale commercial activities. A common feeling among participants was that they were not properly informed about specific packages that awaited them if they returned. Although some of the participants said it would be tough for them to go back to Rwanda since they have become embedded in their communities in South Kivu, they agreed that it would be useful still to have sufficient information where they can use to make up their own minds on what would be the appropriate action to take. Participants used words such as "decide myself", "make my own mind", "think for myself", etc.

Although participants said they were concerned about money matters and how they would cope financially if they returned, their comments suggested they lacked basic knowledge of the actual amount of money paid on arrival and other payments during the demobilization processes which includes the Basic Needs Kit (BNK), the Recognition of Service Allowance (RSA) for those that were formerly members of the Rwandan armed forces and the Reintegration grant paid six months after demobilization (subject to certain re-integration conditions being met). They also lacked knowledge of the processes, sequence and timeframe of demobilization activities on arrival in Rwanda.

Participants said most of the information they had about the reward programme was from people within their socio-ethnic networks. Moreover, they said they had a lot of questions they would love to ask about specifics in a context where they can remain anonymous and their identities protected for fear of attacks by extremist FDLR combatants and commanders who do not want them to return. Participants were also concerned about reintegration within their communities. They believed that neighbours and church members in their former communities that lost relatives in 1994 may want to vent anger on them or make false accusations against them at the *Gacaca* courts.

WG 8: All we need is the truth, not propaganda ... would I have a farm to plant on and rear flocks if we return? How long would we have to remain in Mutobo (camp for returnees) before going home? Would my wife and children be separated from me while in the camp? What assurance can I have that they won't use Gacaca to persecute me like they have done before to other people? Is that not what we've been asking all this time? ... yet no one has given us satisfying answers till today.

WG 4: If I had information from a friend I know personally or relative that has seen everything they do there I think it would make things easier. I would be able to decide myself then. But now it is hard to know what is true from all the propaganda. And it doesn't help when they talk too much.
(Walungu Group)

MG 10: There is no information about current returnees. Most of the people they interview on the programme are those that returned years ago. How about those that returned a month ago or two weeks? And a lot of times those interviews are repeated. It all seems like propaganda.

MG 3: I heard that there is a camp for everybody when you return and you live in the camp for months before they release you to go back to your village. Why should I want to go through such a refugee kind of life in my own country after all they have put me through?
(Mwenga Group)

FG 4: I am doing business at the moment and I have livestock and a farm from which I can feed my family but I do not know how much they would be giving me there until I get my feet on the ground again in Rwanda to be able to take care of my family.

FG 2: Other than that, I think the problem some of us have is that they keep saying that they will help to get us back into our communities, but what we don't know is how people there would take us back. There are people in 1994 that lost their brothers, their parents and children in the same locality, or the same church, how would they receive us? We would be like aliens there and they can attack us or make false testament at the traditional court. How would that be handled? We don't know.
(Fizi Group)

You know sometimes we need to understand that there are some things such as human feelings and thoughts. I know we are can go back and they can help with some money after six months to set up a business, but what do you do in all those six months? Sit down and count the stars? I was not in the army so I won't get paid any gratuity it's only the FRw50,000 which can't last for one month with all the things you need to set up when you arrive. And they expect you survive with that for six months? Six months is not six days. You have to feed, you have to take care of wife and children. But it is not just that, to be fair to myself and to them, a lot of people do not find going back worth thinking about. A lot of the youths are keen on retiring fighting but they don't have anything to go back to in Rwanda.

Another comment from Uvira participant:

Gutahuka keeps saying everything is good now in Rwanda ... angels are singing in Rwanda and gold is raining .... But we all know that cannot be true. Everything cannot just be good good good, there has to be something that is not good. Why not tell us everything and not only the good and good and good all the time.
(Uvira Group)

Dialogue Listeners' Perception of DDRRR and Reintegration in Rwanda

Participants from *Dialogue* listening groups were asked what they thought were the barriers to returning to Rwanda and what they thought about resettling and reintegrating in Rwanda.

Negative Views of Repatriation and Opportunities for Reintegration in Rwanda

Although participants in all contexts studied agreed that things have improved greatly in Rwanda, in terms of economic opportunities, they believed they have been away for far too long to benefit personally from the new economic opportunities in the country. Having been away for so long, they believed that they would be excluded and would have difficulty in coping and forming new business partnerships in Rwanda. The major problem, participants said, was reintegrating not only socially but also economically in Rwanda. Opportunities for growth and personal development were perceived to be bleak in Rwanda.

I have nothing to return to there. But I know there are people that are doing well, buying cars, building houses and making big business, but most of them are Tutsis. They only help themselves. But as soon as they look at your face and see you are not one of them, the door is immediately shut against you and all you can do is stand there and throw nuts against a shut door.
(Uvira Group)

Some people think that because Rwanda is so heavily helped by America, Britain and France, that things would be transparent and that there would equal opportunities for everyone. The truth is most people who are not Tutsis continue to roll on the dirt of poverty and no one cares about them.
(Mwenga Group)

Some of us left Rwanda 16 years now, where would we start from if we were to return? There is nothing there for us now, and we all know that. We are not dreamers.
(Walungu Group)

FD 6: I am yet to see or hear about one person that returned and went on to have a good life, make decent money for himself and his family. Those that have returned are really struggling.

FD 1: It is a tough life out there I can tell you ... because there is not enough for those that are there how much more me. In Rwanda you have to fight for everything, you fight for land to build your house, fight for school to send your children, fight for a stand in the market, fight for a space in the field to feed your goats. What don't you fight for? I'm tired of fighting my brother, I'd rather stay here and when it is time, die here.
(Fizi Group)

Poor Knowledge of Specifics of Resettlement Grants

Dialogue participants generally lacked knowledge of specifics of resettlement grants in Rwanda. Also, they did not show much enthusiasm about the discussion when it came to financial settlements for returnees (unlike in the *Gutahuka* groups). Participants were generally apathetic. But generally (including those in Uvira) lacked knowledge of specific elements of grants and when paid.

It would be difficult to survive with your wife and family there when you have to abandon everything here and relocate to Rwanda. How do you live? What do you eat? It would have been different if they paid reasonable money on arrival and provide some kind of money on a continuous basis, provide land for grazing.
(Walungu Group)

I can't really tell how much is paid, but I know it is not worth anything and they don't pay it to everyone. If they were serious with what they are doing, they would have offered land to those that are farmers or pastoralists.
(Fizi Group)

It is only former military personnel that are given some money like a form of pension. Everyone else goes home without anything.
(Mwenga Group)

I know some amount of money is supposed to be paid when you return but most times they don't pay, they say they have to make sure you were not part of the genocide first before you are paid. And how do they find out? They ask where you were and what you were doing in 1994, and if they feel your face looks like somebody that must have killed people they say ok you go to Gacaca and you won't get paid anything. It is all a trick.
(Uvira Group)

Perception of Justice in the *Gacaca* Court System (Across *Gutahuka* & *Dialogue* Groups)

The Rwandan *Gacaca* traditional courts was a controversial topic during discussions in both listening groups. While the younger participants said they had nothing to fear with the courts, the older ones mainly in Fizi and Mwenga believed that the

Gacaca courts were not transparent but were meant to hunt Hutus and that no one however innocent is safe. While most of the participants insisted they had nothing whatsoever to do with the Rwandan genocide, they still feared victimization. A few of the younger participants said they could not say whether their fathers, now dead, had been involved in the killings and the level of involvement. So they feared they could become victims of a vendetta. Furthermore, in terms of knowledge, information that participants across both listening groups had on the *Gacaca* courts were from socially transmitted or informal sources. And the picture generally was that it is an instrument of persecution. Although the National Service of *Gacaca* Jurisdiction in Rwanda and the Rwandan Ministry of Justice have both assured that justice is restorative and fair, participants remained cautious and suspicious. Moreover, participants displayed lack of accurate knowledge of the way the *Gacaca* justice system actually worked. Most participants felt no one could obtain justice from the *Gacaca* courts because of the way they believe the court is constituted.

Negative Perception and Distrust of Gacaca Justice System across Listening Groups

If I should speak for myself, I was a minor in 1994 so there is no sane way I would be accused of any killings, but the problem I have is that I do not know what my (late) father did or did not do and how he was involved. If I should go back to my village in Rwanda now you never know, somebody may come to me and say "your father did this or that to my mother or to my father or my brother" and then take it on me. For that person, that is his own justice and that is outside the Gacaca justice system.
Walungu (Gutahuka Listening Group)

It is not the court that is a problem for me because I was only a little boy then, so they won't bother me. But I hear stories that people come up with every kind of claim just to avenge on your family so that they can continue to occupy your family land. I think the court is just a way of trying to get back at people.
Fizi (Gutahuka Group)

Who created the Gacaca courts? Was it not Kagame that does not like Hutus? That court is not a real court. A few people sit and decide if you are guilty or not guilty and most times they do not even have evidence but simply because the person that brought the case is crying and pulling their hair, they would say you are guilty. I don't think there is justice in Gacaca.
Mwenga (Dialogue Group)

You can say what you want to say in those (Gacaca) courts but if they want to make you guilty they would. The truth is, Gacaca is all politics. It was created to punish their Hutu enemies.
Mwenga (Gutahuka Group)

All the talk about justice in Gacaca court is a big lie. In the constitution of Rwanda there was nothing like Gacaca. The courts are there and you can have your lawyer to defend you. But in the Gacaca courts, it is anything goes, no lawyer to defend you and the person accusing you ... is also your judge. So how can you ever win?
Uvira (Gutahuka Group)

Very many of our people have fled from Rwanda back to Congo because when they got there they realized that the Tutsi people were using the Gacaca court to persecute Hutu people. All the talk of justice is just a way of deceiving people. We all know that.
Uvira (Dialogue Listening Group)

Perceptions of Victims and Victimhood

Participants were encouraged to talk about their experiences and to reflect on the effects of conflict on everyone in the community and all parties and then discuss who the most severe victims of the conflict were.

Perception of Victimhood in *Gutahuka* Groups

Participants saw the Hutu ethnic group in general as the main victims of the conflict. They lamented that they have been "hunted like preys", "hated", "lied against", etc. since 1994 and the international community has turned a blind eye on their plight. They have tried to form vigilantes to defend themselves but everyone sees them as spoilers and aggressors. Generally, there was a feeling of aloofness concerning what other ethnic groups including Congolese autochthons and Tutsis have suffered.

Perception of Selves as Victims of the Conflict

We (Rwandan Hutus) have suffered a lot, no one has suffered persecution more than us.
(Mwenga Group)

Everybody in the world hates us because they think we all committed genocide and because of that no one wants to speak for us or even help us. But the truth is we are the ones that they have committed genocide against.
(Fizi Group)

More than 1 million Hutus have been killed since 1994 but you won't hear about that on the radio. All you hear is that 1 million Tutsis were killed by Hutus in genocide. The Rwandan government has been carrying out genocide against us for 15 years and no one cares.
(Uvira Group)

Every Hutu child knows he would be lucky to live till the age of 30. It was never this way before. Now we are pursued by MONUC, hunted like preys by FARDC now taken over by Tutsis, everybody is after the Hutu blood.
(Walungu Group)

Perception of Victimhood in *Dialogue* Groups

Across all contexts, participants had varying notions of who they perceived as the worst affected victims of the conflict. While some participants believed the children among them and women among them suffered the most, others felt the men who are targeted for killing are the worst victims. Some others felt the Hutus in general were the worst victims of the conflict.

Mixed Perception of Victimhood

> I don't think there are any people in the world so hated like us. They say we committed genocide but they forget that members of FDLR are mostly in their 20s and must have been only little children in 1994 how could they have committed genocide then?
> **(Walungu Group)**

> Because of how they control the radio, they have made everybody outside this area to think that every Rwandan Hutu in eastern Congo is a member of FDLR and had committed genocide. So we are the most badly affected people.
> **(Uvira Group)**

> I think those that have suffered most are the women, particularly the pregnant women. I helped give birth to a baby in the bush two years ago, but she died. The woman had a disease and was releasing blood for a few days. But she survived. Most don't. It is possible she was even forced (raped).
> **(Mwenga Group)**

> I think everybody, well maybe the children most. Because they have not done any sin to deserve all the suffering they go through.
> **(Fizi Group)**

Perception of Villainity in *Gutahuka* Groups

Participants across all contexts of the study traced the instigators of the conflict to Rwanda and felt that the Tutsi-led Rwandan government has benefited most from the conflict in terms of successfully persecuting all those that posed a political or strategic threat. They also believed that the Rwandan government waged "a self-financed war" against Hutus and the Congolese government of Laurent Kabila for deciding to side with the Hutus. In sum, across all contexts, participants believed that the Tutsi-led Rwandan government was the villain in the conflict and gained most from it.

"Tutsi and Their Government in Rwanda" as Villains

> Paul Kagame has benefited most from all these because he now runs a dictatorship and has either imprisoned or chased on exile all Hutu elites opposed to his policies.
> **(Mwenga Group)**

> The Rwandan government has been the main gainers from the war, not only in terms of chasing out all its enemies, they have made so much money from the war here. Every single money spent

on Rwandan soldiers sent to fight in the Congo, was recouped three times from this same country
through their backhand dealings in raw mineral resources.
(Uvira Group)

Those that caused the war and have gained most are the Tutsi and their government in Rwanda.
They have succeeded in pursuing all Hutus from their homeland, taken over the homes, and now in
Congo they are succeeding in chasing away our people that have managed to make a new life here,
buy land, build houses. They now control the Congolese army and making plenty money from mining.
(Walungu Group)

The Tutsi have won the war. They have the government in Rwanda, they now control the army in
Congo, Uganda and Burundi. They have succeeded in putting Hutus on the flight and those that
they manage to bring back, they have caged. What else can we say (throws hands in demonstration
of feeling of helplessness).
(Fizi Group)

Perception of Villainity in *Dialogue* Groups

Across all contexts, participants had varying beliefs and perceptions of who the villains
of the conflict were. While some participants felt it was Tutsis that have now been integrated into the FARDC, some others felt it was President Joseph Kabila who has succeeded in consolidating his political power, silenced or sent opposition on exile or
succeeded in extraditing opposition figures or threatening them with extradition to
the war crimes tribunal. A few others felt the mining companies have profiteered from
the conflict and used the opportunity to make money from Congo.

Mixed Perception of Villainity

I think it is Nkunda's and Ntaganda's army who have now become part of the FARDC. They now
have the uniform to go after us.
(Mwenga Group)

Go to Shabunda you would see those that have gained most from the war. They own illegal mining
camps there, forcing people to dig costly ores so they can take it and sell in France and America.
Those are the ones making money from the war and want the war to go on forever.
(Walungu Group)

After everything, Joseph Kabila has made the most gain. He came from nowhere and is President
while we keep fighting. Think about it, he has succeeded in quieting everybody that would oppose
him. It is either you committed genocide or you raped women during the war. He is President and
Belgium, France and America love him.
(Uvira Group)

I think ... (Tutsi) people have profited most from this war. Look at Ntaganda, who is he? Now he is
a general in the Congo army just for killing more Hutu people than most other people. There are
several like him.
(Fizi Group)

Opportunities for Civic Engagement and Personal Development
Participants were asked about what they thought about opportunities for contributing to the socio-political development of their communities either by voting, standing in for elections or other actions that can lead to self-development either in Congo or Rwanda.

Perception of Opportunities for Civic Engagement in *Gutahuka* Groups
Across all contexts, participants believed there were no opportunities for civic engagement either in Rwanda or in their communities in South Kivu. Participants said their most pressing need was survival and not civic engagement.

Survival before Civic Engagement

> *You have to survive first before you talk of voting in election or calling a politician.*
> ***(Walungu Group)***

> *When everybody wants you dead or repatriated, where do you start from?*
> ***(Uvira Group)***

> *We try to help ourselves as a people so that we are not exterminated. We build our own maternity hospitals, our own schools and so on, but as for politics we are not interested. I don't even think I can vote here talk less of standing in for election.*
> ***(Fizi Group)***

> *No one thinks about such things, (civic engagement) I do have a (citizenship) card, but that is only for business, when crossing the border, I know I can't use it to vote.*
> ***(Mwenga Group)***

Perception of Opportunities for Civic Engagement in *Dialogue* Groups
As in *Gutahuka* listening groups, participants felt there were minimal opportunities for civic engagement due to restrictions of their citizenship, shibboleths and identity as Hutus. They cannot call on the radio programmes because as soon as they start talking people would know it is a Hutu calling.[21] A common thread found across listening groups was participants' belief that citizenship and identity restrictions prevented civic engagements. This was put forward more forthrightly as a problem in all *Dialogue* groups.

---

21 Hutus pronounce "l" as "r" as in *Banyamurenge* instead of *Banyamulenge*. In South Kivu, the "l" and "r" work as a shibboleth to restrict or grant access for Rwandan Hutus.

Civic Engagement Is Limited by Restrictions of Citizenship and Identity

> *As soon as people know you are not a citizens, a door is shut in front of you. And there is nothing you can really do.*
> ***(Uvira Group)***

> *I once called into on radio programme in 2006 to talk about how the voting was going on our area in Kabare where we lived then. I did not mention I was Hutu, but the announcer said you know you are not supposed to vote, you are not Congolese. I quickly hung up. I can't be involved.*
> ***(Mwenga Group)***

> *As long as we are not citizens here it is difficult to be involved politically.*
> ***(Walungu Group)***

> *We have tried to build schools and hospitals here which is the best we can do for ourselves.*
> ***(Fizi Group)***

PART 2: CONGOLESE AUTOCHTHON FOCUS GROUPS

This part analyses comments from eight focus groups made up of Congolese autochthons in Mwenga, Uvira, Fizi and Walungu contexts. In each context, there were two focus groups representing the two listening groups. As in Hutu focus groups, participants were encouraged to express their views freely and refrain from using offensive language and name callings. They were encouraged to reach a consensus on answers, and where a consensus could not be reached, they were free to present the different positions. As in Hutu groups, in most cases there was a consensus among participants.

Gutahuka Listeners' Perception of Barriers to Peace
Participants across all contexts were asked to discuss among themselves and decide the barriers to peace in South Kivu in order of severity.

FDLR and Hutus – the Greatest Barriers to Peace
FDLR and Hutus were grouped together because in all discussions participants used the two interchangeably. It is essential to emphasize that although all FDLR elements are Hutus not all Hutus are FDLR members. But the two reinforce each other. FDLR militants say they are there to protect Hutus in Congo, while Hutus feel satisfied that there are people fighting their cause. Also, FDLR members prefer Hutu civilians to remain in South Kivu so that they can easily blend back into Hutu civilian

population when retreating from FARDC military onslaughts.[22] In two of the four groups, participants easily reached a consensus that FDLR militants in particular and Rwandan Hutus in general currently living in eastern DRC are the major barriers to peace in South Kivu. In Uvira, it was more argumentative than in the other groups as some members felt Hutus were being unfairly targeted. In Fizi, they felt the FDLR was only a player in the mix and not a barrier because they were there to help protect Hutus who they believed were being persecuted by the Tutsi-dominated army and the CNDP. In all groups, however, Hutus and FDLR came up and were identified by some participants as the main barriers.

> *The FDLR are the problem. Every military operation going on now is targeted at them. There must be a problem with you when everybody is pursuing you.*
> **(Mwenga Group)**

> *They (FDLR combatants) have raped thousands of our women, killed thousands of our young men, stole everything they can steal, they are the ones that have kept us where we are today. The truth is, the sooner they (FDLR) disarm and return to Rwanda the sooner the peace.*
> **(Walungu Group)**

> *When there is a snake under your roof, you sleep with one eye open even if the snake is helping you to chase the rats from your home. That is how it is with the Abacunguzi.[23] We don't hate them but we can't sleep well while they are here.*
> **(Uvira Group)**

> *The Abacunguzi is there for a purpose. I know they have caused every kind of problem. The war is now centred on them. If they disarmed and stayed here, it would be alright. They are part of us.*
> **(Fizi Group)**

The second barrier to peace that was discussed most by participants after the Hutus/FDLR was foreigners in general.

Foreigners (Mainly Rwandans) Are Barriers to Peace

> *The problem is really with Rwandans that want to be Congolese at all costs.*
> **(Uvira Group)**

> *From the time of Leopold till today, the problem of Congo has always been with outsiders coming to kill and plunder. Today it is Rwandans, Chinese, Europeans and Americans.*
> **(Fizi Group)**

---

22 Interview with Paul Wakenge, former AFDL Commander in North Kivu on 29th July 2009.
23 The local name for the armed wing of the FDLR.

Deport all Rwandans including the Banyamulenges and Kinyarwandas and you will see that the Congolese can live in peace and prosperity.
(Mwenga Group)

If all Rwandan foreigners leave South Kivu we will have peace here.
(Mwenga Group)

Myths Perceived as Barriers to Peace

It was interesting to note that in addition to the two main barriers identified above, in all contexts, participants also held various myths about the reasons behind the endurance of the war. The myths varied with contexts but were all based on unsubstantiated rumours.

America is causing the problem so they can come in and take away coltan while we fight. They want to use coltan to rebuild the tower that Osama (bin Laden) destroyed in America.
(Walungu Group)

Rwanda wants to make sure we continue fighting so that they can continue to receive money from America, Britain and France. If we stop fighting, they will stop giving them money that is why they keep causing problems here.
(Mwenga Group)

The truth is Satan and his Demons are the main cause of the problem. The world is coming to an end and the Bible says in the final days, there shall be many wars. Ours is one of them.
(Fizi Group)

The problem is with MONUC's Muslim fighters. They steal UN's weapons and sell to armed groups so they can keep fighting and making trouble to prevent America from buying coltan from here to rebuild the American tower that Osama (bin Laden) and the Muslims bombed.
(Uvira Group)

Dialogue Listeners' Perception of Barriers to Peace

Dialogue listeners' perceptions of barriers to peace varied from context to context, and in Uvira and Fizi, participants could not reach a common position on what they perceived as the chief barrier to peace. But a common thread in all comments across all contexts is the feeling among participants that the government, the Congolese army and the UN had failed in their responsibilities. The most recurring point made across all contexts was a failed mixage/*brassage* system which they believed have prevented the country from having a unified army. Participants that felt the problem was with the FARDC rooted it to the failed mixage programme. They attributed the refusal of FDLR to disarm and the reluctance of the local Mai Mai militias to join the brassage system to distrust of the FARDC and MONUC's inability or unwillingness to protect their communities from attacks.

Failed Mixage and Brassage as Barrier to Peace

> *Ex-fighters that know no other profession other than war have not been given another job so they return to the bushes to join Mai Mai when they do not like the conditions at brassage.*
> *(Fizi Group)*

> *So many FARDC are ex-members of CNDP. They still think like CNDP because they still have the same commanders, the same bags, the same uniform, the same guns …. Their commanders simply called them together and said from today you are no longer CNDP but Congolese army.*
> *(Walungu Group)*

> *There have been no-sense alliances between FARDC and other (armed) groups. Whenever FARDC fight and are unable to win, they go back and sign for peace and make them part of the FARDC. Even after brassage the new soldiers do not respect their new commanders. They do what they want to do. That is why you see all the rape and killing by government army going on here.*
> *(Mwenga Group)*

> *UD 7: They (the FARDC) keep attacking Hutus because they are mostly members of CNDP that have been dressed in FARDC uniform and deployed to areas where there are Hutus.*
> *UD 1: They only call themselves FARDC, but it is CNDP. Everyone knows that.*
> *(Uvira Group)*

The Congolese army dominated discussions in all contexts on barriers to peace. Generally, there was a pattern of aversion for the Congolese army in all contexts. Participants used words such as "weak", "poorly paid", "instrument of oppression", "undisciplined", etc. to describe the national army.

Weak and Fragmented FARDC as a Barrier to Peace

> *The FARDC is too weak to do anything. It can't even defend itself let alone the people.*
> *(Walungu Group)*

> *We have an army that cannot take charge. They are too divided … they are like foufou[24] without starch. Everybody has his own objective – some to kill Hutus, some to steal, some to rape, some others to dig up ores.*
> *(Fizi Group)*

> *The FARDC is responsible for most of the rape and looting cases in Rutshuru and in Mwenge. They are the most undisciplined group of soldiers any country can ever have.*
> *(Uvira Group)*

---

24 Popular Congolese meal made from cassava, maize and/or yam.

They are too fragmented, too disorganized and too poorly paid to fight. The army here has always been an instrument of oppression in this place.
(Mwenga Group)

Gutahuka Listeners' Perceptions of Interventions

Perception of Interventions was assessed based on descriptive and prescriptive trans-formations. The intention was to understand participants' perception of and engage-ment with recent and ongoing local peacebuilding interventions, democratic reforms, new institutions and structures that support governance both at national and provin-cial levels. Prescriptive levels of transformation assessed participants' perceptions of needed interventions in their communities in particular and the DRC in general.

Perception of Descriptive Interventions

Participants were asked what have been done by either the government or MONUC or any other intervention agency to create peace, encourage civic engagement with new democratic values, reforms and institutions to end the conflicts in South Kivu and what they thought of such intervention efforts.

MONUC's Interventions

Across all contexts, participants' perception of descriptive interventions centred on the activities of MONUC in South Kivu. Generally, participants across all contexts were dissatisfied with MONUC's efforts but agreed that the situation could have been worse if UN had not deployed peacekeepers. Although participants presented them as facts, some of the views expressed on MONUC's interventions were either inaccurate or misrepresented.

MONUC Is Not Doing Enough but It Could Have Been Worse

They have helped to conduct elections although it had problems especially in the east, it helped to keep things on the table steady. And they are now trying to get Hutu fighters to return to Rwanda ....
And also they report what is happening in Kinshasa on Okapi.
(Mwenga Group)

The United Nations has put pressure on Kabila to negotiate with some armed groups but that is because they don't want to fight the armed groups themselves.
(Uvira Group)

They have negotiated the peace agreements that ended the war in 2003, that was the best thing they have done. Since then I can't see anything else they have achieved. Sometimes I wonder what they are still doing here.
(Walungu Group)

> MONUC has not been that effective, but I think if they weren't here, Rwanda would have invaded
> this place and killed everybody.
> **(Fizi Group)**

Perception of Opportunities for Civic Engagement

Participants were asked to talk about how and to what extent intervention efforts have enabled them to participate and be more involved in civic duties at the community level such as voting, standing in for election, writing to their representatives, attending town hall meetings, etc. The responses varied across contexts. Generally, responses suggest that participants did not see civic engagement as a priority.

Civic Engagement Is Not the Priority for Now

> Our people have a saying, you use what you have in the stomach to carry what's on your head. If there
> is no food in the stomach, there is no power to go and start pursuing politics. By the time you go to the
> farm, and to the market the day is over. There is no time to do all those things you are talking about.
> **(Walungu Group)**

> All those things are for politicians. We are ordinary people ... You do your best to take care of your-
> self and your family and make sure everything is alright in your home. That is what everybody does
> here, not pursuing politicians about.
> **(Mwenga Group)**

> If you want to start writing to politicians, or calling politicians they won't even answer you. Do you
> think people in Kinshasa even care about what we think here? They are worried about their own
> bank accounts and me I am worried about my own stomach. It is only when you are a big man that
> politicians pick up their phones when you call or even listen to what you have to say.
> **(Fizi Group)**

> Sometimes the NGO people come here on house to house to ask people what they think the govern-
> ment should do. We have answered so many questions in the past, but nothing ever happens after
> that. They don't come back to you after they are gone. Two years, they came here and asked us what
> we think they should do, we mentioned borehole for water, some assistance to the vigilantes and
> a few other things. They left and never came back. So we don't have time for such things anymore.
> **(Uvira Group)**

Perception of Opportunities for Personal development

Participants were also asked if they thought they had enough opportunities to develop themselves, so they can do better in their business, raise their children better and live better lives. Opinions varied across contexts, but a common denominator among the comments is that participants felt it was their responsibility to develop themselves and not the duty of anyone else or the political and social system. Across contexts, participants talked about their belief in doing things for themselves because opportunities are never existent except one pushes through and has the help of God. Generally, participants' views across contexts were rooted in strong religious beliefs as they attributed self-development to God and to family.

The System Offers No Opportunities for Self-development

> Even if you are in America or Britain, if God is not on your side you cannot develop yourself. You can try but what if a bus knocks you down and you die what would happen to all of it?
> **(Uvira Group)**

> We try to help ourselves, look out for each other. If I see an opportunity such as herbs that can cure his (points at another participant) ailment, I get it to him, and that way we develop each other. We help ourselves and God helps us too. That is the way things work here.
> **(Fizi Group)**

> No other person can wipe your bum like yourself, they would feel disgusted. No one can develop me or know my problem like me and my kindred here. So I don't see my help coming from the government or from peacekeepers. My helps is from God.
> **(Walungu Group)**

> The only thing I can say is that sometimes the peacekeepers escort us to markets in Kabare so we can go and sell our produce. But most times we need to come back on our own so it's the same thing. You have to pray and hope nothing happens to you. Other than that I can't see any development for myself from them.
> **(Mwenga Group)**

Gutahuka Listeners' Prescriptive Interventions

Participants were asked what interventions are needed in their communities in particular and the country in general to help fulfil some of their needs and create peace. The most recurring theme across all contexts except in Fizi was that foreigners, mainly Rwandans including ethnic Tutsis and Hutus, are made to leave. In some contexts, they did admit that it may never happen; however, there was a general consensus that if a way is made for all ethnic Rwandans to return to their country and live together in peace there, that there would be peace also in Congo. In Fizi, participants said Hutus should be granted citizenship and allowed to remain and that all military action against them should be stopped.

All Foreigners Should Be Made to Leave then There Shall Be Peace for All

> In Burhinji two brothers were taken hostage by FDLR and tortured heavily. They were only released after they paid big (amount of) money. If they and all the other Rwandans take their trouble and go back, we would be able to build our home again.
> **(Walungu Group)**

In 1995, we opened our doors to them (Hutu refugees), took them in and fed them as if they were our brothers but now they are biting the same fingers that fed them. They brought their hatred and fighting here and now it is like we have a snake in our roof that we cannot remove.
(Uvira Group)

Tutsi people fight wherever they go, they have fought us, they have fought the Hutu, they have fought the pygmies ... everyone. I know it would never happen in my life time, but if they are all forced to return to Rwanda we would have a solution.
(Mwenga Group)

Military operation against the Abacunguzi is not working, it is the civilians that are suffering. Most of the FDLR fighters they said they killed during KIMIA II or captured are Hutu civilians who have settled here peacefully and integrated into a new life in their communities. The military operation should stop and Hutus should be asked to remain here peacefully. After all, we accepted and allowed the Banyamulenges to remain and even gave them citizenship, so why not do the same thing for the Hutu people who are even more like us.
(Fizi Group)

Imagination of Future Relationships with other groups

As part of perceptions of prescriptive transformations, *Gutahuka* participants were asked about what they perceived would be the nature of their relationship with other groups in the future and their imagination of a unified Congolese army involving all the ethnic groups in the country. Across all contexts except in Fizi, participants said they did not think it would ever be possible for all ethnic groups to integrate and live together peacefully as a community. Also, participants said it would be impossible to have a unified army involving all the ethnic groups because they thought it would be difficult to get all the groups to transcend their personal interests and that of their ethnic groups and work together within a unified Congolese security force. In Fizi, although participants said it would be difficult to get all the groups together under the same army commander, they believed it was not impossible. Moreover, the female participants said the entire *brassage* system was biased against them; hence, they did not see any place in the army for women.

Communal Integration Unimaginable: It Is Impossible to See All the Ethnic Groups Living Together in Peace

I can't even imagine, everybody living here together, Tutsis, Hutus and us. The hyena and the fowl would have to play together first before that happens.
(Mwenga Group)

Let us be honest, that would never happen, everybody has his own plans and the truth is we are not the same. So that division would always be there.
(Uvira Group)

I think it is easier to say it is possible than for it to actually happen. I don't see it happening – not in my lifetime.
(Walungu Group)

There was, however, a totally different opinion in Fizi:

We have lived together here for some time, the Banyamulenges have lived here, I know they could be troublesome, but most of them mind their own business and do their jobs. The Hutus are hard-working and we would always need them. Most of the decent maternity hospitals here were built by them and schools as well. So I think it is possible to live together in peace.
(Fizi Group)

Military Integration Unworkable: Many Factors (Mainly Ethnic) Prevent Army Integration

What integration? It won't happen because go to the army today you would find people that want to have Ugandan or Rwandan army to work with them. But there are some true Congolese soldiers that are not happy. So I don't expect them to last together as a unit.
(Walungu Group)

UG 4: Brassage is all politics, CNDP still have their command structures intact even when they integrate with FARDC. So it is impossible to have an army that has Hutus, Tutsis, Mai Mai fighters all working together

UG 10: It (brassage) discriminates against women and the whole army and reintegration pro-grammes do not include women who were somehow involved maybe as forced sex agents or spies. There are women forced to be cooking for them and when they all go for brassage, the women are left to fend for themselves. The brassage does not let in those women.
(Uvira Group)

Government is partial towards CNDP because they can't win them. In Shabunda they are hunting FDLR but in Chondo CNDP still mount roadblocks and collect tributes. A unified army of all ethnic groups here is never going to happen.
(Mwenga Group)

FG 2: As at today, I don't think there is any true Congolese son that would normally want to carry out commands from a Rwandan Commander even with all the citizenship talk. But first if there is peace at the community, and everybody lives together then we can move from there to the army. Anything is possible.

FG 8: I agree with him. Who would have thought only a few years ago, that Congo army can fight alongside the Rwandan army, but it happened. I know there are people that are not happy with it, but it happened.
(Fizi Group)

Dialogue Listeners' Perceptions of Interventions

As in *Gutahuka* listening groups, *Dialogue* participants were asked about what they thought about current intervention efforts to transform the conflicts and achieve peace and stability.

Perception of Descriptive Interventions

Comments varied across contexts. A common theme that recurred in all the groups, however, was government's and MONUC's negotiations with armed groups to resolve issues and the challenges thereof. Participants said such negotiations should involve all the armed groups including the FDLR and the local Mai Mai militias.

Negotiating with Armed Groups Is Good, but Should Be More Comprehensive

> If there is no cooperation with all the armed groups I think the cooperation with the other ones would be useless because the fighting would continue. The leaders in Congo and Rwanda have to sit down with FDLR and talk. That is what FDLR is asking for.
> *(Mwenga Group)*

> The government has signed agreement with all the forces except FDLR and some local Mai Mai vigilantes, and I wonder why the selection and discrimination. If they do away with the double standards, then we can move forward.
> *(Uvira Group)*

> The government and the United Nations have negotiated with different fighting groups and in some cases have been successful in securing agreements. Sometimes, they fight with them, sometimes they invite them over for discussion. The fighting has not always worked because they run back into the villages and start maiming civilians. So the UN has to do more talking and less fighting.
> *(Walungu Group)*

> The brassage system has helped to bring fighters together and help to get them to repent. But it would be good if they extended it to Hutus as well.
> *(Fizi Group)*

Perception of Opportunities for Civic Engagement

As in *Gutahuka* listening groups, participants were asked to talk about how and to what extent intervention efforts have enabled them to participate and be more involved in civic duties at the community level such as voting, standing in for election, volunteering, making views known through the media, writing to their representatives, attending town hall meetings, etc. Responses varied across contexts, but there were consistent expressions of optimism across all contexts. Although the participants agreed that more still needed to be done, they also indicated that they were willing to be more involved in political and social activities if their efforts would bring about positive changes to their communities. They said it was their "responsibility", an "obligation" to take part in discussions and/or actions that can help to achieve the common good.

Civic Engagement – a Responsibility, a Social Obligation

One of the things I've begun to do at the moment is to call during the call-in programmes on radio, the only problem is that it is costly. But it is my responsibility. If I don't do it who would? We can't leave it and hope that somehow those up there would know what we think.
(Walungu Group)

I recently took part in a conflict resolution meeting that MONUC organized here. I felt very good about it because I was able to talk about some things that we do not like about their work here. I wish there was more of such opportunities.
(Uvira Group)

My church is involved in de-mining activities. Although it is not in Fizi, but it is something that we should all do. It is an obligation really. We come together to build schools, maternity hospitals and so on, because the government is just not there, so we have to fend for ourselves.
(Fizi Group)

It is part of our duty to help build our community.
(Mwenga Group)

Perception of Opportunities for Personal Development
In terms of opportunities for personal development, there was generally the feeling among participants that if the government took care of the basic infrastructural needs such as roads and electricity supply and provide security, there would be space for growth. Each context had different impressions of what needed to be changed, but they all agreed that if specific changes were made, there were genuine opportunities for growth.

There Are Opportunities

I repair broken radio sets now but I know I can do more. If there are roads and security for people to bring their radio sets from far I can make some more money.
(Uvira Group)

> *We are doing our best here. There are a number of self-help projects that we have put together from our association contributions, like the pineapple farms we are doing now. If things are stable, we can even start exporting to Europe.*
> **(Fizi Group)**

> *The problem we've been having is travelling safely from here to Bukavu or Goma, but if there is better security we can expand our farms and sell more. Yes I would say there would be more opportunities if there is security on the roads.*
> **(Walungu Group)**

> *MD 5: I hear the government has signed contracts with China to build roads, and bridges to connect the country. If they can do that it would be really good. So people here can travel and trade easily...*

> *MD 1: But there has to be peace first.*

> *MD 5: I am on your side.*
> **(Mwenga Group)**

Perception of Prescriptive levels of Interventions

As in *Gutahuka* listening groups, participants were asked what they believed needed to be done by any of the agencies so they can realize their collective potentials and aspirations as a community and achieve peace and progress. The most emphasized theme across all contexts was credible political leadership.

Credible Leadership Is Needed

> *If there was no corruption among the political and business leaders there are a lot we can achieve in Congo.*
> **(Uvira Group)**

> *Congo is a rich country, but corruption has finished us. That is one thing that needs to be sorted before we can go far.*
> **(Mwenga Group)**

> *People say foreigners are the problem here, but I think it is our leaders. They are the ones that let in the foreigners in the first place because of what their pocket is gaining from it.*
> **(Fizi Group)**

> *After (Patrice) Lumumba we've not had a leader that genuinely cared for the people. It's all about their pockets first. That is what is holding us back.*
> **(Walungu Group)**

Imagination of Future Relationships with Other groups

As in *Gutahuka* listening groups, participants were asked about what they imagined their relationship with other ethnic groups would be in the future.

Community Integration: Participants felt the problem that would prevent integration would be the problem of citizenship. If citizenship issues are resolved once and for all, it would be possible to know who should remain and who should not. That way, communities could decide to forge ahead together as a people.

The Citizenship Question Need to Be Resolved Once and for All

If we know that from today, for example, all Rwandans Tutsi or Hutu that have lived in this country say for 10 years or were born here can be given (citizenship) card then we can say, it's up to us to live together as a people. But the problem is that it has not been resolved.
(Uvira Group)

Most of the hospitals here, schools and so on here are built by Hutu self-help groups. They are good neighbours; we've never really had problems with them. They are part of our community.
(Fizi Group)

My father told me that Hutu and Tutsi people used to come here to farm and feed their livestock and even live here peacefully. But that was before Mobutu started playing politics with citizenship. I think citizenship problems will prevent integration.
(Walungu Group)

It would be easier if we all knew who is citizen and who is not. Most of the Hutus can't go back to Rwandan and we understand that. If they are given the chance to be citizens, it would be possible for them to integrate here easily.
(Fizi Group)

Security Forces Integration: As in *Gutahuka* listening groups, participants believed a lot needed to be done to integrate the various factions in the army and that it would take time.

A Fully Integrated Army Can Bring Peace If the Divisions Are Transcended

The brassage should include everybody. Else we would keep talking about this every day. A genuine brassage can help to integrate the army.
(Uvira Group)

The problem with the army is that most times they are not paid. At the moment they are owed wages for several months. The young men in the Mai Mai don't want to join the army when they know they won't get paid. If they get this done properly, such as the wages, ensure discipline and have commanders that everybody can respect, then it would be possible to integrate everyone that bears arms.
(Fizi Group)

We can have a united army if they drop all the interests and work together as one country. But that would take a long time.
(Walungu Group)

It is unjust when they say CNDP can join brassage and FDLR cannot. They should either allow everybody that wants to join to do so or decide that if you were an ex-combatant you cannot join the army.
(Mwenga Group)

Perception of Victims and Victimhood

Participants were encouraged to reflect on their experiences of victimhood and to discuss the effects of the conflict on everyone in the community and all parties and then discuss who were the most severely affected by the conflict.

Perception of Victimhood in *Gutahuka* Groups

There was no agreement across contexts on worst victims of the conflict. But participants agreed with the women participants that pregnant women suffered badly. Across all contexts, the comments on women victims were put forward very emotionally by women participants and the male participants did not object with the women's position.

Abused and Impregnated Women the Worst Victims

Women have suffered so badly in this war. Raped and impregnated, they still have to run with their pregnancy.
(Fizi Group)

I can't tell the story of women in this war, it is too sad. Nobody talks about us. But women have suffered most in this war. Women have been used as sex slaves and as soon as they become pregnant, they are left behind.
(Mwenga Group)

Let's think about what women have suffered in this war. The truth is there are very few women that have not known abuse.
(Uvira Group)

I hope we would be able to tell out stories someday. Women have really suffered in this war.
(Walungu Group)

Perception of Victimhood in *Dialogue* Groups

Participants had varying views of who they believed to be the worst victims of the conflict. But the most recurring victims across all contexts were Hutu refugees. Pregnant women were also mentioned in three of the four contexts.

Hutus as Victims of Conflict

> It is hard not to feel for them (Hutus) ... haunted and hated by everyone.
> **(Fizi Group)**

> I think Hutus are the most hated people. But most of them are very hardworking.
> **(Mwenga Group)**

> A genocide has been committed against them (Hutus) but everyone is talking about Tutsi genocide.
> **(Uvira Group)**

> I know we have suffered, but no one can ever tell the Hutu story, what they have gone through since 1994.
> **(Walungu Group)**

Mixed Perceptions of Villainity

Those that were responsible and have gained most from the conflict was a topic that was intensely debated across all groups. In *Gutahuka* listening groups, there was no pattern. Views ranged from Rwandan government (Uvira), mining entrepreneurs (Walungu), guerrilla entrepreneurs that eventually transformed into politicians (Fizi), and foreigners in general (Mwenga).

In the *Dialogue* Groups, participants had varying views of who they thought gained most from the war. But the most recurring theme across contexts was corrupt politicians in Kinshasa.

Corrupt Politicians Are the Villains

> You would see them (villains) in Kinshasa with the shiny cars and big houses.
> **(Mwenga Group)**

> Go to Kinshasa you would see them – polished skin, fat belly and fat face. Most politicians have a back hand in the mining business.
> **(Uvira Group)**

> It is hard to see a politician who has not gained in one way or the other from the war.
> **(Fizi Group)**

> The richest people in this country are not business people but politicians. They have had their hands in everything.
> **(Walungu Group)**

10 No Intention to Return to Rwanda

This chapter explores how *Gutahuka* – the UN's programme on Radio Okapi that seeks to convince FDLR fighters to disarm – influences Rwandan Hutu listeners to return to Rwanda as prescribed in the programme. On a broader level, it explores how Psyops can be used to influence groups to voluntarily lay down their arms and participate in a disarmament, repatriation and reintegration programme.

As pointed out earlier, *Gutahuka* seeks to convince Rwandan Hutus particularly members of the FDLR to voluntarily join the DDRRR process and repatriate to Rwanda. I have drawn on Ajzen's (1985, 1991) Theory of Planned Behaviour (TPB) to interpret data from focus group discussions conducted among Hutu networks in South Kivu Province. TPB has been used as a tool both for designing and evaluating behaviour change communication campaigns. TPB is Ajzen's extension of the Theory of Reasoned Action (TRA) (Fishbein 1967). The central element in TPB is an individual's intention to perform a behaviour desired by a source. Building on TRA, TPB postulates three conceptually independent determinants of behavioural intentions. Whereas TRA postulates two independent determinants – Attitude Towards the Behaviour and Subjective Norm – TPB introduces a third element as an antecedent for behavioural intention – Perceived Behavioural Control. Perceived behavioural control draws on past or present experience and anticipated impediments or obstacles in assessing the ease or difficulty in performing the desired behaviour. As a general rule, TPB prescribes that the higher the degree of positive attitude and subjective norms with respect to the intended behaviour, the greater the perceived behavioural control and the stronger the individual's intention to perform the behaviour (Ajzen 1988, 1991). Basically, TPB assumes that behaviour is predicated on the formation of an intention to perform a desired behaviour and that intention is a function of three motivational influences namely: Attitudes, Subjective Norms and Perceived Behavioural Control. Furthermore, non-motivational factors that have the potentials of conditioning the behaviour are represented by actual control over the behaviour (Actual Behavioural Control). Please see Table 10.1 for a full summary of the interpretative approach adopted.

Table 10.1: Summary of Interpretative Approach

Theoretical Framework	Theory of Planned Behaviour (Ajzen 1985, 1991)
Main dependent construct	Planned Behaviour: Repatriation to Rwanda
Main independent constructs	Attitude Towards Behaviour, Subjective Norm, Perceived Behavioural Control
Summary of main interfering variables envisaged	Perception of Rwanda; perception of opportunities for growth and personal development in Rwanda; knowledge of DDRRR processes; relational fears in terms of re-integration and living side by side with former Tutsi "enemies"; fear of victimization.

TPB fitted the study mainly because it evaluates "behavioural intentions". Although it may not necessarily translate to actual behaviour, intention, as Ajzen (1991), and Francis et al. (2004) have both argued, can be used as a proximal measure for behaviour. This is important to the research because the research question is not intended to measure actual behaviour of participants in terms of repatriation to Rwanda but to determine the effectiveness of the communicative approach of *Gutahuka* to potentially convince Hutu FDLR combatants to disarm and join the DDRRR process. MONUC believes that *Gutahuka* has significantly contributed to the actual repatriation of 1564 FDLR combatants along with 2187 dependents in 2009. Interviews and comments of Hirondelle Foundation leaders as seen earlier in this chapter express their belief drawn from previous experiences that an Informative Approach would achieve more sustainable rewards. This research question therefore seeks to find out whether *Gutahuka* as it is currently designed is capable of convincing its Hutu Targets to repatriate. In answering the question therefore, the work interprets the comments from focus group discussions to explore Hutus' (including ex-combatants) normative beliefs and the referents thereof that are more likely to apply the most social pressure with respect to the behavioural outcomes desired by the creators of *Gutahuka*. The aim of this section therefore is to use the tools in TPB to interpret the relative strength of focus group participants' normative beliefs with respect to each referent as well as the motivation to comply with each referent's social pressure. The process will explain if and how *Gutahuka* can influence Rwandan Hutus, particularly FDLR combatants to voluntarily repatriate to Rwanda for the DDRRR processes as envisaged by MONUC. Another interesting element in TPB unlike other theories such as TRA is that it gives room to explore both external and internal cognitive factors that can potentially impede or impel behavioural intention. Adopting and slightly adapting the model fitted the research question. Although TPB is normally used to predict behaviour, it can also be used to explain behaviour or why particular targets adopted or did not adopt a certain behaviour after exposure to influence and how specific attitudes, subjective norms, perceived behavioural control factors and actual behavioural control factors might explain Targets' adoption or otherwise of a desired behaviour (please see Renzi and Klobas 2002). In its intents and purposes, RQ1 was not particularly designed to predict behaviour in terms of whether Rwandan Hutus and ex-combatants would voluntarily repatriate or not. Rather, the intended purpose was to explain factors that can potentially impede or impel *Gutahuka*'s influence on participants' intention to repatriate to Rwanda. RQ1 therefore seeks to determine the conceptually independent determinants of Hutu's intention to repatriate in relation to *Gutahuka*.

Behavioural intention is important to the work because Hutus that participated in the focus group are yet to repatriate to Rwanda. Conceptually, they are still in their decision-making process, unlike those that have already repatriated or those that are still in the fighting ranks. Those still in the fighting ranks have probably made up their minds not to return hence would not be valid subjects for the study. Focus Group participants included ex-FDLR combatants. Although they have voluntarily quitted fighting, they are yet to take up MONUC's repatriation offer. They currently live in South Kivu along with their dependents, extended family members among Hutu civilian population. Most of them are ex-refugees who fled to the DRC during the Rwandan conflicts of 1994. The groups researched therefore are at the strategic middle point between two behavioural extremes – repatriation to Rwanda and returning to the bush to continue the "struggle". At this strategic midpoint, their behaviour can swing in any direction depending on the stimulating factors. They can either return to the forests to continue the fight or take up MONUC's repatriation offer; alternatively, they can decide to do nothing, settle into civilian live in the DRC as immigrants and see what turns out in future. Whatever the case, findings can explain reasons for the successes or failures of *Gutahuka* in achieving its strategic communications objectives and the emerging implications for the design of such communication strategies in future.

Essentially, the main dependent construct for this research question is the "behavioural intention" of return to Rwanda. As shown in Figure 10.1, the main independent constructs are Attitude Towards Behaviour, Subjective Norms and Perceived Behavioural Control.

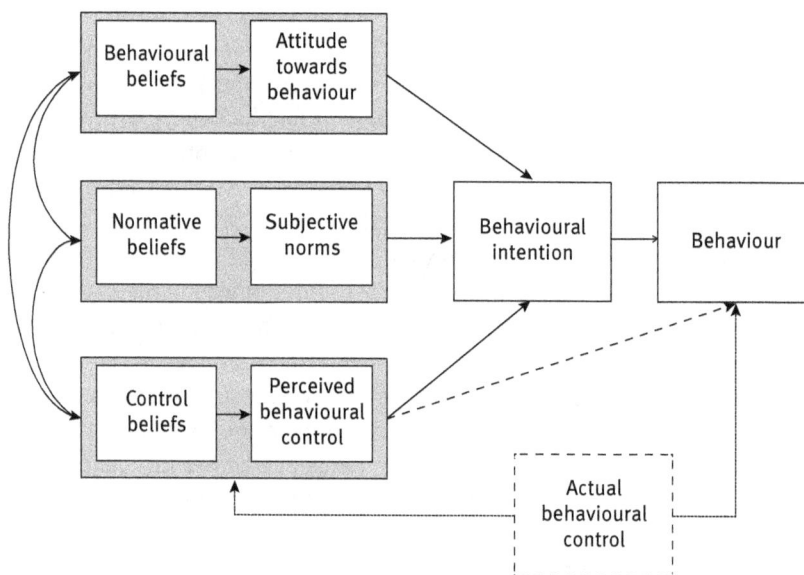

Figure 10.1: Theory of Planned Behaviour (Ajzen 2002)

10.1 Defining Determinants of Planned Behaviour

TPB states that behavioural intentions are the sum of an individual's attitude towards the referent behaviour; the subjective norms weighing in support or against the performance of the referent behaviour and the Target's perception of the ease with which the behaviour can be performed. Attitude towards behaviour is operationalized as the Target's positive or negative feelings about performing the referent behaviour. It is established by assessing the Target's beliefs regarding the consequences arising from the behaviour and an evaluation of the desirability of such consequences (Ajzen 1991). Ajzen expresses attitude as the sum of the individual consequence X desirability assessments for all expected consequences of the behaviour. On this study, this will be assessed based on focus group comments of Hutus that portray their behavioural beliefs.

10.2 Hutu Participants' Attitude towards Repatriation to Rwanda

The measures in this work were indirect or belief-based. This is because the variables in the model are psychological or internal constructs. So instead of asking participants specific or direct questions about their behavioural beliefs and outcome evaluations, it was preferable to engage them in discussions so that they can talk about not only their beliefs and evaluations of outcomes of their beliefs but also the bases for such beliefs so that the cognitive processes involved in their evaluation can be understood. Underlying cognitive structures were established and correlated appropriately to the research questions and for comparison with other participants across the different contexts of the study.

Hutu Participants' Normative Beliefs Regarding Consequences of Returning and Desirability Evaluations

The process of coding quotations and defining concepts for interpretation of qualitative data was drawn from comparative methods of qualitative data analyses espoused in Glaser and Strauss (1967). This involved coding quotations from analysed texts of participants' comments that exemplify the concepts, comparing and combining similar quotations across texts to establish patterns. It builds on the pattern matching and coding procedures suggested by Trochim (1985) and Miles and Huberman (1994).

To identify Hutu participants' normative beliefs about consequences of returning and evaluation of the desirability thereof, I coded quotations into concepts from participants' comments on the following discussion topics:
1. socio-political reforms and justice systems in Rwanda
2. reintegration in Rwanda
3. opportunities for personal development in Rwanda

The concepts were coded from comments in both *Gutahuka* and *Dialogue* Hutu listening groups for comparative purposes across the four contexts of the study. The intention was to identify specific elements of normative beliefs shared/unshared by participants across contexts and listening groups. Emerging concepts of consequences of repatriation represent the second degree variables of "Attitude Toward Behaviour" and are further coded in terms of desirability or undesirability and tagged accordingly. The researcher's coding outcomes matched with that of two PhD colleagues that also independently coded the comments. Table 10.2 summarizes the attitudes of Hutus across listening groups and contexts to returning (please see Appendix 2 for the full table). The variables column shows the emerging concepts, identified by all coders as undesirable. An "x" mark in the columns indicates that the concept was expressed by the group under which it is marked.

Table 10.2: Hutu Expressions of Consequences of Repatriation. *G= Gutahuka* group; *D=Dialogue* group.

Attitude	Variables (Concepts)	Fizi		Mwenga		Uvira		Walungu	
		G	*D*	*G*	*D*	*G*	*D*	*G*	*D*
Consequences of Repatriation	**Uncertainty**	x	x					x	
	Gacaca **Persecution**	x		x	x	x	x	x	
	Reintegration fears	x							
	Money worries		x		x	x			x
	No hopes for Personal Development		x		x	x	x		x

As shown in Table 10.2, participants had varying undesirable evaluations of the consequences of returning to Rwanda. Across listening groups, the most recurring undesirable concept is participants' perception of the *Gacaca* justice system in Rwanda. Six out of eight focus groups (in both listening groups) expressed the undesirability of the *Gacaca* justice process as a consequence of repatriation. Participants feared that the *Gacaca* justice system is designed to persecute Hutus that return. This fear was expressed in all *Gutahuka* groups and two out of four *Dialogue* groups. Participants' perception that if they take MONUC's offer, they would eventually suffer victimization is strong across listening groups. Its prevalence in all contexts suggests that this fear is not treated in *Gutahuka*. Invariably, it is a factor that participants cared about highly and would need to be convinced that if they returned, they would not be victimized. *Gutahuka* as a programme does not guarantee that returnees would not be prosecuted in the *Gacaca* courts, but it gives assurances that returnees will be given a fair hearing if ever referred to the traditional courts. Among Hutu communities in South Kivu, there are rumours of returnees being convicted by the courts based on false testimonies. Such rumours thrive because of lack of adequate and reliable information in South Kivu on exactly what the courts stand for and the processes involved in their judgments.

Undesirable Consequences of Repatriation across Listening Groups

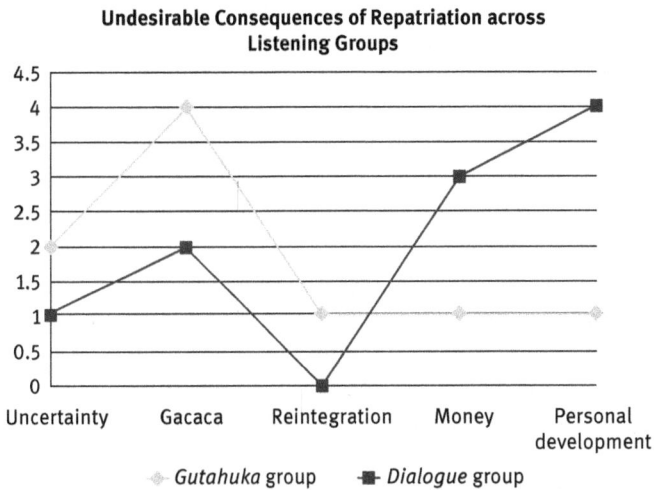

Figure 10.2: Undesirable Consequences of Repatriation

Two *Dialogue* groups (Walungu and Fizi) did not express fear of the *Gacaca* justice system but were worried about Money Matters, the uncertainties thereof as well as absence of opportunities for personal development in Rwanda. Perception of opportunities for personal development is another high factor in participants' behavioural beliefs about consequences of returning. Five out of eight Hutu listening groups believed there is nothing for them to return to in Rwanda. Interestingly, out of the five groups, only one *Gutahuka* group (Uvira) believed there was nothing to go back to Rwanda. All four *Dialogue* listening groups believed there was nothing for them in Rwanda, hence no reason to return (please see Figure 10.2).

Ajzen (1988) has written that among beliefs that ultimately determine intention and action is a set that deals with the presence or absence of requisite resources and opportunities. These beliefs, according to him, may be based in part on previous experiences or influenced by second hand or socially transmitted information by friends or close Others. This is the case in participants' thinking about the *Gacaca* court. Although participants did not have any direct experience with the *Gacaca* justice system as they obviously are yet to return to Rwanda, their behavioural beliefs about the system are influenced by their exposure to second hand information about the traditional courts. *Gutahuka* has failed in treating or correcting this (mis)information as evident in the pattern of prevalence of this behavioural belief across all Hutu *Gutahuka* listening groups. Behavioural Intention or, in this case, Intention to Repatriate is not supported by adequate information that can treat the fear generated by second hand influences on perceptions about *Gacaca*. Ajzen corroborates that behaviour is a function "of salient information, or beliefs, relevant to the behaviour" (1988, 134).

Reintegration is the lowest concept across listening groups. Only one out of eight groups expressed reintegration in Rwanda as an undesirable consequence of returning. What this shows is that in both listening groups participants do not believe living side by side with Tutsis is impossible or a problem for that matter. This is underscored by the fact that historically, the two groups have existed and lived side by side with each other – exchanging trade and inter-marrying until the crises of 1994. A shared history, common language, intermarriage, common cultures, a common way of life, etc. are some of the factors that both ethnic groups have in common. This suggests that the factors that divide the two ethnic groups are more political than cultural and can therefore be transcended. A programme that draws and builds on narratives of shared values, shared beliefs and culture of the Hutus and Tutsis can thus open up a sphere for mutual engagement and dialogue on the common good. It can also stimulate discussions and collective imaginations of future interdependence and mutually rewarding relationships.

Furthermore, compared with *Dialogue* listeners, *Gutahuka* listeners were less worried about personal development in Rwanda. Whereas all participants in *Dialogue* groups believed there was nothing to return to in Rwanda, only one *Gutahuka* group expressed personal development as a restraining or undesirable factor. This shows that *Gutahuka* is successful in portraying availability of opportunities for Hutu returnees to achieve their personal development goals. This has been a dominant element in *Gutahuka's* portrayal of returnees interviewed in the programme. Some of the repatriatees interviewed expressed their happiness with the life they have returned to in Rwanda in terms of being able to participate in local political, economic and social activities. Some of those interviewed are known to be occupying strategic political positions in Rwanda. For example, Major General Paul Rwarakabije,[25] a former Commander-in-Chief of the armed wing of FDLR and now a Commissioner at the Rwandan Demobilisation and Reintegration Commission (RDRC), has been interviewed several times on *Gutahuka* and generally portrayed as an example of a former FDLR operative who repatriated and went on to have a successful career back home in Rwanda. In the *Gutahuka* episode of 26 November 2009, this was said of him:

> Like other ex-combatants already reintegrated into Rwandan society, Major General Rwarakabije is currently a commissioner of the Rwanda Demobilization and Reintegration Commission, a testament that anyone can obtain a senior position in Rwanda irrespective of your ethic group and social status.

---

25 It is noteworthy that General Paul Rwarakabije has not been implicated in the Rwandan genocide. Although he was, at the time of the genocide, a FAR Lt. Col., according to the Human Rights Watch report Vol. 13, No.8 (A) of December 2001 "Observing the Rules of War?" he served "in one of the units least implicated in the genocide killings and is not accused of reprehensible acts" (p.7).

Several other former FDLR commanders now have "juicy" political positions in Rwanda such as Jerome Ngendahimana, appointed Military Assistant to RDF's Chief in Command and also Vice President of a newly created government commission. Another example is General Seraphim Bizimungu who has been recognized as a General in the Rwandan Army despite the fact the he was promoted to General by a splinter group of the FDLR, the Military Command for Change (CMC), only a few weeks before his repatriation in 2006. It is a key GoR D&R strategy to appoint repatriated FDLR Commanders into key political positions particularly in the RDRC in order to appeal to other commanders to repatriate (Romkema and Veenhoop 2007). The expectation is that if more commanders repatriate, FDLR fighters would be demotivated and eventually surrender or quit fighting. As stated earlier, *Gutahuka* frequently interviews such repatriated Commanders to show that those that choose to return can look forward to a fulfilling personal life in Rwanda. Representations of the personal successes of repatriated ex-FDLR Commanders evidenced in their appointment into key political positions in Rwanda and supported with appropriate verbal accomplishments in *Gutahuka* have significant impacts on participants' attitude towards repatriating to Rwanda. They do not perceive personal development as an undesirable consequence of repatriation unlike listeners of *Dialogue*. The only exception however was the Uvira group that remained untreated. It seems contradictory that *Gutahuka* participants in Uvira, being the most informed on DDRRR processes of all contexts, did not believe they had anything to return to in Rwanda. These contradictions are more contextual than conceptual. In Uvira, there have been several movements of Hutus to and from Rwanda and a lot of interaction between participants and their kindred that have visited and returned from Rwanda. Socially transmitted information is exchanged through this channel. The rumour on ground is that it is only former FDLR Commanders who were successful in negotiating a good repatriation deal that are rewarded with political appointments. Their part of the deal involved repatriating their entire divisions, brigades or battalions (as the case may be) in exchange for amnesty and political positions.[26] A key source in the FDLR who insisted on anonymity told the author in Bukavu that the FDLR recruits and other lower-ranked elements that cannot negotiate such a deal return to a life of difficulty and persecution in Rwanda. Follow-up interviews with select participants in Uvira revealed that this argument is generally believed among Hutus in Uvira.

In summary (please see Figure 10.2), through its creative representation of the personal successes of Hutu repatriatees, *Gutahuka* is successful in convincing listeners that Personal Development is not an Undesirable Consequence of returning.

---

[26] Interview with a former FDLR Major in Uvira (17. 02. 2010) who preferred not to be named and independently confirmed by Paul Wakenge (former AFDL Commander, South Kivu).

These representations send two categories of messages: firstly that in Rwanda, there is no discrimination against Hutus, and secondly that there are enabling conditions for combatants to return and achieve their personal development goals. The major failure of *Gutahuka* in influencing the attitude of Hutus towards repatriation is in its untreatment of fears of persecution in the *Gacaca* justice system. Across all *Gutahuka* listening groups, the belief is that the *Gacaca* is not fair, is stage-managed and is specifically created to persecute Hutus that repatriate.

Subjective Norms

TPB defines Subjective Norms as the Target's perception of whether a Referent Other or people important to the Targets think the behaviour should be performed. The opinion of any given referent is weighted by the motivation that an individual has to comply with the wishes of that referent. Normative beliefs of participants are viewed as determining subjective norms (Ajzen 1988). Theoretically, TPB expresses subjective norms as a function of the individual perception X motivation assessments for all relevant Referents. In this work, it is assessed based on participants' focus group comments in relation to the proposition of relevant Referents. As in Attitudes, subjective Norms were measured indirectly during the focus groups. Rather than answering direct questions about their normative beliefs in relation to their normative Other, participants spoke freely about what they felt about returning, their perceived barriers to returning and most importantly about their perception of prescriptive norms or what they felt needed to be done to achieve peace in their communities and the country at large. Commonly held beliefs were elicited from participants' comments, grouped into themes and matched with appropriate normative referents.

Normative Beliefs of Hutu *Gutahuka* Listeners

Normative beliefs of Hutu *Gutahuka* and *Dialogue* listeners were elicited from participants' comments on discussions on Prescriptive Interventions and Barriers to Peace during focus group discussions. These were varied with MONUC's normative appeals in *Gutahuka*. In Table 10.3, *Gutahuka* Norms column contains quotations from *Gutahuka* episodes that relate to the statements of normative belief expressed during focus groups (shown in normative Belief column). In the referents column, there is an X mark on the referent(s) from which each normative was extracted. In the graph (Figure 10.3) that follows, each referent was scored 10 points for each compliant normative belief expressed.

Table 10.3: Hutus' Normative Beliefs and Referents

Normative Belief	*Gutahuka's* Injunctive, Subjective and Descriptive Norms	Referents		
		Hutu *Gutahuka* Listening Group	Hutu *Dialogue* Listening Group	MONUC
MONUC is a barrier to Peace	"(MONUC) are there to protect (and) help you re-join your family in Rwanda." (*Gutahuka,* 17. 09. 2008)	X		
Weak GoDRC is a barrier to Peace	"(FDLR) militants are destroying the peace in the land." (*Gutahuka,* 17. 09. 2008)		X	
Hutus should be encouraged to remain in the DRC	"Return to Rwanda before it is too late." (*Gutahuka,* 04. 04. 2008)	X	X	
Hutus should be encouraged to integrate in the DRC	"UNHCR will assist to repatriate Hutu non-fighters home (to Rwanda)." (*Gutahuka,* 18. 05. 2009)	X	X	
Hutus have strong reasons not to return	"You have nothing to fear in returning. I feel safe here (in Rwanda)." (*Gutahuka* interview 12. 11. 2008)	X	X	
Rwandan government is a barrier to Peace, FDLR will keep fighting	"...fighting (is) not the way to right any grievance." -Major General Paul Rwarakabije, ex-FDLR Commander (*Gutahuka,* 26. 11. 2009)	X		
GoDRC should negotiate with FDLR	"I am advising Commander Iyamuremye Gaston and others to open a discussion with MONUC, the DR Congo army, the FARDC, and the International Community to allow FDLR combatants return home peacefully." -Major General Paul Rwarakabije, ex-FDLR commander (*Gutahuka,* 26. 11. 2009)		X	X
FARDC is a barrier to Peace	"The Congolese army is working hard to pursue and stop FDLR militants." (*Gutahuka,* 02. 11. 2008)		X	

Of the eight normative beliefs in the two Hutu listening groups, only one complied with MONUC's normative appeal – FDLR should negotiate with the GoDRC. This belief was expressed in all Hutu *Dialogue* listening groups. It was only mentioned passively by one of the participants in one of the *Gutahuka* listening groups and because of that it did not pass through the methods used in selecting and representing quotations from transcripts of focus groups.

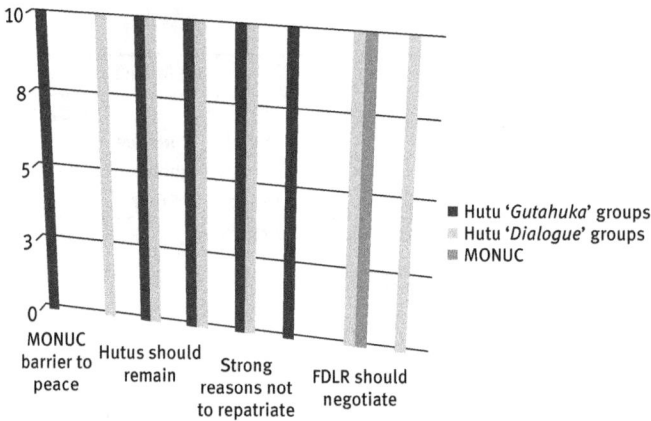

Figure 10.3: Referents of Hutus' Normative Beliefs

None of the Norms – Descriptive, Injunctive and Subjective – expressed in *Gutahuka* exerted any significant social pressure on Hutu listeners (see Figure 10.3). Instead, *Dialogue* listeners across all contexts felt the need to include the FDLR in negotiations both with MONUC and the GoDRC. The implication is that *Gutahuka*'s appeal to normative influence is feeble and ineffective in exerting social pressure on Hutus to voluntarily repatriate. Essentially, the motivation to comply with MONUC's normative appeals was low despite MONUC's usage of ex-FDLR commanders and militants and its use of injunctive norms that prescribe consequences for non-compliance. Although *Gutahuka*'s three-fold normative appeal is referenced by fellow Hutus – including former armed comrades and Commanders – participants' motivation to comply was low. A key reason is the spatial and psychological distance of MONUC's normative referents from *Gutahuka*'s target audience. The former Commanders interviewed on *Gutahuka* are distant *influentials* and do not have any direct bearing on the present personal circumstances and social affiliations of targets. It is unlikely that this would have been the case when participants were still within the spatial sphere of influence of their Commanders or their repatriated comrades at arms. The lack of influence is significant, and while it is at odds with MONUC's opinion about the success of *Gutahuka*, it corroborates Construal-level theories' argument that distant events or individuals are represented as abstract, intangible and unobservable concepts in contrast to close events or individuals represented as concrete and specific concepts (Fujita et al. 2005; Trope and Liberman 2003; Liberman and Trope 1998). More recent researches have shown construal-level differences associated with psychological and social distances such as in power hierarchies and spatial distances between a Target's current location and the referents' locations. (Williams and Bargh 2008; Fujita and Han 2009; Fujita et al. 2006; Smith and Trope 2006). In the cases studied in this research, there is evidence of both psychological and spatial distances between

Gutahuka's normative referents and Targets. This however is not the only reason for participants' low motivation to comply with the programme's normative appeal, after all, there is also a spatial distance and, to some extent, psychological distance between members of Hutu networks across contexts, yet they still shared normative beliefs. A deeper look at control factors that influence beliefs and behaviours of participants vis-a-vis *Gutahuka* appeals may provide further illumination.

The second emerging implication is that *Dialogue* listeners believed it was needful for FDLR hierarchy to negotiate a peaceful solution with MONUC and/or the GoDRC. Despite not being directly exposed to *Gutahuka*, *Dialogue* groups' exposure to interactive and informative programme contents created a context for exploration of solutions that were more transactional in nature – a trait that was unique to *Dialogue* groups and consistent across contexts. This is discussed in more detail in RQ 2.

Perceived Behavioural Control

TPB defines Behavioural control as the Target's perception of the difficulties of performing a prescribed behaviour. TPB views the control that reactors or respondents have over their behaviour as lying on a continuum from behaviours that are easily performed to those requiring considerable efforts or resources. Ideational factors such as fear and knowledge, or the lack thereof, are elements of perceived behavioural control. Behavioural control also includes actions taken by the external controlling agents to impel a specific behaviour (Ajzen 1991, 2002).

To impel Hutus to repatriate, MONUC employed or supported various other non-military pressures described earlier in this chapter. Military pressure was also exerted on FDLR elements by FARDC and RDF with logistical supports from MONUC as well as from the Tutsi-dominated armed group the CNDP. Two major military operations were carried out by FARDC and supported by MONUC against FDLR during the course of the research: Operation *Kimia II* and Operation *Umoja Wetu*. The later involved a joint military operation with Rwandan security forces. Participants were affected in varying degrees. Prior to the military onslaughts on FDLR, participants identified themselves freely as Hutus; however, due to intimidation and fear of attacks by FARDC troops, they resorted to keeping a low profile and insisted on anonymity during the research. Mwenga and Walungu were particularly affected. There were significant military and non-military pressures to control behavioural intention albeit at varying degrees across contexts. For example, there were more non-military pressures in Uvira than in the other contexts. Participants in Uvira were constantly exposed to face-to-face contacts with MONUC's field sensitization officers during the course of the research project. This afforded participants there the opportunity to ask questions about their concerns and seek clarifications about specific elements of the repatriation programme. The outcome of these encounters was evident in Uvira *Gutahuka* listeners' more detailed knowledge of specifics of the DDRRR including available incentives for repatriating. Another reason is their exposure to the programme *Isange Mubanyu*. Interestingly, although they both lived within the same context, Hutu *Dialogue* listeners in Uvira were not as informed about DDRRR processes as *Gutahuka* listeners even though they had access to the same variable information sources that the *Gutahuka* group had. This is attributable to the interest in repatriation that *Gutahuka* programme generated among its listeners. Although *Gutahuka* participants across all contexts said the programme did not give them enough information about specific details of the DDRRR processes particularly regarding the sequence, processes and economic rewards of returning to Rwanda, the programme did create a longing for information about the homeland. This impelled participants in Uvira who had access to other information sources to seek these and use them for their desired purpose. This supports Blumler and Katz's uses and gratification theory that media users have different needs and hence actively seek out media sources that best fulfil their yearnings (1974). Indeed, media choices are not an end, but a means to an end. In Uvira, *Gutahuka* served the purpose of generating a quest among participants for more information, but its impact was limited because participants generally believed MONUC was sending the wrong message. Several of the Hutu participants, for example, said they had integrated into the community, married a Congolese and had quit fighting in the FDLR and hence should be encouraged to remain not told to repatriate. For listeners in Uvira, access to multiple sources of information engendered an active search for other media (including inter-personal sources) that would be more useful to their quest. In the other cases, participants that listened to *Gutahuka* had poor knowledge not only of the DDRRR processes but also of positive political changes in Rwanda.

Although there have been significant political changes in Rwanda, the highly polarizing politics that created divisions between Hutus and Tutsis in the 1980s and early 90s are consistently re-told in Hutu communities in South Kivu; hence, even those that were too young then to understand and those that were not born then have strong feelings about the political events. Although they were probably too young to have understood much of the political disharmony between Hutus and Tutsis back in the early 90s, young participants in *Gutahuka* focus groups spoke passionately about Tutsi hatred for Hutus and consistently referred to the Rwandan government as "Tutsi government". Although they have not had direct experience of any discrimination in Rwanda, their belief that the Rwandan government is anti-Hutu and pro-Tutsi is impelled by socially gained knowledge or influence from social groups and local influentials over the years. Such beliefs combine with the other factors to create interferences for *Gutahuka's* behaviour change objectives.

Moreover, aside from not fulfilling the information needs of its targets, participants' comments showed there is indeed a crisis of message in *Gutahuka*. Although convinced that there are opportunities for personal development in Rwanda, *Gutahuka* listeners believed they had even stronger reasons not to repatriate and would rather create a new life peacefully in Congo where they have developed strong ties, friendship and livelihood and in several cases inter-married or co-habited with the Congolese. But more importantly, they were not convinced that Rwanda's *Gacaca* justice system would not be used as a tool to persecute them if they decide to return. Essentially, *Gutahuka's* message of Repatriation does not exert enough influence on listeners' behavioural intention for two main reasons. Firstly, participants' distrust of *Gacaca* and fear of judicial persecution have not been treated in the programme. Secondly, participants believe they can settle and integrate in the DRC where they have developed close family ties and social networks rather than going back to start what they believe is a new life in Rwanda. These beliefs have not been sufficiently treated in *Gutahuka*.

10.3 Emerging Issues

An interesting element in the research was the convergence of opinions concerning repatriation across all contexts of the two listening groups studied. Although contexts varied, the ethnic network (in this case Hutus) was constant. Responses among the two listening groups were dissimilar; indeed, there was more congruence in responses across contexts than across the two listening groups. A shared history, constant interaction at the various hierarchical structures inherent in the Hutu network as well as a collective consumption of media messages did not create a convergence of views between the two listening groups on the critical topics discussed.

Dialogue participants displayed lesser knowledge of specifics of DDRRR. Also, they believed Rwanda had nothing to offer them. They were more engaged with political and socio-economic developments in the DRC and more interested in GoDRC's interventions. *Dialogue* participants have come to expect more from the GoDRC and believe it can be responsive. This opens a sphere for political participation and more civic engagement with nascent democratic reforms. The problem however is that there is no context for civic engagement due to restrictions of citizenship and identity which is not aided by *Gutahuka's* dominant discourse of "go back home". Despite these restrictions, however, participants showed high knowledge and interest in domestic political and economic affairs of the DRC. The interest was more on the DRC because it is where they believe they can have opportunities for personal growth and fulfilment.

In summary, the following key findings were made:

1. **Attitudes:** There are marked differences in perceptions of undesirable consequences of repatriation between *Gutahuka* and *Dialogue* listening groups. While *Gutahuka* listeners' most undesirable consequences are the Rwandan *Gacaca* Justice System and Uncertainty, *Dialogue* listeners were more worried about Money Matters and opportunities for Personal Development in Rwanda.

2. **Subjective Norms:** None of *Gutahuka* listeners' normative beliefs complied with any of MONUC's normative appeals, whereas *Dialogue* listeners' normative beliefs on FDLR negotiations complied with MONUC's appeal to subjective norms.

3. **Perceived Behavioural Control**: Both listening groups were exposed to the same external (military and political) pressures; however, *Dialogue* listeners were more optimistic about the ability of the GoDRC to respond to their needs or issues than *Gutahuka* listeners.

In conclusion, behavioural intentions within the context of a deeply divided society are defined by members' normative beliefs and influences of psychologically and spatially close referents. In the Hutu communitarian settings researched, members are rewarded for allegiance to the network, group norms and group values, interdependence and cooperation. Rewards take the form of information sharing, commerce and protection. This creates strong affinities among network members even across contexts. Across contexts, and although pressured by external factors, the Hutus believe their identity is pre-eminent and a recognition of their collective identity is essential to their survival as individuals and as a people. Findings suggest that group identity is not isolated from the Other, but it is fluid and is constantly negotiated and determined alongside the Other according to group needs, aspirations and perceptions. The nature and perception of groups are defined by their interactions with the Other group(s) and the nature of information they are exposed to. They constantly co-evolve with their social and political environments and the emerging imperatives or dynamics of their relationships with the other groups. The nature of information they need in their co-evolution processes and how they engage with such information is equally co-evolving. When conflicts arise with the Other for example, group behaviour and responses are negotiated in line with their constantly evolving perception of the Other, the variegated identity earlier negotiated and the contending issues. An understanding of these intersections and ways and means meanings are shared within ethnic networks is an important window for designing information intervention contents for conflict transformation.

Furthermore, the normative beliefs, reference groups and motivation to comply with pressures from each reference group within a given context and time determine the metaphors around which the thoughts and practices of the network are negotiated. In the research, the metaphors around which the thoughts and discursive practices of Rwandan Hutu groups in South Kivu were organized determined their language structure and dominant narratives and in turn how they shared meaning or engaged with the intervention messages of MONUC. In each context studied, historical and contextual metaphors defined how participants expressed their views, how *Gutahuka* and other DDRRR sensitization activities were deconstructed and the various ways and means through which participants sought alternative mediated or socially transmitted information to affirm or repudiate their normative beliefs and/or intentions. Basically, metaphors and associated inferences that underlied the internal communication patterns of Hutu ethnic networks were not the same with those that underlied their communication with cultural outsiders even within the same contexts and also with spatially distant referents. These metaphors include a discursive history of war, of guilt, of genocide, of asylum, of fugitivity, of refugeeism, of dialecti-cal shibboleths that restrict citizenship and its rewards, and of constantly struggling against resistance from autochthonous groups and the haunts of Tutsi-dominated armed groups. Though un-expressed, these metaphors make up the discursive for-mations that interfere with the contents of *Gutahuka*'s normative appeals. Indeed, the Hutus' collective history of shared frustrations, shared struggle, shared hopes for a better life *somewhere* and a shared sense of persecution and guilt are formations they do not and cannot share with the outsider intervener. These unshared epistemes con-taminate or defect meaning sharing with the outsider. Meanings and the negotiations thereof thus become ambiguated and restricted. These, in addition to negative per-ceptions of the credibility of MONUC's peacekeepers, shield individuals in the Hutu network from the influence of MONUC's behaviour-change messages. However, they were more open to information which they could use to collectively (re)negotiate their future, behavioural intentions and even survival as a people. For them, information is a key element in their survival kit. Some of the participants spend a substantial part of their income on strong-signal radio sets and batteries so they can listen to the BBC World Service, VOA and RFI for information they normally would not be able to access on the local news sources. An approach that rigorously provides information to fulfil this basic survival need is essential.

For targets that are already keen to return, *Gutahuka* offers them hope and re-assurance that

1. It is the "right" decision to make – *those that made the same decision previously are happy about it.*
2. Help is available – *MONUC is on hand to extract them and take them safely to Rwanda where they would be reinserted into their communities.*
3. There is no need to delay – repatriation has to be done now before it is too late.

Gutahuka however had limited impacts on targets that were yet to make a decision about whether to voluntarily repatriate or not. For these ones, the knowledge and information from which they can make an informed decision to repatriate seem lost within the normative appeal elements of *Gutahuka*.

Finally, a prudent approach to behavioural change for Hutus therefore can be achieved at two fronts – *Informational* and *Referential*. Firstly, participants' behavioural intention is defined not only by group pressures but also by a collective sense of uncertainty about what the Rwandan homeland holds for them. This can be treated with rigorous and objective information. Furthermore, rigorous information to dispel the myths and false stories about *Gacaca* justice system in the homeland can also provide a useful resource for achieving impacts. Secondly, interveners can work from the "inside" through social means of information sharing. Opinion leaders, family heads, pastors, priests, leaders of age-grade and other self-help associations, etc. have the potentials to exert more normative influence on behaviour and attitudes than the physically and socially distant normative referents used in *Gutahuka*.

11 Impacts of Dialogue Entre Congolais

This chapter explores how the programme *Dialogue Entre Congolais* (*Dialogue* here-after) influences the perception of Congolese autochthons concerning descriptive levels of transformation and their attitude towards Rwandan Hutus. More broadly, it explores how media interventions that only provide "objective information" can influence the audience's engagement with new democratic values and attitudes in a post-conflict setting.

Designing focus group discussion topics to elicit Autochthon participants' perception of descriptive levels of transformation was critical to the entire research because of its implications on how groups perceive post-conflict changes and the role of the media therein. The core direction of the discussion and the research question itself was derived from Lederach's (1995) analysis of conflict transformation processes. According to Lederach, conflict transforms perceptions of self, the Other and the issues in contention. The consequence usually is a foggy understanding of the Other group's intentions. Actions could be misinterpreted which could in turn (re) escalate the conflict. Intervention media takes on the role of treating "deviances" to perception of self, the Other and the issues in contention.

Another impact of conflicts on communication patterns of affected groups is that it decreases their ability to articulate their beliefs and intentions in a manner that is credible and devoid of propaganda and rhetoric (Lederach 1995, 1997). Thus in conflict situations where parties fail to share meaning in a peaceful or objective manner, perceptions of the Other are susceptible to manipulation by group leaders. Descriptive languages such as "enemy", "oppressors", "rebels", etc. are used against the Other and languages such as "freedom fighters", "liberators", etc. are used to describe self (Lederach 1995; Volkan 1990; Kelman 1965). In such cases, reconstructed images of the enemy prevail and potentially dominate public discussions and perceptions.

The research component described in this chapter sought to understand more clearly the communication patterns that can potentially transform a conflict group's perception of self, the Other and the contending issues that impel the conflict either towards escalation or de-escalation. Potentially, findings can enhance a deeper awareness of conflict dynamics not necessarily as purveyed by intervention media but as perceived by consumers of intervention media, who also happen to be among the victims of the conflict.

11.1 Topical Issues Treated in *Dialogue*

During the listenership treatment which covered the period from 4 December 2008 to 6 January 2010, a total of 284 new episodes of *Dialogue* were broadcast on Radio Okapi and 284 repeat broadcasts. In each episode, the moderator introduced the topic or topics for discussion for the day and discussed the background and the reasons the topic(s) selected were important to the Congolese. Usually discussion topics were derived from recent events that had been reported on the news. Some episodes dealt with more than one topical question. A salient example is the episode of 26 December 2008 which dealt with four topical questions: the resignation of Prime Minister Antoine Gizenga, the implications of the appointment of Adolphe Muzito as replacement, the resumption of war in the eastern region of the country and the implications of the Nairobi negotiations between representatives of the government and the CNDP.

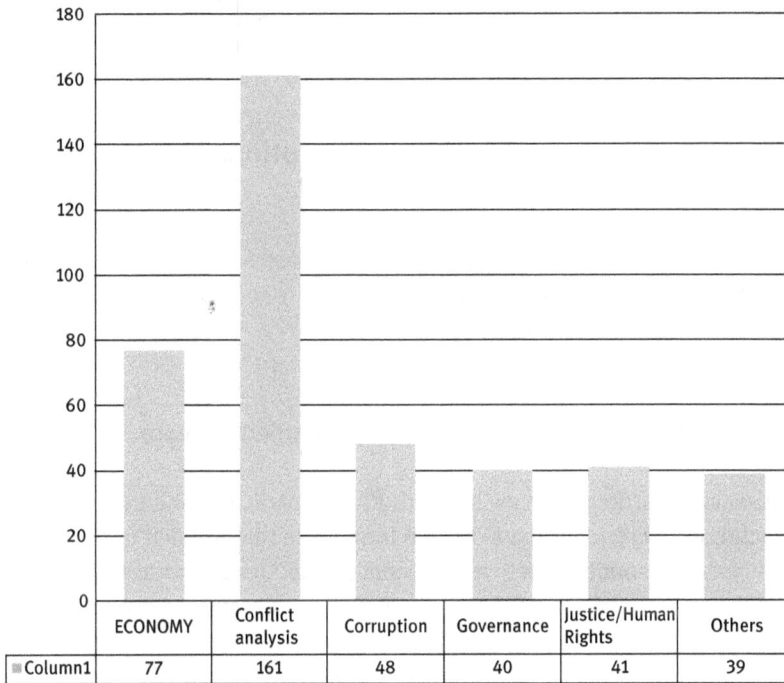

	ECONOMY	Conflict analysis	Corruption	Governance	Justice/Human Rights	Others
Column1	77	161	48	40	41	39

Figure 11.1: Themes of "*Dialogue*" Episodes Participants Listened To *(between 4 December 2008 and 6 January 2010) Note: some episode topics contained more than one theme; thus, total number of themes is higher than total number of episodic topics broadcast during the period.*

Another example is the episode of 18 December 2008 which dealt with two topical questions: the then ongoing talks between the CNDP and the GoDRC, and the problem of corruption in the National Parliament. A third example is the episode of 20 January 2009 where two topics were discussed: the implications of the deployment of two battalions of Rwandan troops in North Kivu (including explanation of why the troops were in the DRC), and French President Sarkozy's proposal to resolve the crises in eastern DRC and help manage the wealth in the eastern region. In all

284 episodes, 335 topics were discussed. Out of these, 406 themes were identified and coded accordingly. Analyses of the episodic themes during the period showed the DRC Conflict was the most discussed issue (48% of episodic topics). This was followed by the Economy which made up of 23% of issues discussed, followed by Corruption issues at 14% and Governance, Justice, Human Rights and other topics at 12% each. Themes were coded from online episodic descriptions of *Dialogue* broadcast on Radio Okapi's website (www.radiookapi.net) during the period. Autochthon participants across all contexts of the study listened to an average of 47 episodes during the listenership monitoring. Although participants were not asked to state the episode they listened to, the researcher believed that they were exposed to a higher number of conflict episodes in relation to other themes. As shown in Figure 11.1, a total of 161 episodes discussed Conflict issues representing 48% of all episodic topics.

11.2 Discussion of *Dialogue* Listeners' Perceptions of Descriptive Transformations

This part will discuss *Dialogue* listeners' perceptions of barriers to peace and conflict transformation processes. Their focus group comments are compared with *Gutahuka* listeners who functioned as control group in this case.

Factuality, Logicality and Objectivity in Perceptions of Barriers to Peace

In their discussion of barriers to peace in South Kivu in particular and in the DRC in general, autochthon *Dialogue* listeners differed from those that listened to *Gutahuka*. *Dialogue* participants' comments were more factual, more logical and more objective than those of *Gutahuka* participants. Although they did not easily reach a consensus on all issues discussed, comments were less emotional and anecdotal than in *Gutahuka* groups but significantly richer in fact and breadth of analyses. For example, in the Walungu *Dialogue* group when participants talked about the failed *brassage* and *mixage* system as being a barrier to peace, they attributed the failure to too many serving FARDC soldiers having been former members of the Tutsi armed group, the CNDP. A participant proceeded to support this position logically in describing why it is a problem:

> *They still think like CNDP, because they still have the same commanders ... the same uniform, the same guns.*

> *Their commanders simply called them together and said from today you are no longer CNDP but Congolese army.*

These are all facts. A former AFDL Commander and Intelligence Officer corroborated the participant's comment and said former CNDP fighters mixed into the FARDC were rarely re-trained. In most cases, he said, they continued in the FARDC under the same commanders and command structure brought in from the CNDP.

Generally, *Dialogue* participants based their opinions on objective facts and there is also a pattern of their statements following a logical progression – from statement of the issue, a position and an argument or reason to support the position. An example is from a comment from Uvira autochthon focus group. In supporting, the group's position that failed *mixage* and *brassage* is a barrier to peace, the participant, although not a Hutu himself, pointed out that one of the impediments to peace is that FARDC soldiers keep attacking Hutus, *"because they* (FARDC soldiers) *are mostly members of CNDP that have been dressed in FARDC uniform and deployed to areas where there are Hutus"* (Participant Comments at Uvira Autochthon *Dialogue* Group).[27]

The salient element in the above participant's comments is that they are factual and presented logically. Moreover, the last comment being from a non-Hutu is significant because of its objectivity which was rarely found among *Gutahuka* listeners. Across all contexts, there were rarely any instances of *Gutahuka* listeners speaking in support of or expressing a form of solidarity or understanding with the Hutus in their expressions of barriers to peace except in Fizi. This can be explained contextually. In Fizi, there is a very close-knit relationship between the Congolese community and Hutu settlers. "Fizians" (as Autochthons in Fizi are called) generally believe Hutus are very hardworking people, and it is common to have a Hutu as a handyman working in the farms or the herds. There are also a number of self-help projects created by Hutus that are also used by Congolese autochthons – such as maternity clinics, primary schools, herbal healing homes, etc. Aside from Fizi group, *Gutahuka* listeners were generally apathetic towards Hutus and mostly attributed barriers to peace to the refusal of the FDLR (made up of Hutus) to disarm.

In terms of factuality, *Gutahuka* listening control groups based their opinion that the FDLR is the main barrier to peace mostly on anecdotal evidence. For example, in Mwenga, a participant said the FDLR is the problem because:

> *Every military operation going on now is targeted at them.*

And added:

> *There must be a problem with you when everybody is pursuing you.*

The reasoning that because every military operation is targeted at the FDLR is proof they are a barrier to peace is rather simplistic and departs from the pattern found in

---

27 Again, I crosschecked this information with Paul Wakenge. Most ex-CNDP members of the FARDC are deployed to North and South Kivu not necessarily for political reasons, but because the FARDC has a policy of deploying soldiers around areas they originate from or are familiar with.

Dialogue groups. Another example is the catalogue of myths expressed as barriers to peace by participants in all contexts of *Gutahuka* listenership. The myths ranged from the US government being responsible for the conflicts for political ends to Satan and Demons working to create problems.

A pattern of informed analyses and breadth of logic evident in *Dialogue* listening groups reflects the nature of the programme *Dialogue*. The programme is fundamentally debates-based. The first political show of its kind in the DRC, discussants on *Dialogue* are drawn from various fields of endeavours – ranging from Politics to the academia – usually those well informed on the topic discussed. The discussants, who usually have opposing views, rigorously debate the issues and probe the meaning behind the news and current events.

The emerging implication is that consistent exposure to radio programmes that debate issues dispassionately and logically encourages listeners to follow, not necessarily the same reasoning, but the same pattern of dispassionate and logical analyses. That all *Dialogue* groups found it more difficult to reach a consensus on their views of barriers to peace suggests disparate views or perceptions of the issues. This suggests that *Dialogue* has no direct impact on their reasoning, but on the way they reason. There is no evidence of *Dialogue* influencing participants' thoughts on barriers to peace. Indeed, this is not the objective of the programme – according to Hirondelle Foundation's Radio Okapi Programme Officer, Caroline Vuilemin, the programme is not intended to pass on a particular belief or form of normative influence on behaviour but to stimulate debates on the common good.

In addition, *Dialogue* participants' comments departed from the opinions of the control group who also attributed barriers to peace to the presence of foreigners (mainly Rwandans) in the DRC. Showing undertones of objectivity, *Dialogue* participants spoke of a weak and fragmented national army as another barrier to peace. Expressions such as "too divided" (Fizi), "too weak" (Walungu), "undisciplined" (Uvira), "disorganized" and "too poorly paid" (Mwenga) were used to describe the FARDC.

What was lacking however among *Dialogue* participants was a common construction of systemic solutions to what they perceived as barriers to peace. Although participants expressed their perceptions of what should be done to transform the conflict when asked, they did not identify "fixes" to what they perceived as a failed brassage/mixage system such as training for new recruits or a more transparent D&R policy. This can be seen as one of the deficiencies of the approach in *Dialogue*. It debates the problem, not the solution. Pundits on the programme argue extensively on the issues that confront the country, but not on ways and means of solving the issues. The emerging implication is that while an Informative Approach that draws on participatory debates on the common good is useful in stimulating objective understanding of the problems and logical expressions thereof, it lacks a context for a collective exploration and expression of the way forward – a critical element in post-conflict settings. Moreover, Hirondelle Foundation's leaders seem to be overly concerned with providing a platform for an objective understanding of the problem to the detriment of a collective construction of the solution. While acknowledging the imperatives of a factual understanding of the problems and a dispassionate expression thereof, an approach that impels the community to look within itself and draw on its cultural or spiritual foundations to logically understand not only its problems but also the solutions can help a society emerging from deep conflicts to explore new realities and narratives that depart from the ones that drive most conflicts.

Perception of Prescriptive Transformations

When asked about their beliefs concerning what needed to be done to achieve peace and development in their communities in particular and the country in general, an interesting pattern emerges in *Dialogue* groups' comments. The comments reflect the salient themes in the programme *Dialogue*. Participants did not express specific ways and means through which sustainable conflict transformation (or peace and development) can be achieved in their communities or in the region, but in all contexts they talked about structural elements which they linked to poor leadership both at regional and national levels. In two of the contexts (Uvira and Mwenga), corruption was specifically mentioned as one of the main impediments to conflict transformation – a salient topic on *Dialogue*. This pattern significantly departs from the control group where participants across contexts mostly talked about relational issues of *autochthony* and *allochthony*. In the main, *Gutahuka* listeners reasoned that if foreigners (primarily Rwandan Hutus) left the country, there would be peace – reflecting the underlying meaning of *Gutahuka's* "go back home" message.

The emerging implication here is that *Dialogue* participants perceived prescriptive transformations along the trajectory of structural interventions not necessarily within the rubric of immediate issue or relational concerns such as presence of foreigners, but on the imperatives of credible political leadership. While immediate issue or relational concerns are by no means less important or less urgent, an understanding of the role of credible leadership in transforming the conflicts of the DRC suggests a collective consciousness of the role of a legitimate or democratically elected government in transforming deep-seated socio-political issues. This is important in a country that has seen over 40 years of corrupt authoritarian government out of 50 years of independence. It suggests a new appreciation of values of good governance and accountability. The sharp contrasts between their beliefs and those of their contemporaries and in some cases neighbours and other close Others that listened to *Gutahuka* during the period validate the influence of the programmes on participants' opinions regarding issues that concern them and their normative beliefs about transformation. As noted earlier in this chapter, a shared context, constant interaction at the various hierarchical structures and normative formations inherent within the autochthon networks was not strong enough to converge the normative beliefs of the two listening groups on the critical topics discussed. It also has implications not only on debates on the impacts of radio on audience perceptions in conflict and post-conflict societies but also on debates on the nature of media impacts on audiences, which will be discussed in greater detail later.

Engagement with New Democratic Values and Reforms

In addition to patterns of more factual, logical and objective expressions of perceptions of barriers to peace and a deeper understanding of structural conflict transformation factors, a third pattern, perception of civic engagement was investigated in relation to *Gutahuka* control groups. Firstly, *Dialogue* participants' comments showed a collective sense of responsibility and ownership of democratic reforms. They used words such as "my responsibility" (Walungu Group), "an obligation" (Fizi Group), "our community" (Mwenga) when commenting on their engagement with community self-help projects and new democratic processes. There were also evidence of participants' involvement in civic duties and other active expressions of civic engagement during the course of the programme. For example, in Walungu, a participant said he has started calling-in during phone-in programmes on the local radio although he said it was expensive to make the phone calls, but added "If I don't do it who would? We can't leave it and hope that somehow those up there would know what we think" (Walungu Group). In Uvira, a *Dialogue* participant said he has recently (during the course of the listenership) taken part in a conflict resolution meeting organized by MONUC's JPT where he had opportunity to talk about communal issues of interest and wished there were more of such opportunities. Also, a *Dialogue* participant in Fizi said his church is involved in de-mining activities, but although he is not directly involved since it is not in his hometown, he believed it was an obligation to take part in community efforts such as building schools, maternal care and birth centres, among others. Across all contexts, *Dialogue* participants perceived themselves as stakeholders in their society's wellbeing. Another interesting pattern is that participants in *Dialogue* groups all linked opportunities for personal development to stability, peace and development in their region, expressions used included: "if there are roads and security ..." (Uvira group); "if things are stable..." (Fizi group); "security on the roads..." (Walungu group); "there has to be peace first" (Mwenga group).

Secondly, there is pattern among the *Dialogue* participants or groups that perceived civic engagement as needful – they also had a positive perception of opportunities for their personal development in the DRC as well as a sense of optimism or hope for a better future for their communities. This cannot be said to be the case with *Gutahuka* listeners who in all contexts were more inclined towards short-term needs such as "food in the stomach" (Walungu group), "worried about my own stomach" (Fizi group), etc. The implication is that *Dialogue* listeners linked attainment of their personal development goals with a stable society in the DRC. Stability is constructed within frames of not only absence of war, but also infrastructural development – roads, bridges as well as general security. This explains their perception of themselves as stakeholders in their community's wellbeing. Patterns in beliefs expressed in *Gutahuka* groups in both networks are fundamentally different. Participants did not talk about any civic engagement activity there were involved in but in their comments suggested that they perceived politicians as being responsible for the wellbeing of their community and that the political system offered no opportunities for civic engagement.

Expressions of normative beliefs about new democratic values and descriptive interventions by Hutu *Dialogue* listeners show a pattern that matches those of autochthon listeners. In their discussion of descriptive interventions, firstly Hutu *Dialogue* listeners displayed very good knowledge of ongoing intervention efforts of the DRC government (although they believed the interventions were weak and half-hearted); secondly there was a pattern of Hutu *Dialogue* listeners claiming a stake or ownership of transformation processes. Although they all acknowledged that political participation for them is limited by their identity and restricted citizenship, they were as optimistic as the autochthon *Dialogue* groups of the GoDRC's ability to fix the issues if things were done right. Unlike *Gutahuka* listeners across both networks, Hutu *Dialogue* listeners across contexts saw intervention activities within the trajectory of the DRC's elected government. This supports patterns observed among Autochthon listeners who saw credible political leadership as an essential element in conflict transformation processes. Among both autochthon and Hutu *Dialogue* listeners, there is a strong pattern of engagement, a sense of ownership and relatively greater factual, logical and objective expression of issues. This is because the format of *Dialogue* encourages popular participation in decision-making processes, engagement in the democratic processes and collective discussion of the common good.

Dialogue represents a transactional media regime that draws on communitarian media values. It seeks to collectively negotiate social construction of the common good and engages Radio Okapi as a member of the community – constantly debating and exploring the common good. Constant exposure of community members to *Dialogue* created a new reality or new sets of mediated norms, built not necessarily on the historically dysfunctional patterns of social relations or solely on the subjective norms of political elites or guerrilla entrepreneurs, but on a reconditioning of objective and subjective norms using the tools of credible and interactive media. Objective norms are ongoing events which constitute the bases or backdrop for discussions in *Dialogue*. Subjective norms purveyed by elites are refined into a more transactional mode – involving debates on the issues rather than the top-down purvey of subjective norms in *Gutahuka*. These have implications on contemporary debates on the normative role of the media particularly in crises societies in terms of its influence on beliefs and attitudes towards the normative Other.

Moreover, autochthon *Dialogue* listeners expressed a more favourable attitude towards Rwandan Hutus than did autochthon *Gutahuka* listeners. When asked about what they imagined their relationship with the ethnic Other would look like in future,

Dialogue participants, as in earlier patterns observed, were specific in describing what they perceived would be an impediment to social or community integration. Again, there was a pattern of *Dialogue* participants talking about the problems or impediments albeit in way that showed objectivity. The most talked about impediment across contexts was Citizenship. The issue for them was not necessarily about Hutus or Tutsis remaining but absence of a systematic framework and transparency of regulations for attaining citizenship which, as pointed out in earlier chapters of this work, has been used as a political tool by previous governments. There was the underlying reasoning among participants across contexts that when crises of citizenship are resolved, communities could then decide to forge ahead together as a people.

The most revealing expressions of *Dialogue* participants' attitude towards Hutus was in their comments about who they felt were the worst victims of the conflicts. There was an interesting pattern across all contexts of autochthon *Dialogue* listenership groups. All groups talked about Hutu refugees as being among the worst victims of the conflict. The empathy with Hutus was strong among participants and evident in their tone. For example, in Fizi, a participant said "It is hard not to feel for them (Hutus) ... haunted and hated by everyone". In Uvira, a participant expressed a view that is very rarely expressed among non-Hutus: "genocide has been committed against them (Hutu) but everyone is talking about Tutsi genocide". In Walungu, participants said no one can ever tell what Hutus have gone through since they fled Rwanda in 1994. These sentiments were in contrast with those expressed by the control *Gutahuka* listening groups. In the autochthon *Gutahuka* groups, there was no mention of Hutus as victims of the conflict at all. But women (mainly pregnant women) were identified as worst victims. Also, with exceptions in Fizi, autochthon *Gutahuka* listeners across all contexts wanted all Rwandans – both Hutu and Tutsis – to leave. When asked to talk about their imagination of future relationships with other ethnic groups, again except in Fizi, *Gutahuka* listeners said they did not think it would ever be possible for all ethnic groups to integrate and live together peacefully as a community. They also said it would not be possible to have a unified army involving all the ethnic groups because they thought it would be difficult to get all the groups to transcend their personal interests and that of their ethnic groups to work together within a unified Congolese security force. Again, there was an exception in Fizi on this. Overall, participants across listening groups in Fizi felt far more comfortable with the ethnic Other than participants in the other contexts. This is because, as pointed out before, in Fizi, there has been a history of mutual relationship between Hutus and autochthons not only in inter-marriage but also in trade. For years, both groups have lived side by side with each other and conflicts have been very minimal between them. Indeed, MONUC does not have a JPT, TOB or COB deployment in Fizi. This illustrates the relative calm in the territory when compared with the other towns. The history of mutual alliance between both groups goes deeper beyond the reach of media influence to perception of the ethnic Other. This is treated in more detail later in this document.

In summary, there is a strongly noticeable pattern of contrasts between both listening groups' perceptions of Hutus. There is a pattern of empathy and constructive engagement evident in *Dialogue* listeners' attitude towards not only Hutus but also the ethnic Other in general, but most noticeably among the Hutus. Perceptions of Hutus as victims of the conflict reflect a sense of fellow-feeling with the Hutu refugees in their communities. Granted, expressions of sympathy may not necessarily reflect actual attitude of listeners towards Hutus, but it is suggestive of what they think about the Hutus which in turn inform attitude. Furthermore, the discussion approach used in the focus groups was designed to measure attitudes through cognitive processes and not direct questioning. So participants did not have to answer direct attitude measurement questions such as "what do you think of the Hutu?". But they had the latitude to talk about whoever they felt were affected or afflicted most by the DRC war, for example. A pattern in answers across contexts suggest a linkage between the programme listened and perceptions of victimhood and victims of the conflict. *Dialogue* participants expressed the need for a process where Hutus can access Congolese citizenship. This further shows that they have a positive attitude towards Hutus in contrast with *Gutahuka* listeners who believed integration both at the community level and within the army was impossible. Indeed, *Dialogue* can positively influence regular autochthon listeners' attitude towards Rwandan Hutus. This is attributed to the transactional nature of the programme. The programme is based on a model that illustrates mass communication as a horizontal or transactional process. By creating a platform for rigorous debates of key issues that confront the community as a whole, the programme encourages audiences to participate in evaluating the current situation, to perceive the current situation based on the different positions debated and to interpret the debates in a way that fits their own peculiar episteme. As shall be discussed later in this chapter, this interpretation can either lead to convergence or divergence within the communication network (Rogers and Kincaid 1981; Kincaid 1993; Rogers 1995).

11.3 Process of Perception Change in *Dialogue* Groups

This section will show that *Dialogue* influenced perceptions and attitudes of listeners through a transactional process of exposure to information about the current situation, ideation, interpretation and (re)evaluation of ongoing events or current situation to achieve changes in personal perceptions.

Exposure to Current Situation

Dialogue participants were exposed to the *objective reality* of ongoing events at local, national and regional levels (or current situation) with its implicit inter-relationships by first talking about the event to create a background to the debates. Participants were also directly exposed to some of the events through either the media or during their daily lives.

Ideation

Ideation involves evolution of knowledge of the issues in contention as selected, clarified and discussed on *Dialogue*. It connotes a knowledge process that evolves along with exposure to ongoing events, clarification, discussion and personal evaluation of the issues debated on *Dialogue*. Ideation was achieved at three transactional levels: first, direct exposure to ongoing events or objective reality; second, exposure to clarifications and discussions in *Dialogue*; and third, through a process of personal evaluation and re-evaluation conditioned by personal interpretation, clarifications, discussants' perspectives and proposals on *Dialogue* (see Figure 11.2). Ideation was not constant but dynamic – constantly changing along with a constantly changing objective reality and the (re)evaluation thereof. Constantly evolving events and debates arguing for different sides of the issues not only enhanced ideation but also led to series of evaluations and re-evaluations both at personal and group levels. In the perception process, ideation was constantly refined by exposure to real-world events (and the variables that underlie them), as well as exposure to reconstructed versions or debates of some of those events on *Dialogue*. Exposure to reconstructed realities in turn conditioned participants' interpretation of objective realities. There were indeed cases where participants used the same arguments, logic and phrases used by their preferred *Dialogue* discussants to buttress their points during focus group discussions. The process of ideation also underlined participants' understanding and interpretation of the issues which led to either their disbelieving or affirmation of previous beliefs or even adoption of a whole new set of beliefs. Importantly, knowledge derived from clarified discussions of issues on *Dialogue* enhanced an understanding of the Other's issues, hence potentially achieving mutual understanding and agreement.

Re-Evaluation of Current Situation

Three salient elements in *Dialogue* defined participants' constantly evolving evaluation of realities: clarifications of topics (in *Dialogue*, discussion issues are first explained and the background information provided); *Dialogue* discussants' expressions of their discursive perceptions of the issues clarified based on their own world view; and proposal for a way forward on the issues – usually summed up by the moderator. Throughout the process of listening, each participant's impressions of the issues and related phenomena were constantly redefined along with their understanding and interpretation of the issues. Understanding and personal Interpretation of the issues were influenced by each participant's re-evaluation of the issues after exposure and greater knowledge. Comments at focus groups reflected not only a greater depth of knowledge on issues but a larger breadth of analyses by individual participants on the issues.

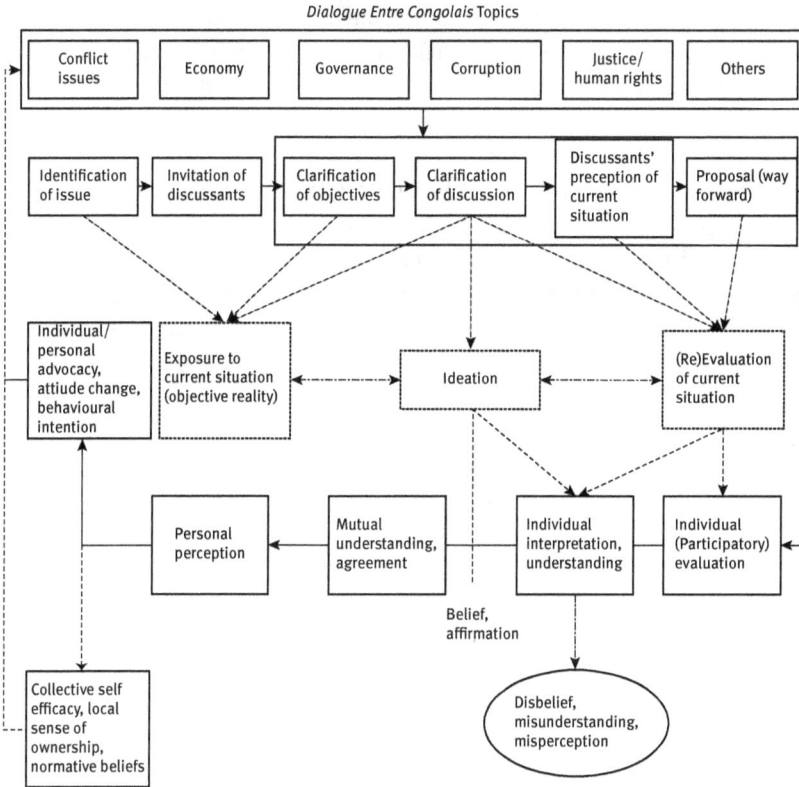

Dialogue Entre Congolais Topics

Conflict issues	Economy	Governance	Corruption	Justice/ human rights	Others

Identification of issue	Invitation of discussants	Clarification of objectives	Clarification of discussion	Discussants' perception of current situation	Proposal (way forward)

Individual/ personal advocacy, attiude change, behavioural intention	Exposure to current situation (objective reality)	Ideation	(Re)Evaluation of current situation

Personal perception	Mutual understanding, agreement	Individual interpretation, understanding	Individual (Participatory) evaluation

Belief, affirmation

Collective self efficacy, local sense of ownership, normative beliefs

Disbelief, misunderstanding, misperception

Figure 11.2: Process of Perception Change in *Dialogue* Groups

Personal Perception

Personal Perception of the issues relating to conflict transformation processes, intervention mechanisms and the impediments thereof reflected not necessarily the views purveyed by discussants on *Dialogue* but a new stream of perception borne out of personal interpretation, mutual agreement and understanding. As pointed out earlier, conflict transforms perceptions of self, the Other and the issues in contention (Lederach 1995, 1997). Lederach's works have shown that a salient impact of conflict on the communication patterns of conflict groups is a decreased ability to articulate one's intentions in a manner that is credible and devoid of propaganda and rhetoric. When compared with the control group, *Dialogue*-treated participants shared meaning in a more robust and reflective manner. Moreover, individual participants re-engaged with the ethnic Other based, not on negative descriptive languages found in the control groups' expressions, but on an objective and logical evaluation of the self, the Other and the contending issues such as citizenship and barriers to peace. At personal levels, personal advocacy was noticed in participants' comments about various community engagement activities they had become involved in since their participation in the research. At group levels, although there were lesser agreements on topics discussed, there was a greater level of collective self-efficacy, and collective sense of ownership of transformation processes.

In summary, *Dialogue* discussions were horizontal and transactional. They enabled individual- and group-level evaluation and re-evaluation of the different positions purveyed by discussants. New levels of perception that emerged from understanding and belief promoted individual advocacy, perception and attitudinal change. In situations where the new thinking are transmitted through social or informal means within the community, social impact can be achieved through collective self-efficacy which in turn can have actual effects on the events discussed on *Dialogue*.

12 "Hutus are the ones that have kept us where we are today": When Psyops Backfire

Radio is a ubiquitous medium. Anyone can listen to a program broadcast on radio. When radio is then used to target a particular audience, what kind of impacts can Group A's exposure to Psyops contents designed for Group B have on perceptions and attitudes of Group A towards Group B? Drawing on the case in the DRC, a study of how exposure of Autochthons to *Gutahuka* affected Autochthons' attitudes towards Hutu provides strong insights on potential impacts of contents meant for the Other.

Congolese autochthons exposed to *Gutahuka* expressed more awareness of the ethnic and political divisions that can deter future social and political relationships. Across contexts, except in Fizi with its peculiar socio-cultural blend of Hutus and autochthons, *Gutahuka*-exposed autochthons were pessimistic about possibilities of a unified Congolese army involving all the ethnic groups including settled Hutus. This contrasts with opinions of *Dialogue* listeners who recommended that questions of citizenship be resolved once and for all to enable communities to integrate peacefully. Generally, *Dialogue* participants perceived there were opportunities for integration and a mutually rewarding relationship across ethnic groups if issues of identity and citizenship were resolved. A salient pattern of difference in beliefs between the listening groups is that *Dialogue* listeners showed more empathy towards Hutus than listeners of *Gutahuka*. In discussing their perceptions of Victimhood, autochthon listeners of *Gutahuka* did not see Hutus as victims of the conflict, whereas autochthon *Dialogue* listeners across all contexts believed Hutus were among the main victims of the conflict implying as it were, a greater sense of empathy towards the Hutus. In one of the *Gutahuka* groups (Mwenga), Hutus were even identified as the Villains. *Dialogue* listeners' perception of villainity centred on corrupt politicians.

It had been envisaged at the beginning of the study that exposure to the Other's programme would deepen an understanding and empathy with the Other's issues, but the reverse has been the case in autochthon listeners of *Gutahuka*. They perceived Hutus as the problem and expressed the normative appeal in *Gutahuka* that peace in the DRC is linked to FDLR militants (embedded in Hutu communities) repatriating to Rwanda. Interestingly, Hutu *Dialogue* listeners had mixed perceptions of Victimhood and villainity that did not show any particular pattern. Again, this reflects the discursive and analytical nature of the programme *Dialogue*.

Beliefs expressed by autochthon listeners of *Gutahuka* have far reaching implications on contentious debates on the impacts of exposure to contents meant for the Other in deeply divided societies and the overarching debates on the role of the media in reinforcing dominant power relations in the society. There have been a retinue of interesting scholarly works that support the position that the media convey mainstream outlooks and normative beliefs about behaviour (Barak 1994; Signorielli and Morgan 1989; Gerbner et al. 1982; among others). Indeed, Barak (1994) has observed how media contents identify heroes, villains and neutral characters and associate them with specific traits, beliefs or forms of behaviour and in other cases label and stigmatize certain activities and individuals or groups as antisocial, deviant or undesirable. He posits that such associations have relative implications on social control. Also, Mutz (1998) has written brilliantly on the "impersonal" nature of influence by media portrayals of attitudes, beliefs or experiences of collectives outside an individual's personal life space. She has argued for "impersonal influence" to be taken more seriously because of its potential to expand contemporary understanding of social influence processes from media portrayals of indirect associations. This research provides important evidence within the spheres of Barak's (1994) "symbolic deviance" and Mutz' (1998) "impersonal influence". By constantly calling on FDLR militants to repatriate, *Gutahuka* labels or stigmatizes Hutus in general as deviant and undesirable. This is because there is a social reality that associates the FDLR with Hutus and vice versa, which in turn creates unspoken assumptions and cognitive framing of the Hutu Other as "foreign", "unwelcome", "deviant" and "undesirable" among autochthon listeners of the programme. Although autochthons are not the target audience for the programme, they are as exposed if not more exposed to it as the targets themselves – more exposed because FDLR militants in the forests are prevented by their commanders from listening to the programme for fear they would be convinced to surrender. Obviously, Radio is not selective in its reach; hence, audiences who are not targets of a particular intervention programme but are exposed to it do end up consuming the programme. In the case of *Gutahuka*, although MONUC presents the programme in Kinyarwanda, the language spoken among Hutus in Rwanda, most Congolese in the Kivus understand and speak Kinyarwanda fluently having lived side by side with Rwandans for several years. For non-targets, *Gutahuka's* messages constructs "symbolic deviance" – involving unspoken assumptions, associations and framing of the FDLR combatant as an "unwelcome" or undesirable Hutu. This in turn impugns on non-targets' perception of the Hutu Other. The "Otherization" of Hutus is further deepened by media reports of joint military activities against the FDLR. An autochthon *Gutahuka* group member in Mwenga, quoted earlier, said of Hutus: "there must be a problem with you when everybody is pursuing you". The result is what Barak (1994) terms "symbolic punishment" through stigmatization or labelling of the Hutu Other as antisocial, deviant or undesirable. Such negativity may not be expressed explicitly in *Gutahuka* but dynamic interactions of Gutahuka's messages and implicit normative appeals with unspoken assumptions rooted in an epistemic association of the FDLR with Hutu and vice versa lead to the construction of symbolic deviance not intended by the programme creators. Although *Gutahuka's* messages and normative appeals are intended to restore peace in South Kivu by achieving voluntary repatriation of FDLR elements and Hutu civilians, they do have negative implications on social relations between autochthons and the Hutu Other when considered against the backdrop of a social reality or discursive formation that associates the FDLR with Hutu and vice versa – an association taken for granted or unaccounted for in the programme. By problematizing the FDLR–Hutu, *Gutahuka* created or deepened animosity towards Hutus among autochthon listeners in three of the four contexts researched. In the fourth context, Fizi, there is a historical reality that supports a mutual alliance and cordial relations between the autochthons and Hutus. This in turn is supported by local influentials that purvey localized subjective realities or norms. Fizi Participants' engagements with objective realities or ongoing events and with the mediated reality of *Gutahuka* were thus conditioned by stronger historical and subjective realities which make up the discursive formation of their society (see Figure 12.1).

In the other contexts, however, *Gutahuka* further reinforces the dominant power relations by depicting the FDLR as the problem and not the breakdown in social relations and other structural causes of the conflict. The result has been a "we–they" cognitioning and expression of relations between the autochthon "self" and the Hutu Other. This is evident in a comment by an autochthon *Gutahuka* listener in Walungu:

> They (Hutus) have raped thousands of our women, killed thousands of our young men, stole every-thing they can steal, they are the ones that have kept us where we are today.

The calibration of the Hutu as a normative Other is only evident among autochthon *Gutahuka* listening groups. Although living within the same contexts with Hutus, and having regular interpersonal interactions with them, perception of Hutus in three of the contexts seems to be influenced more deeply from *Gutahuka* representations of the FDLR/Hutus than from their day-to-day interactions with them. This corroborates Mutz' position that people respond "to a media-constructed pseudoenvironment – rather than their immediate personal experiences or those of friends and acquaintances" (1998, 6).

At a broader level, media (re)constructed reality is not necessarily about the direct persuasive or influence potentials of media messages that set out to change behaviour or a viewpoint. Mediated reality is the media superstructure's refinement of the subjective reality (or opinions or experience of influential collectives) purveyed by elites or political/military actors to influence citizens (as in the case of purveyors of subjective norms in *Gutahuka*). Because of the media's expertise in matters that are beyond the realm of citizens' personal experiences, they are perceived as more reliable sources of information. Mutz (1998) has argued that media content is particularly well suited and used as a credible channel of information about such collective subjective realities. Essentially, in the context of a violently divided society where, as Lederach has written, perceptions of self, the Other and the issues in contention are constantly altered resulting in a "contaminated" interpretation and understanding of the Other's intentions, media intervention contents have strong potential impacts even on non-Target listeners. As findings have shown, non-Target listeners exposed to contents aimed at changing the behaviour of the ethnic Other resulted in more negative perceptions of the Other compared with participants that listened to a political debate programme – *Dialogue*. In the communities researched, participants were exposed to a communicative sphere that drew on four contending realities with varying degrees of potential impacts on interpretation and engagement with mediated contents: Historical Reality, Objective Reality, Subjective Reality and Mediated Reality.

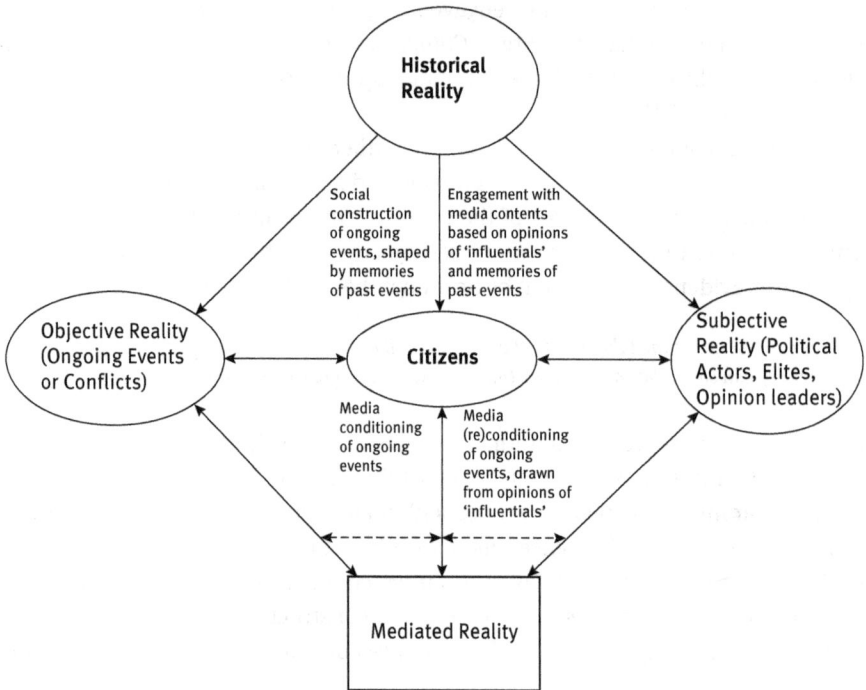

Figure 12.1: Contending Realities in Conflict Settings

12.1 Contending Realities in Narrative Frameworks of *Dialogue* and *Gutahuka*

Participants' comments during focus groups show that communication patterns of groups researched were overwhelmingly rooted in their memory or knowledge of previous conflicts, events or interrelationships. Historical realities define the epistemes within which metaphors around which the thoughts, discursive practices and communication patterns of each network are negotiated. Hugh Mail (2004) has argued that collective memories is a salient element that should be of interest to conflict transformers because memories of past conflicts determine groups' expectations in future relationships and significantly determine their behaviour towards the Other and how meaning is shared. In this study, key influentials or purveyors of subjective realities were themselves influenced by historical realities which in turn infected their communication patterns. Participants in the focus groups were at the intersection of a triad of realities that in addition to other factors defined their perceptions. Those exposed to a mediated reality that did not provide a platform for objectively engaging and debating out the historical and subjective realities in the triad were subjected to the normative influences of those realities in their engagement with media contents. Exposure to the Others' media contents within a communicative sphere or intersection that is hostile to the Other created a stronger negative opinion of the ethnic Other. The tendency to blame the Hutu Other for the misfortune of the autochthon-self was intensified with exposure to the Hutu Other's behaviour change messages. In each context studied, historical realities to a remarkable extent defined how participants expressed their views, how programme messages were interpreted and the various ways they sought alternative mediated or socially transmitted information that met their peculiar needs. Exceptions were found however among participants exposed to a media platform where the contending realities were confronted and debated.

Through the programme *Dialogue,* Radio Okapi performs more than mere cognitive functions of providing objective information. The programme also undertakes interpretative functions including analyses, evaluation, assessments and comments. Discussants in some cases are not only the authors of the cognitive and interpretative elements of *Dialogue* but also the authors of the very issues they seek to interpret. Through the programme, they are able to present their arguments within their own narrative frameworks. Their narrative frameworks are different from the narrative frameworks in Radio Okapi's news discourses with its inherent gate-keeping appendages. Arguably, this represents the liberal democratic role of Radio Okapi in the DRC. By mediating objective realities of ongoing events and subjective realities purveyed by political elites, *Dialogue* provides elites a raw forum to criticize policy decisions and to comment on other issues of popular concern while also affording citizens an opportunity to participate in the questioning, evaluation and interpretation processes.

13 Revisiting Unfinished Debates on Information Intervention

While there have been increasing interests on the role of the media in transforming conflicts in crises states, until now, impacts of actual media intervention Information Operations activities in ongoing conflicts have remained under-studied. Emerging implications of findings and their pinpoints to contemporary and future practice and research will be further discussed and summed up in this chapter.

In this work, Information Intervention has been defined more expansively to include public diplomacy activities of external state and non-state actors (including NGOs, IGOs, religious organizations, etc.) aimed at transforming conflicts and building peace in crises states. This breadth of definition encompasses Public Information Operations of the UN in Peace Support Operations. Seen within this breadth, Information Intervention as a concept has proliferated particularly in crises states where NGOs, Western Strategic Communications Consulting companies, foreign governments, etc. are involved directly and/or in partnership or contracts with the UN in running broadcast stations, creating programmes intended to inform and change local attitudes and perceptions as well as various other strategic communication functions. Despite this proliferation, there has been no clearly defined framework for specific and time-referenced actions drawn from detailed evaluation of an ongoing information intervention programme to understand areas of successes and areas of failures in each conflict phase. There has also been the issue of who has the legitimacy and the "social license" to carry out or manage information intervention functions in crises states. This is particularly more pertinent in an era that the UN has increasingly outsourced its information intervention operations and various other elements of its PIO to NGOs and Strategic Communications Consulting companies. Hitherto such functions were traditionally core activities of the UN's Department of Public Information or the Public Information Unit of the specific UN Mission. Hirondelle Foundation currently runs Radio Okapi, the largest UN Mission radio in history; *Miraya FM* in conjunction with the UN Mission in Sudan; *Radio Ndeke Luka* in Central African Republic, a successor of the UN MINURCA Radio; *Cotton Tree News* in Sierra Leone in conjunction with United Nations Integrated Peacebuilding Office in Sierra Leone; and *Star Radio* in Liberia. Moreover, a number of NGOs based in the global north such as Search for Common Ground and Radio Benevolencija have created hundreds of transformational and reconciliation radio programmes targeted at groups in divided societies across Africa. In terms of collaboration with consulting companies, in November 2009, the UN Support Office for AMISOM (UNSOA) awarded a $7.25 million a year contract to a consulting consortium led by UK-based PR firm Bell Pottinger to, among other strategic communications activities, run a radio station for the Somalia peace mission. The new outsourcing of UN Information Intervention functions has until now escaped the radar of communications scholars.

The consequence has been that information intervention has remained under-theorized and limited to operational level discourses and ad hoc practices based on expediency.

Another consequence has been that scholars and practitioners in the field are yet to build synergies to evaluate practices, identify lessons and theorize so that frameworks for analyses and modules can be built for ongoing and future operations. Such synergies can create a better understanding of the imperatives and criteria for selecting an appropriate partner or contractor to work with the UN in its evolving policy of outsourcing key components of its Mission Public Information Operations. Audiences' perceptions of the partnering organizations, their ideological leanings, profit-status and information-giving philosophy deserve to be more rigorously engaged with – not only by practitioners but also by scholars.

A third consequence, as this study has shown, has been confusion over the approach to information intervention practice that really works. A knowledge base of the nature of impacts of each approach can guide procurement specialists at the UN on criteria for selecting partners or contractors to plan and implement the UN's Information Intervention operations in crises states. What obtains at the moment is a tendency to improvise at each case and phase of media intervention which inevitably results in clashes of ideological approaches at some of the most intricate and volatile intersections of intervention; more so when ideologically disparate organizations (such as the UN/NGOs/Consulting Companies) work together. This research therefore (re)stimulates debates on Information Intervention particularly relating to whose right or duty it is to impart information in a crises society when it becomes a humanitarian need, the nature of information provided and the nature of outcomes and impacts triggered.

For UN Missions, particularly those with Chapter VII mandates, there is an emerging proclivity to hire Military Information experts as consultants to design and implement information intervention programmes.[28] The likely consequence is that techniques of military information activities such as Deception Operations may be used as a key strategy of information intervention. Philip M. Taylor (2002) in a typically authoritative style has compared and contrasted techniques of information intervention and military information and observes that although both techniques emphasize the importance of information to strategy during times of conflict, they should not be mixed. He acknowledges that when information becomes an element of strategy in a post-conflict situation (like in the case of MONUC's information approach to DDRRR), and not merely an undifferentiated product of public sphere, it becomes difficult if not hypocritical to apply traditional thinking on free expression. Drawing on comparable cases from NATO information campaigns in Kosovo aimed at trans-

---

[28] For example, part of the consortium that won UNSOA's Public Information contract is Albany Associates. Most of their consultants and Directors are former military information experts.

forming ethnic hatred, Taylor observes that information warfare and the techniques thereof are slowly becoming part of the arsenal used during post-conflict information interventions. This indeed is the case in the DRC and in the current unfolding case in Somalia. It is propelled by a new sensitivity to the imperatives of adopting effective communication strategies in supporting mission objectives – ranging from prevention of ethnic clashes to transforming ethnic and religious hatred in divided societies. The danger however is that information intervention contents run the risk of being perceived locally as an external propaganda tool meant to serve the interests of its foreign originators. Hence, any corresponding media development effort would be viewed with suspicion with far-reaching consequences on the credibility of the entire intervention operation. Moreover, as this research has shown, contents may unwittingly create more wedges between groups if Information Intervention contents are not informed by a detailed knowledge of local epistemes and metaphors that underlie communications and intergroup relations. At such cases, Information Interveners may unwittingly become a part of the conflict they seek to transform. To avoid this, Price (2000) has made a case for UN collaboration with NGOs in information intervention either as partners or as watchdogs. This work has shown that UN collaboration with an NGO is not without its own problems and that the UN and NGOs do not necessarily see eye to eye ideologically. IGOs generally and the UN in particular have philosophies that are different from those of NGOs and both adopt different ideological approaches to dealing with conflicts especially where the UN is involved in a Chapter VII peacekeeping mandate. In the DRC, for example, this research has shown that although the UN and Hirondelle Foundation have worked together since 2002, asymmetric approaches, caused not only by differences in ideologies but also by differences in operational objectives, have tended to elicit disparate responses to Radio Okapi's programming contents. The study has shown that within Radio Okapi, there are two contending media ideologies – an Informative Approach favoured by Hirondelle Foundation and a Behaviour Change Communication Approach preferred by MONUC. These contending approaches are evident in the two intervention programmes studied in this work – *Dialogue Entre Congolais* produced by Hirondelle Foundation and *Gutahuka* produced by MONUC. Exposure to each of the programmes had varying impacts on participants' perceptions of barriers to peace, descriptive and prescriptive interventions, victimhood and villainity, attitudes towards the ethnic Other and knowledge of MONUC's DDRRR processes. Findings show that although *Gutahuka* could be effective in reassuring Hutu groups that were already keen on returning to Rwanda that help is available, it is less effective in persuading undecided ex-combatants and Hutus to repatriate. This, among other reasons, is because their apprehensions about the Rwandan *Gacaca* justice system and fear of judicial persecution if they returned to Rwanda have not been sufficiently treated and transformed on the programme. Also, although listeners believed *Gutahuka's* normative appeal that there were opportunities for personal development in the Rwandan homeland if they returned, participants expressed uncertainties over a range of issues – from the unknown to access to land and other renewable resources – suggesting that the programme was lacking in compelling information. Furthermore, the programme reinforced Hutu participants' hostility towards the Tutsi Other culminating in participants' descriptions of the Rwandan government as "Tutsi government".

Radio is a ubiquitous medium – generally received by all within the reach of the transmitting station. Hence, there are possibilities that non-Targets may be exposed to behaviour-change contents not meant for them. This study engaged with the question of how disparate networks operating within homogenous contexts engage with information products meant for the Other. There is evidence in this research that exposure of non-targets to behaviour change contents meant for the Other creates hostility against the targets. Congolese autochthons exposed to *Gutahuka* during the period did not develop a sense of affinity with the Hutus as envisaged, but hostility. Across contexts, they expressed the belief that if Hutus and all Rwandans left the DRC, there would be peace – reflective of the normative appeals in *Gutahuka* that portray the armed group, the FDLR, as barriers to peace. Epistemic associations between the FDLR and the Hutu impelled autochthon participants to express sentiments of undesirability regarding not only the FDLR but also the Otherised Hutu. Here was arguably one of the sharpest contrasts between perceptions of Autochthon listeners of *Dialogue* and their *Gutahuka* listening counterparts. Autochthon *Dialogue* listeners were more empathetic with what they saw as plight of the Hutus. Across all contexts of the study, they identified Hutus as one of the main victims of the war and expressed emotions of empathy to their plight. Among the *Gutahuka* listeners, there was no mention of Hutus at all (even passively) as victims of the conflict. The emerging implication is that *Dialogue* listeners were more analytical of the conflict situation and the dynamics thereof including issues of causality, victimhood and villainity, and the various military operations targeted at the FDLR (but inevitably also fatally affecting Hutu civilians and refugees) as a basis for their perception of Hutus as victims. *Gutahuka* listeners on the other hand perceived the various military operations against the FDLR as evidence of the undesirability of not just the FDLR but also the Hutu. Simply put, the same objective reality of military operations against the FDLR elicited two fundamentally different perceptions from listeners within the same network and contexts based on the nature of intervention programmes each was exposed to. Two critical implications emerge. Firstly, hate contents are not only the ones that are overtly hateful. Messages targeted at specific groups for the purpose of achieving behavioural change can lead to alienation and hostility towards the Target group by the Other (non-target) groups exposed to the messages. The implication is that media intervention contents that purvey a narrative without first understanding how it interacts with other epistemic narratives, metaphors and historical realities on ground run the risk of deepening rifts between groups and escalating the conflict. Another implication is that contextually associated individuals or social groups do not always have homogenous interpretation, perception and/or decoding of media messages. At the core of these discursive perceptions is the ideological orientation of messages audiences are exposed to and how they interact with historical and subjective realities on ground. Whereas *Gutahuka* called on FDLR militants to disarm and return, *Dialogue* encouraged objective and pluralistic analyses of the conflict including the crises situation and the underlying issues within a narrative framework that demands of listeners a level of iterative evaluation, understanding and interpretation to achieve individual and collective belief or disbelief. This can explain why *Dialogue* listeners across contexts and networks perceived failed interventions of the DRC government as one of the main barriers to peace. This shows that *Dialogue* listeners' construction of conflict transformation processes and conflict multipliers rest on the activities or inactivities of the democratically elected government in the DRC and not the presence of Hutu "foreigners". Though dissatisfied with the intervention activities of the government, *Dialogue* listeners' responses showed they perceived the government as endowed with the legitimacy and political licence needed to tackle the problems. An essential starting point in the democratic process in the DRC – a country that has experienced over 40 years of brutal military rule out of about 50 years of self rule – is a recognition of the legitimacy of the democratically elected government and the new institutions set up to support democracy and good governance. Importantly, *Dialogue* participants' discussions of prescriptions for conflict transformation centred on specific actions the government and its institutions (primarily the armed forces) could take to achieve peace. Interestingly, autochthon *Dialogue* listeners did not see any ethnic group as a barrier to peace, neither indeed did Hutu *Dialogue* listeners. Whereas Hutu *Gutahuka* listeners saw the "Tutsi government" of Rwanda as the greatest barrier to peace, Hutu *Dialogue* listeners saw the inactions of the Congolese government as barriers to peace – corroborating the perception of autochthon *Dialogue* listeners of the GoDRC's legitimacy and capability to live up to its mandate if supported and if issues of corruption are solved.

Another interesting element in the research was the Uvira factor. *Gutahuka* participants in Uvira context were more knowledgeable of DDRRR processes when compared with the other contexts. This has already been attributed to their additional exposure to various other sources of information about DDRRR through their own personal search. Uvira *Dialogue* listeners however did not have as much information or go out in search of DDRRR information although they had the same access with their *Gutahuka* compatriots. I have explained this as evidence of Blumler and Katz' (1974) Uses and Gratification Theory. *Gutahuka* participants, on their own, actively sought available sources of information on a topic that their involvement in the listenership treatment had generated a cognitive interest in.

13.1 Final Word

Contemporary works on Information Intervention have tended to concentrate on rationalizing intervention. There have been far lesser studies on the nature of intervention, the framework for intervention and the composition of interveners. Krug and Price (2002) have made a compelling case for and proposed a module that can be generically applied in post-conflict settings. But their module is focused primarily on regulatory frameworks and issues of governmentality, media reform and governance. This work extends the frontiers of the discussion by exploring not only the actual contents of intervention media but also the impacts of specific contents on groups in societies violently divided along ethnic cleavages. Today, information intervention or public diplomacy activities by external NGOs and IGOs as a tool for Peacebuilding or preventing genocide has become normatively acceptable in international settings. As previously noted, UNSOA has recently outsourced a major PIO component to a communication consulting consortium after an openly advertised bidding process which drew tenders from NGOs including Hirondelle Foundation. While various factors determine the outcome of UN procurement processes, the UN's decision to award the contract to a private consulting consortium is instructive. If anything, it suggests that the UN is becoming more confident with its new outsourcing of public information components which started with the outsourcing of Radio Okapi to Hirondelle Foundation in 2002. Part of the UNSOA outsourcing deal is a Radio component – Radio Bar-Kulan which is run by Okapi Consulting – a member of the consortium[29]. Along this trajectory, this study moves the debates from questions of legitimacy of media intervention to questions of who should intervene as well as the nature and effectiveness of specific media intervention contents and their impacts in real-world settings. Furthermore, the methodological approach used in the study moves the debates beyond prediction models and/or retrospective rationalizations frequently used in media impact evaluation processes of this nature. The research was built on real time, real-world subjects and contexts involving working with real people within real contexts of an ongoing conflict setting – intact with emotions of fear, anger and guilt as well as rumours and other socially transmitted information which have potentials of affecting audience engagements. Findings provide instruments with which operational researchers or media intervention practitioners can compare predictions and rationalize impacts as they happen, in future conflicts. Furthermore, findings have implications on contemporary understanding of the relative importance of communication models and their interactions within ongoing or future conflict settings where the media have been used as a tool for violence or for transformation and Peacebuilding.

Furthermore, this study is a reminder that Radio as a communication medium is still a powerful tool of mass communication and indeed worthy of continued research. In an era where the Internet is the main buzz-word, researchers and research funders have been understandably more attracted to new media and internet communications. With increasing interest and research funding going the way of online deliberation

---

29 Okapi Consulting has nothing to do with Radio Okapi. It is a South African–based private consulting company headed by David Smith, former MONUC's Chief of Public Information.

spaces, radio research is once again threatened with a return to the doghouse, to borrow Hilmes' (2002) parody. As a radio enthusiast I note this with a heavy heart, the study of radio has not been particularly attractive to twenty-first century media scholars and indeed funders. The disinterest dates back a bit more. In the past four decades, the study of popular culture has bloomed. But this bloom has unfortunately excluded Radio. Michele Hilmes attributes what she calls the negative "academic legitimation" of radio since the 1960s to the medium's "cultural marginality" and "low brow roots" (2002, 6). Generally, since the late 1960s, Radio was increasingly being considered as low profile and inferior to other more technologically enhanced media such as Television. By the 1970s, as Hilmes has noted, industrially, culturally, historiographically and theoretically, radio had been rendered invisible by the temper of the times. But Radio's ostensible degeneration into a "vast cultural wasteland" (Squier 2003, 1) did not apparently affect international Radio because it actually bloomed during the cold war as a tool for propaganda and public diplomacy. During the cold war, Radio Free Europe, the VOA, the BBC and other international broadcasters expanded and took on more strategic importance in the international affairs departments of sponsor nations. Rawnsley has substantially filled the gaps on the use of Radio as a propaganda tool during the cold war (1999, 1996). As a tool for psyops, public and cultural diplomacy, Surrogate Radio continues to occupy the attention of key Western Governments and their intelligence agencies in borderlands including Afghanistan, Iraq, Iran, Zimbabwe, etc. This work calls to mind that in Africa, beyond the realms of Western Government's use of Radio for strategic purposes, Radio remains the most popular medium of communication and frequently used by the UN, NGOs and governments to reach citizens. Its misuse during the Rwandan genocide demonstrates its potentials. A strong oral tradition, a social and cultural fondness for story-telling and devotion to radio borne out of absence of diverse other means of mass communication makes radio a potentially powerful tool for transforming conflicts in Africa. Moreover, Radio impels the pan-African philosophy of *Ubuntu* – inspiring sharing, commonality and communitarianism. Group listenerships to radio in rural areas provide a meeting point for exchange of stories and affinity, but more importantly a key anchor point for sharing – sharing not only the radio receiver and the listening processes but also meaning. This study has once again drawn attention to this reality about Africa and harps on the imperatives of designing Information Intervention approaches that draw on these factors. The approach has to depart from the Western perception of an individualized Radio audience or "listener". Ethnographic observation of radio listeners in Uvira showed that radio audiences are not aggregates of individuals but are social entities bound together by shared histories, cultural ties and local epistemes. Media messages are consumed not individually, but collectively. Meaning is collectively negotiated and shared among culturally inter-dependent beings. This has far reaching implications for designing information contents for audiences in rural Africa. Current Western libertarian approach of seeking to achieve psychological impacts on "individuals" need to give way to a more interactive approach aimed at achieving social impacts. The implication of findings in this study is that contents for African audiences need to draw and build on the rich oral traditions and traditionally trans-actional processes of information and meaning sharing. Such contents should first map existing narratives to identify conflicting messages. Secondly explore, using par-ticipatory processes, new narratives that transcend historical realities within which conflict parties weave their narratives. Thirdly design the new narratives within an interactive framework that engages with and challenges conflicting ones.

Within the realm of Public Diplomacy, Information Intervention figures promi-nently, not as an appendage for explaining mandates or rationalizing an interven-tion, but as a virile tool for stimulating public debates on the common good. And within military spheres of Psyops, information intervention figures not only as a force multiplier but as a key component of strategy. This study emphasizes the need to keep the approaches that underlie both doctrines far apart particularly during the post-conflict reconstruction phase. In summary, findings of this study show that in violently divided societies, Information Intervention approaches aimed at achieving attitudinal and/or behavioural change by appealing to social norms can be ineffective if not counter-productive. But an informative approach involving the use of narratives that stimulate discursive discussions on the common good, a collectively imagined future and issues of good governance can open up a sphere for participation, social interaction and civic engagement.

Methodologically, lessons learned abound. To transcend culturally constrained spaces of meaning sharing, peer researchers were used to monitor listenership and conduct the focus group discussions. The narratives from focus groups were detailed and authentic. In its frankness and truth, comments by participants were neither unduly polite nor rude but buttressed a non-rhetorical exposure of participants' views on issues that they felt strongly about. Moreover, it gave them a sense of empower-ment – they felt they could narrate their own stories their own way. It was a recreation of contextually organic social conversations and comments were recorded and tran-scribed verbatim. Participants retained their assured anonymity as each comment was assigned a code rather than a name. The methodological setback with most qual-itative studies involving groups in divided societies is that cultural outsiders try to chisel out insider information from an insider who believes he does not have any stake in the outsider's work. The result has been the tendency for the insider group to be polite by sharing what they perceive the outsider wants to hear or to be rude by being verbally aggressive in expressing sentiments about the Other. This study underscores the imperatives of a participatory approach to media impact research particularly in divided societies in Africa. A participatory approach not only in research but also in developing Information Intervention contents can give audiences a greater sense of ownership and empowerment. It can also result in a more robust engagement.

Future studies emerging from this work will explore the ways and means through which violently divided societies share meaning or tell their own stories and the narrative frameworks within which such meanings or stories are told. In societies divided by conflicts, several factors contribute to contending narratives which in turn infect groups' perceptions, attitudes and actions against or for the Other. The narratives are usually drawn from historical realities and/or from ideologies emerging from ethnic or religious beliefs. An ethnographic research that studies and draws on the contending narratives of divided societies to explore ways of creating, alongside the community members, narrative frameworks and new narratives that dwell not on the hurts of the past but on a common imagination of a shared future is imperative.

13.2 End Note: Reflections of an Outsider Researcher

Conducting research in the DRC is a tough task especially when it is carried out by an "outsider". Socio-ethnic profiling is common in the Kivus. Profiling cuts across every fibre of social life and may range from profiling the ethnic identity of the corner shop owner to the ethnic identity of President Kabila's mother. Public and private discourse on both historical and contemporary issues are underlined and most times parochially limited by the social, ethnic, political and sometimes religious issues that have kept this society divided for so long. As a cultural outsider, I knew that attempting to break into the mix would be a difficult task. The issue was well summed by my South Kivu friend in Leyton, East London, Paul Inongo when he asked me during one of our heated arguments about the cause of the conflict in the DRC. "Do you want to be told what you want to hear or do you want to do a real proper research in Kivu and know what those people truly think?", he asked. The Congolese, he told me, have a way of being polite to foreigners – telling them niceties just to get them off their backs, and added, "I think that is one of the main problems NGO and UN researchers face when they go there. They rush through things having already decided what they are looking for. The folks sense their hurry and simply tell them what they want to hear, get paid an honorarium and off they go". For the first time all evening, Paul got me thinking seriously about my research method and my identity as a researcher in South Kivu.

A lot has been written about researching deeply divided societies and the dilemma of the "insider" and "outsider" researcher. Herman (2001) has written of the impermeable identity wall standing between the outsider and the divided society researched. Taylor (1967) has written about the normative and attitudinal neutrality of the insider or outsider researcher and how subjectivity by insiders and compunction by outsiders can contaminate research findings. This has led postmodernists in recent decades to make a case for a more hermeneutic disclosure of not only the researcher's identity but also the researcher's personal opinion regarding the society and the conflict. This is because for postmodernists the research is viewed with subjective lenses – from the research data to the analyses thereof especially when viewed from the lenses of power relations (please see Foucault 1982; Hermann 2001).

As an outsider researching a violently divided society with a rather unfair share of intricate power bases, I tended more on the positivist or empiricist school. For an outsider without any personal stakes in the DRC conflict, my initial thinking was that there would not be any shadow of personal value and/or attitudes from the study or the object of research. My intention was to completely isolate my identity as an "outsider" including my normative stance on the DRC conflict from the research itself. But it was not as easy as I had thought it would be. Firstly, because as an African, I have come to feel that every conflict in Africa and its social effects is my conflict – a story I relate to in several ways, having grown up and lived in the volatile Niger-Delta region of Nigeria. I have also been an eye-witness to the social effects of injustices occasioned by unwholesome alliances between corrupt government and transnational extracting corporations. The lines between the positivist school (with its implicit demands for objectivity) and the hermeneutic school with its normative requirement for reflexivity became more blurred for me the more I knew about the human suffering in eastern DRC caused by the conflict. As an African with my own baggage unevenly laced with my own strong personal story, I could not remain aloof to the tragedies and avoidable human suffering in eastern DRC. For once, I felt the sense of Gourevitch's (1998) "involved outsider". Irrespective of what epistemological school – positivist or hermeneutic I professed – I longed to be what Hermann (2001) describes as a "participating observer" not in terms of making myself the subject of my study or being prejudiced. Rather, working in the background to see and report how the people here could research their own problems, reflect on their own situation and identify the gaps themselves. Though I was an "outsider", I shared the same feeling, the same need, like the ordinary men and women from the Kivus who opened their homes to me and shared their stories of frustrated hopes with me, for the return of peace so that the prosperity this region is naturally blessed with can for the first time be of benefit to all its people. But I determined never to allow my position between the positivist and hermeneutic epistemological traditions to influence my research or become the problematique. But it made me to adopt a research design that engaged more with the communities and networks I researched – a participatory method that involved the researched in the research.

Moreover, I was determined from the very beginning to deterritorialize the study. Since it was participatory, I decided to entrust most of the responsibility to my Research Assistant, Serge Sakombi. Simply out of exuberance I codenamed him *Eagle Finger*. He became known by that codename within the entire research team. Serge has extensive experience. At the age of 21, he was a Commander with the AFDL, the rebel group that overthrew the totalitarian regime of Mobutu Sese Seko in 1997. His extensive contacts in South Kivu and insights were invaluable.

Eagle Finger was tasked with the responsibility of recruiting eight more research assistants – two (one from each network) from each cellule. Cellule represents networks in context, for example, Hutu network in Fizi context is a cellule; autochthonous community in Fizi is another cellule. The Cellule Research Assistants (CRAs) or Peer

Researchers would go on to play a very critical role in the research – mobilizing participants, visiting them at home as often as possible (without appearing to put pressure), monitoring and ensuring that each participant listened to the radio programme assigned and reporting back to *Eagle Finger* who would then report to me once every month. To fulfil this responsibility, the CRAs[30] had to be socially engaged and embedded in their cellules. Aside from taking care of the practical but very important elements of the study (such as visiting participants at home and monitoring listenership), my use of Peer Researchers also helped to break down the "impermeable identity wall" (Herman 2001, 77).

The identity of the researcher has implications on the conceptualization, analyses and methodology used in researching violently divided societies (Smyth and Robinson 2001). My research involved potentially dealing with members of guerrilla movements particularly the elusive FDLR. There was the possibility that some of them could be former members of the Rwandan Interahamwe genocidaires. Their elusiveness, constant mobility and distrust of non-members in general created an impregnable wall for a foreign researcher. This made the use of an insider peer researcher invaluable. Being a researcher after the positivist tradition, I felt it necessary to keep informal, social contacts with either side of the network divide as minimal as possible. The Peer Researchers helped me achieve this by creating the link. This work would not have been possible without them.

---

30 CRAs and Peer Researchers are used interchangeably throughout this book.

Appendix 1

Radio Okapi Penetration Rate in Kinshasa (Total Penetration 64.3%)

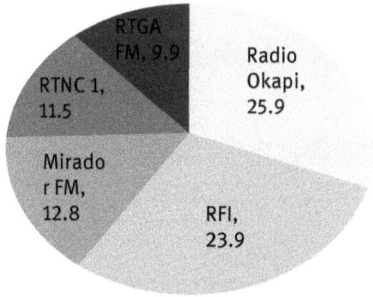

Source: IMMAR Institut de Sondage (2006)

Radio Okapi Penetration Rate in Matadi (Total Penetration: 67.2%)

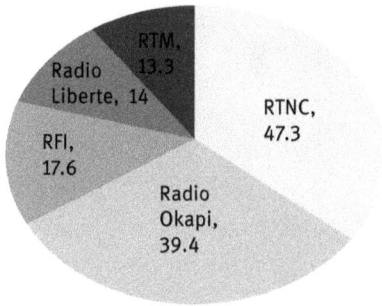

Source: IMMAR Institut de Sondage (2006)

Radio Okapi Penetration Rate in Kisangani (Total Penetration 54.5%)

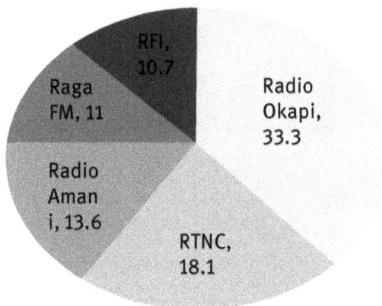

Source: IMMAR Institut de Sondage (2006)

Radio Okapi Penetration Rate in Lubumbashi (Total Penetration: 76.1%)

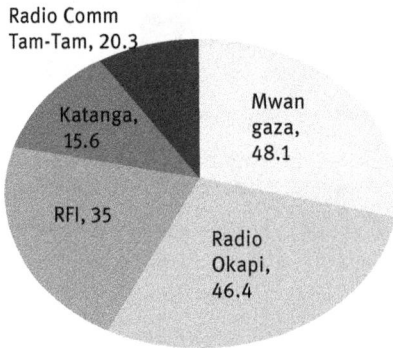

Radio Comm
Tam-Tam, 20.3

Katanga,
15.6

Mwan
gaza,
48.1

RFI, 35

Radio
Okapi,
46.4

Source: IMMAR Institut de Sondage (2006)

Radio Okapi Penetration Rate in Bukavu (Total Penetration 68.9%)

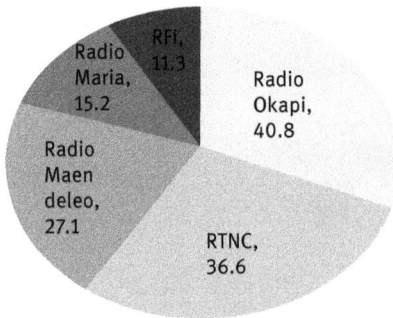

Radio
Maria,
15.2

RFI,
11.3

Radio
Okapi,
40.8

Radio
Maen
deleo,
27.1

RTNC,
36.6

Source: IMMAR Institut de Sondage (2006)

Appendix 2

Hutu Expressions of Consequences of Repatriation

Variables (concepts)	Fizi		Mwenga		Uvira		Walungu	
	Gutahuka	Dialogue	Gutahuka	Dialogue	Gutahuka	Dialogue	Gutahuka	Dialogue
Uncertainty	"I have livestock and a farm … but I do not know how much they would be giving me there until I get my feet on the ground … to take care of my family."	"I am yet to see or hear about one person that returned and went on to have a good life."					"All we need is the truth, not propaganda. … would I have a farm to plant on…?" "If I had information from a friend I know personally or relative that has seen everything they do there…. I would be able to decide myself then."	
Gacaca Persecution	"I hear stories that people come up with every kind of claim just to avenge on your family. …"		"…if they want to make you guilty they would. … *Gacaca* is all politics. It was created to punish their Hutu enemies."	"*(Gacaca)* is not a real court … I don't think there is justice in Gacaca."	"All the talk about justice in *Gacaca* court is a big lie. …the person accusing you … is also your judge.	"… Tutsi people (are) using *Gacaca* court to persecute Hutu people. …"	"What assurance can I have that they won't use Gacaca to persecute me like they have done before to other people? …"	

Appendix 2: (continued)

Variables (concepts)	Fizi		Mwenga		Uvira		Walungu	
	Gutahuka	Dialogue	Gutahuka	Dialogue	Gutahuka	Dialogue	Gutahuka	Dialogue
	The court is just a way of trying to get back at people."				So how can you ever win?"	All the talk of justice is just a way of deceiving people."	no one has given us satisfying answers."	
Reintegration Fears		"They say they will help to get us back into our communities, but what we don't know is how people there would take us back ... how would they receive us? ... we would be like aliens there and they can attack us."						
Money Worries		"I can't really tell how much is paid, but I know it is not worth anything and they don't pay it to everyone."	"It is only former military personnel that are given some money like al form of pension. Everyone else	"I was not in the army so I won't get paid any gratuity it's only the FRw50,000 which can't last				"How do you live? What do you eat? It would have been different if they paid reasonable money on arrival

Appendix 2: (continued)

Variables (concepts)	Fizi		Mwenga		Uvira		Walungu	
	Gutahuka	Dialogue	Gutahuka	Dialogue	Gutahuka	Dialogue	Gutahuka	Dialogue
				goes home without anything."	for one month ..."			and provide some kind of money on a continuous basis."
No Hopes for Personal Development		"It is a tough life out there ... I'd rather stay here and when it is time, die here."		"Thousands of Hutus ... have intermarried here, ... they know there is nothing for them in Rwanda."	"A lot of people do not find going back worth thinking about .... Youths don't have anything to go back to in Rwanda.	"I have nothing to return to there ... (Rwanda)."		"There is nothing there for us now, and we all know that."

Bibliography

Primary Sources

Newspapers/Press Releases

Le Lushois, September 10, 1992
Mukuba, August 22, 1992
Le Katangais, August 14, 1992
La Tribune, August 16, September 24, 1992
La Cheminee, August 17–24, *1992*
Le Liberateur-Ujamaa, December 26, 1994
Le Potential, June 1996–December 1996
MONUC News, 12 April 2010. 'MONUC Helpline for Former Rebels'. Issue 282.
MONUC Press Release, 26 November 2009. 'Rwanda: Former FDLR Commander Calls on Compatriots in the DRC to Abandon Armed Struggle'. MONUC.
MONUC Press Release, 28 September 2009. 'Surrenders and Repatriations of FDLR Combatants Increase as MONUC Step Up DDRRR Efforts'. MONUC.

United Nations Official Documents

Security Council Resolutions

S/RES/1925(2010) Resolution 1925
S/RES/1906(2009) Resolution 1906
S/RES/1896(2009) Resolution 1896
S/RES/1857(2008) Resolution 1857
S/RES/1856(2008) Resolution 1856
S/RES/1843(2008) Resolution 1843
S/RES/1807(2008) Resolution 1807
S/RES/1799(2008) Resolution 1799
S/RES/1797(2008) Resolution 1797
S/RES/1794(2007) Resolution 1794
S/RES/1771(2007) Resolution 1771
S/RES/1768(2007) Resolution 1768
S/RES/1756(2007) Resolution 1756
S/RES/1751(2007) Resolution 1751
S/RES/1742(2007) Resolution 1742
S/RES/1736(2006) Resolution 1736
S/RES/1711(2006) Resolution 1711
S/RES/1698(2006) Resolution 1698
S/RES/1693(2006) Resolution 1693
S/RES/1671(2006) Resolution 1671
S/RES/1669(2006) Resolution 1669
S/RES/1654(2006) Resolution 1654
S/RES/1649(2005) Resolution 1649

S/RES/1635(2005) Resolution 1635
S/RES/1628(2005) Resolution 1628
S/RES/1621(2005) Resolution 1621
S/RES/1616(2005) Resolution 1616
S/RES/1596(2005) Resolution 1596
S/RES/1592(2005) Resolution 1592
S/RES/1565(2004) Resolution 1564
S/RES/1555(2004) Resolution 1555
S/RES/1552(2004) Resolution 1552
S/RES/1533(2004) Resolution 1533
S/RES/1522(2004) Resolution 1522
S/RES/1501(2003) Resolution 1501
S/RES/1499(2003) Resolution 1499
S/RES/1489(2003) Resolution 1489
S/RES/1468(2003) Resolution 1468
S/RES/1457(2003) Resolution 1457
S/RES/1399(2002) Resolution 1399
S/RES/1417(2002) Resolution 1417
S/RES/1445(2002) Resolution 1445
S/RES/1376(2001) Resolution 1376
S/RES/1355(2001) Resolution 1355
S/RES/1341(2001) Resolution 1341
S/RES/1332(2000) Resolution 1332
S/RES/1323(2000) Resolution 1323
S/RES/1316(2000) Resolution 1316
S/RES/1304(2000) Resolution 1304
S/RES/1291(2000) Resolution 1291
S/RES/1279(1999) Resolution 1279
S/RES/1279(1999) Resolution 1273
S/RES/1258(1999) Resolution 1258
S/RES/1234(1999) Resolution 1234

United Nations Documents/Agreements/Reports

A/RES/13(I) (February 13, 1946). United Nations General Assembly Resolution 13(I), Annex I,
*Recommendations of the Technical Advisory Committee on Information Concerning the
Policies, Functions and Organisation of the Department of the Department of Public
Information.*

Lusaka Ceasefire Agreement (July 10, 1999). Democratic Republic of Congo: Lusaka Ceasefire
Agreement.

S/2009/623 (4 December 2009). Thirtieth Report of the Secretary-General on the United Nations
Organization Mission in the Democratic Republic of the Congo.

S/2009/603 (23 November 2009). United Nations Security Council Report of the Group of Experts on
the Democratic Republic of the Congo.

S/2009/472 (18 September 2009). Twenty-Ninth Report of the Secretary-General on the United
Nations Organization Mission in the Democratic Republic of the Congo.

S/1999/790 (15 July 1999). UN Security Council, Report of the Secretary-General on the Situation in
the Democratic Republic of the Congo.

S/2009/335 (30 June 2009). Twenty-Eighth Report on the United Nations Organization Mission in the Democratic Republic of the Congo.

S/2009/253 (14 May 2009). Letter dated 14 May 2009 from the Chairman of the Security Council Committee established pursuant to Resolution 1533 (2004) concerning the Democratic Republic of the Congo addressed to the President of the Security Council. (Group of Experts' interim report concerning the operations of the FDLR in the DRC.)

S/2009/160 (27 March 2009). Twenty-Seventh Report of the Secretary-General on the United Nations Organization Mission in the Democratic Republic of the Congo.

S/2008/728 (21 November 2008). Fourth Special Report of the Secretary-General on the United Nations Organization Mission in the Democratic Republic of the Congo.

S/2008/433 (3 July 2008). Twenty-Sixth Report of the Secretary-General on the United Nations Organization Mission in the Democratic Republic of the Congo.

S/2008/434 (11 February 2008). Report of the Security Council Mission on the Electoral Process in the Democratic Republic of the Congo.

S/2007/671 (14 November 2007). Twenty-Fourth Report of the Secretary-General on the United Nations Organization Mission in the Democratic Republic of the Congo.

S/2007/423 (16 July 2007). Letter dated 16 July 2007 from the Chairman of the Security Council Committee established pursuant to Resolution 1533 (2004) concerning the Democratic Republic of the Congo addressed to the President of the Security Council. (Group of Experts report stating that sanctions imposed on the DRC have rarely had the intended coercive effect but recommended suspension of flights by all airlines that are found to be violating regulations, enhancing controls of natural resources and strengthening border control.)

S/2007/156 (20 March 2007). Twenty-Third Report of the Secretary-General on the United Nations Organization Mission in the Democratic Republic of the Congo.

S/2007/40 (25 January 2007). Letter dated 25 January 2007 from the Chairman of the Security Council Committee established pursuant to Resolution 1533 (2004) concerning the Democratic Republic of the Congo addressed to the President of the Security Council.

S/2006/310 (22 May 2006). Report of the Secretary-General Pursuant to Paragraphs 10 and 14 of Security Council Resolution 1649 (2005).

S/2006/53 (27 January 2006). Letter dated 26 January 2006 from the Chairman of the Security Council Committee established pursuant to Resolution 1533 (2004) concerning the Democratic Republic of the Congo addressed to the President of the Security Council.

S/2005/436 (26 July 2005). Letter dated 26 July 2005 from the Chairman of the Security Council Committee established pursuant to Resolution 1533 (2004) concerning the Democratic Republic of the Congo addressed to the President of the Security Council.

S/2005/320/Add.1 (12 July 2005). Special Report of the Secretary-General on Elections in the Democratic Republic of the Congo.

S/2005/320 (26 May 2005). Special Report of the Secretary-General on Elections in the Democratic Republic of the Congo.

S/2005/30 (25 January 2005). Letter dated 25 January 2005 from the Chairman of the Security Council Committee established pursuant to resolution 1533 (2004) concerning the Democratic Republic of the Congo addressed to the President of the Security Council.

S/2004/650 (16 August 2004). Third Special Report of the Secretary-General on the United Nations Organization Mission in the Democratic Republic of the Congo.

S/2004/551 (15 July 2004). Letter dated 15 July 2004 from the Chairman of the Security Council Committee established pursuant to Resolution 1533 (2004) concerning the Democratic Republic of the Congo addressed to the President of the Security Council.

S/2003/1027 (23 October 2003). Letter dated 23 October from the Secretary-General addressed to the President of the Security Council. (A report of the Panel of Experts on Illegal Exploitation of Natural Resources.)

S/2003/566 (27 May 2003). Second Special Report of the Secretary-General on the United Nations Organization Mission in the Democratic Republic of the Congo.

S/2002/1005 (10 September 2002). Special Report of the Secretary-General on the United Nations Organization Mission in the Democratic Republic of the Congo.

S/2001/357 (2001). Report of the Panel of Experts on the Illegal Exploitation of Natural Resources and Other Forms of Wealth of the Democratic Republic of the Congo.

S/2000/30 (17 January 2000). Report of the Secretary-General on the United Nations Organisation Mission in the Democratic Republic of Congo.

S/2000/330 (18 April 2000). Second Report of the Secretary-General on the United Nations Organisation Mission in the Democratic Republic of Congo.

S/1999/1116 (1 November 1999). Second Report of the Secretary-General on the United Nations Prelimanary Deployment in the Democratic Republic of Congo.

S/1999/790 (15 July 1999). Report of the Secretary-General on the United Nations Prelimanary Deployment in the Democratic Republic of Congo.

United Nations (24 October 1945). *Chapter VII: Action with respect to Threats to the Peace, Breaches of the Peace, and Acts of Aggression.* In United Nations Charter. New York: UN. http://www.un.org/en/documents/charter/chapter7.html (accessed on 1 December 2010).

Special Reports

Annan, K., 1997. Strengthening of the United Nations System. UN Doc. A/51/829, New York, March 17.

Annan, K., 2000. We The Peoples: The Role of the United Nations in the Twenty-First Century: Report of the Secretary-General. UN Doc. A/54/2000, New York.

Annan, K., 2002. To Help Us Make the World a Better Place. UN Doc. SG/SM/8277 PI/1428, New York, June 18.

Annan, K., 2003. Secretary-General's Remarks at UNICEF Goodwill Gala. Beverly Hills, Calif., December 3. http://www.un.org/apps/sg/sgstats.asp?nid=671 (accessed on 14 June 2008).

Annan, K., 2004. *A More Secure World: Our Shared Responsibility.* New York: United Nations.

BBC World Service Trust, 2006. *African Media Development Initiative (AMDI) Research Summary Report.* London: BBC World Service Trust.

Boutros-Ghali, B., 1992. *An Agenda for Peace.* New York: UN Department of Public Informaiton.

Boutros-Ghali, B., 1995. *Supplement to an Agenda for Peace.* New York: UN Department of Public Information.

Brahimi, L., et al, 2000. *Report of the Panel of United Nations Peace Operations.* New York: General Assembly, A/55/305 S/2000/809.

Carnegie Commission on Preventing Deadly Conflict, 1997. *Preventing Deadly Conflict: Final Report.* Washington, DC: Carnegie Commission on Preventing Deadly Conflict.

Charbonneau, L., 'Peacekeepers may have committed sex abuse in Congo', *Reuters*, 13 August 2008. http://africa.reuters.com/top/news/usnBAN325952.html (accessed on 14 September 2009).

Crisis Group, 2009. *Congo: A Comprehensive Strategy to Disarm the FDLR.* Africa Report No. 151, July 9.

Feeley, R., and Thomas-Jensen, C., 2008. *Past Due: Remove the FDLR from Eastern Congo.* Enough Strategy Paper, No. 22, June

Gambino, A. W., 2008. *Congo: Securing Peace, Sustaining Progress.* Council on Foreign Relations Special Report No. 40, October.

Garreton, R., 2001. *Report on the Situation of Human Rights in the DRC.* Geneva: United Nations.

Hänggi, H., and Scherrer, V. (Eds.), 2007. *Security Sector Reform and UN Integrated Missions: Experience from Burundi, the Democratic Republic of Congo, Haiti, and Kosovo.* Geneva: Geneva Centre for the Democratic Control of Armed Forces (DCAF).

Human Rights Watch, 2000. *Eastern Congo Ravaged: Killing Civilians and Silencing Protest.* Vol. 12, No. 3(A).

Human Rights Watch, 2001. *Rwanda: Observing the Rules of War?* Vol. 13, No. 8(A).

IMMAR Institut de Sondage, 2006. *Etude Médias en RDC.* Lausanne: Fondation Hirondelle.

International Commission on Intervention and State Sovereignty (ICISS), 2001. *The Responsibility to Protect.* Ottawa: International Development Research Council.

International Crisis Group, 2003. *Rwandan Hutu Rebels in the Congo: A New Approach to Disarmament and Reintegration.* ICG Africa Report No. 63, May 23.

International Crisis Group, 2007. *Congo: Consolidating the Peace.* ICG Africa Report No. 128, July 5.

International Crisis Group, 2009. *Congo: Five Priorities for a Peacebuilding Strategy.* Africa Report No. 150, May 11.

International Crisis Group, 2009. *Congo: A Comprehensive Strategy to Disarm the FDLR,* ICG Africa Report No. 151, July 9.

International Rescue Committee, 2008. *Mortality in the Democratic Republic of Congo: An Ongoing Crisis,* International Rescue Committee, January 2008.

Journalistes en Danger, 1999. *La liberte de la presse en Republique Democratique du Congo* (Kinshasa: Unpublished).

Journalistes en Danger, 2000. *Republique Democratique du Congo: vers une nouvelle strategie pour la liberte d' expression* (Kinshasa: Unpublished).

Journalistes en Danger, 2000. *Report on the Freedom of the Press* (Kinshasa: Unpublished).

Journalistes en Danger, 2000. *Vers une nouvelle strategie pour la liberte d' expression en RDC* (Kinshasa: Unpublished).

Journalistes en Danger, 2001. *L' affaire RTKM: Un espace de liberte pluriel confisque* (Kinshasa: Unpublished).

Minorities at Risk Project, 2004. *Chronology for Hutus in the Dem. Rep. of the Congo.* http://www.unhcr.org/refworld/docid/469f387fc.html (accessed December 2009).

Moffat, J., 2003. *Complexity Theory and Network Centric Warfare.* Washington DC: Command and Control Research Program (CCRP) Publication Series.

OCHA, 2009. *DRC: Humanitarian Situation in South Kivu.* Situation Report. United Nations Office for the Coordination of Humanitarian Affairs, No. 2. 29 March 2009.

Orme, B., 2010. *Broadcasting in UN Blue: The Unexamined Past and Uncertain Future of Peacekeeping Radio.* Centre for International Media Assistance, 16 February, 2010.

Prendergast, J., and Atama, N., 2009. *Eastern Congo: An Action Plan to End the World's Deadliest War,* Enough, 16 July 2009. www.enoughproject.org/publications/eastern-congo-action-plan-end-worldsdeadliest-war (accessed on 01.12.2009).

Radio Okapi, 2006. *Values of Fondation Hirondelle and Radio Okapi.* Lausanne

Reporters sans frontières, 1999. *The Heavy Toll of Laurent-Désiré Kabila: Over 80 Journalists Jailed.* RSF Special Report, September.

Romkema, H., and Veenhoop, D., 2007. *Opportunities and Constraints for the Disarmament & Repatriation of Foreign Armed Groups in the Democratic Republic of Congo. The cases of the*

FDLR, FNL and ADF/NALU. Multi Country Demobilization and Recovery Program. http://www. wilsoncenter.org/events/docs/MDRPDRCCOFSStudy_Final_ENGL.pdf (accessed on 21 December 2009).

Rumsfeld, D., 2005. *Strategy for Homeland Defence and Civil Support*. Washington, DC: US Department of Defence.

United Nations DPKO Lessons Learned Unit, 1996. *Comprehensive Report on Lessons Learned from UNAMIR*, December.

US Office of the Chairman of the Joint Chiefs of Staff, 2001. *Department of Defence Dictionary of Military and Associated Terms*. Joint Publication 1–02, 12 April 2001 (as amended through 19 August 2009). Washington, DC: CJCS.

US Office of the Chairman of the Joint Chiefs of Staff, 2010. *Psychological Operations*. Joint Publication 3–13.2, 7 January 2010. Washington, DC: CJCS.

US President, 2002. *The National Security Strategy of the United States of America*, Washington, DC: White House. http://www.whitehouse.gov/nsc/nss.pdf (accessed on 23 December 2007).

Vinck, P., Pham, P., Baldo, S., Shigekane, R., 2008. *Living with Fear: A Population-Based Survey on Attitudes about Peace, Justice and Social Reconstruction in Eastern Democratic Republic of Congo*. International Centre for Transitional Justice. August 2008. *http://escholarship.org/uc/item/9738b4pm* (accessed on 14 November 2009).

Zeebroek, X., 2008. *The United Nations Mission in the Democratic Republic of Congo: Searching for the Missing Peace*. Fundación para las Relaciones Internacionales y el Diálogo Exterior (FRIDE), Working Paper 66, July 2008.

Internet Resources

Digital Congo, *http://www.digitalcongo.net/*
DRC, Office of the President, *http://www.presidentrdc.cd/*
DRC blogs, gossips, and News, *http://congosiasa.blogspot.com/*
DRC Permanent Mission to the UN, *http://www.un.int/drcongo/*
FDLR, *www.fdlr.org*
Hirondelle Foundation, *www.hirondelle.org*
International Crisis Group, *www.crisisgroup.org*
International Rescue Committee, *http://www.theirc.org*
Le Potentiel Newspaper, www.lepotentiel.com
Mai Mai Militia, *http://www.congo-mai-mai.net/Tribune*
MONUC, *www.monuc.org*, *http://www.un.org/en/peacekeeping/missions/monuc/*
Radio Okapi, *www.radiookapi.net*
Reporters Without Borders, *http://en.rsf.org/*
UN System, *www.unsystem.org*
United Nations, *www.un.org*
UN Department of Public Information, *http://www.un.org/dpi/ngosection/index.asp*
UN Department of Peacekeeping Operations, *http://www.un.org/en/peacekeeping/*
UN Procurement Division, https://www.un.org/Depts/ptd/about-us/contacts (accessed on 29 July 2016)
UN Statistical Databases, http://unstats.un.org/unsd/databases.htm (Website accessed on 1 December 2010)

Radio Outputs

Gutahuka on Radio Okapi (episodes from 12. 09. 2007–30. 04. 2010)
Dialogue Entre Congolais on Radio Okapi (episodes from 12. 09. 2007–30. 04. 2010)

Key Informants

Below are the names and affiliations of key informants in this study that agreed to be named. There were several other key informants that are not listed here out of respect for their insistence on being anonymous either for security reasons or because they were not authorized to speak on behalf of their organisations.

Baroni, Dario – Deputy Director, Fondation Hirondelle, Lausanne, Switzerland.
Etter, Jean-Marie – President, Fondation Hirondelle, Lausanne, Switzerland.
Husi, Jean-Pierre – Director of Sustainability, Fondation Hirondelle, Lausanne, Switzerland.
Kinyenya, Amuri – Co-ordinator, Lusu-Lega North-West Region (a South Kivu socio-cultural organisation).
Mounoubai, Madnodje – Spokesman, Public Information Department, MONUC, Kinshasa, DRC.
Sakombi, Serge – Former AFDL & MAI MAI Commander – South Kivu, DRC.
Vuillemin, Caroline – Director of Operations & Former Radio Okapi Programme Officer, Fondation Hirondelle, Lausanne, Switzerland.
Wakenge, Paul – Former AFDL Commander and Intelligence Officer, DRC.

Secondary Sources

Books

Afoaku, O., 2002. 'Congo's rebels: Their origins, motivations, and strategies'. In John F. Clark (Ed.), *The Africa Stakes of the Congo War* (pp. 109–128). New York: Palgrave Macmillan Press.
Ajzen, I., 1985. 'From intentions to actions: A theory of planned behavior'. In J. Kuhl & J. Beckman (eds.), *Action-Control: From Cognition to Behavior*. Heidelberg: Springer (pp. 11–39).
Ajzen, I., 1987. 'Attitudes, traits, and actions: Dispositional prediction of behavior in personality and social psychology'. In L. Berkowitz (ed.), *Advances in Experimental Social Psychology*. New York: Academic Press (Vol. 20, pp. 1–63).
Ajzen, I., 1988. *Attitudes, Personality, and Behavior*. Milton-Keynes, England: Open University Press & Chicago, IL: Dorsey Press.
Ajzen, I., & Fishbein, M., 1980. *Understanding Attitudes and Predicting Social Behaviour*. New Jersey: Prentice-Hall.
Alexei A. (ed), 1999. *Comprehending and Mastering African Conflicts: The Search For Sustainable Peace and Good Governance*. Colorado: Lynne Renner Publishers Inc.
Alleyne, M. D., 2003. *Global Lies? Propaganda, the UN and World Order*. Basingstoke: Palgrave Macmillan.
Avruch, K., Narel, J. L., & Siegel, P. C., 2000. *Information campaigns for Peace Operations*. Washington, D.C.: DoD C4ISR Cooperative Research Program

Barak, G., 1994. 'Media, society and criminology'. In G. Barak (ed.), *Media, Process, and the Social Construction of Crime: Studies in Newsmaking Criminology*. New York: Garland Publishing Inc (pp. 3–45).

Belcher, S., 1999. *Epic Traditions of Africa*. Bloomington, IN: Indiana University Press.

Bell, D., 1991. *Communitarianism and Its Critics*. Oxford: Clarendon Press.

Bellah, R., Madsen, R., Sullivan, W., Swidler, A., & Tipton, S., 1991. *The Good Society*. New York: Vintage.

Bellah, R. N., Madsen, R., Sullivan, W. M., Swidler, A., & Tipton, S. M., 1985. *Habits of the heart: Individualism and Commitment in American life*. New York: Harper & Row.

Bellamy, A.J., Williams, P., & Griffin, S., 2004. *Understanding Peacekeeping*. Cambridge: Polity Press & Blackwell Publishing.

Bentham, J., 1995. 'Panopticon (Preface)'. In Miran Bozovic (ed.), *The Panopticon Writings*, London: Verso. (pp. 29–95).

Blinderman, E., 2002. 'International Law and Information Intervention'. In M. Price & M. Thompson, *Forging Peace: Intervention, Human Rights and Management of Media Space*. Edinburgh: Edinburgh University Press Ltd.

Blumler J. G., & Katz, E., 1974. *The Uses of Mass Communication*. Newbury Park, CA: Sage.

Botombele (1976). *Cultural Policy in the Republic of Zaire: A Study*. Paris: UNESCO.

Botwe-Asamoah, K., 2005. *Kwame Nkrumah's Politico-Cultural Thought and Policies: an African-Centered Paradigm for the Second Phase of the African Revolution*. New York: Routledge.

Braeckman, C., 1996. *Terreur Africaine: Burundi, Rwanda, Zaire - Les Racines de la Violence*. Paris: Fayard.

Bryant, J., & Thompson, S., 2002. *Fundamentals of Media Effects*. Boston: McGraw Hill.

Campbell, D. T., 1966. 'Pattern matching as an essential in distal knowing'. In K. R. Hammond (ed.), *The Psychology of Egon Brunswick*. New York: Holt, Rinehart and Winston.

Carruthers, S. L., 2000. *The Media at War: Communication and Conflict in the Twentieth Century*. New York: St. Martin's Press.

Christians, C. G., Ferré, J. P., & Fackler, P. M., 1993. *Good News: Social Ethics and the Press*. New York: Oxford University Press.

Cook, T. D., & Campbell, D.T., 1989. *Quasi-Experimentation: Design and Analysis Issues for Field Settings*. Chicago: Rand McNally.

Cornet, J., 1971. *Art of Africa: Treasures from the Congo*. New York: Phaidon.

Curran, J., 2002. *Media and Power*. London: Routledge.

Curran, J., & Lerner, D., 1978. *Propaganda in War and Crisis*. London: Macmillan

Dahl, R. A., 1989. *Democracy and Its Critics*. New Haven: Yale University Press.

Deleuze, G., & Guattari, F., 1987. *A Thousand Plateaus* (trans. and edited by B. Massumi) Minneapolis: University of Minnesota Press.

Derrida, J., 2005. *Rogues: Two Essays on Reason, Meridian, Crossing Aesthetics*. Stanford, CA: Stanford University Press.

Dewey, J., 1988a. 'Practical democracy: Review of Walter Lippmann's The Phantom Public'. In J. A. Boydston (ed.), *John Dewey: The Later Works, 1925–1953*. Carbondale, IL: Southern Illinois University Press.

Dewey, J., 1988b. 'The public and its problems'. In J. A. Boydston (ed.), *John Dewey: The Later Works, 1925–1953*. Carbondale, IL: Southern Illinois University Press.

Dillon, M., 2004. 'The security of governance'. In W. Larner & W. Walters (ed.), *Global Governmentality*. London: Routledge.

Dillon, M., & Neal, A. W. (eds.), 2008. *Foucault on Politics, Security and War*. Basingstoke: Palgrave Macmillan.

Dobrzeniecki, K., 2008. 'A Janus-faced view of the electronic governance between Foucault and Habermas'. In E. Schweighofer (ed.), *Legal Informatics and e-Governance as Tools for the Knowledge Society*. Zaragoza: Prensas Universitarias de Zaragoza. (LEFIS Series; 2)

Dollard J., Doob, L. W., Miller, N. E., Mowrer, O. H., & Sears, R. R. 1939. *Frustration and Aggression*. New Haven: Yale University Press.

Domeniconi, M., 2004. 'How a radio station keeps population informed: Complex return to normality in DR Congo'. In B. James (ed.), *Media: Conflict Prevention and Reconstruction*. Paris: UNESCO.

Duffield M., 2001. *Global Governance and the New Wars: The Merging of Development and Security*. New York: Zed Books

Eagly, A, & Chaiken, S., 1993. *The Psychology of Attitudes*. Fort Worth, TX: Harcourt Brace Jovanovich.

Etzioni, A. (ed.), 1993. *New Communitarian Thinking: Persons, Virtues, Institutions, and Communities*. Charlottesville, VA: University Virginia Press.

Fairclough, N., 1995. *Critical Discourse Analysis*. New York: Longman.

Figueroa, M. E., Kincaid, D. L., Rani, M., & Lewis, G., 2002. *Communication for Social Change: A Framework for Measuring the Process and Its Outcomes*. New York: The Rockefeller Foundation.

Fishbein, M., & Ajzen, I., 1975. *Belief, Attitude, Intention and Behavior: An Introduction to Theory and Research*. Reading, MA: Addison-Wesley.

Fishbein, M., 1967. 'Attitude and the prediction of behavior'. In M. Fishbein (ed.), Readings in Attitude Theory and Measurement. New York: Wiley (pp. 477–492).

Fiske, S. E., 2005. 'Social Cognition and the Normality of Prejudgement'. In J. F. Dovidio, P. Glick, & L. A. Rudman (eds.), *On the Nature of Prejudice: Fifty Years after Allport*. Malden, MA: Blackwell Publishing.

Foucault, M., 2001. *Fearless Speech*. J. Pearson (ed.). Los Angeles, CA: Semiotext(e)/MIT Press.

Foucault, M., 1991. *Discipline and Punish: The Birth of the Prison*. London: Penguin Books.

Foucault, M., 1998. *The Will to Knowledge: The History of Sexuality Volume 1*. London: Penguin Books.

Foucault, M., 2000. 'Confronting governments: Human Rights'. In *Essential World of Foucault* 38 *1954-1984: Volume 3, Power*. ed James D Faubian, 474–75. London: Penguin Books.

Foucault, M., 2003. *Society Must Be Defended: Lectures at the College de France, 1975–76*. London: Alan Lane, The Penguin Press.

Francis J. J., Eccles, M., Johnston, M., Walker, A., Grimshaw, J., Foy, R., Kaner, E. F. S., Smith L., Bonetti, D., 2004. *Constructing Questionnaires Based on the Theory of Planned Behaviour*. Newcastle: CHSR, University of Newcastle.

Frère, M.-S., & Marthoz, J. P., 2007. *The Media and Conflicts in Central Africa*. London: Lynne Reinner Publishers.

Furniss, G. & Liz, G. (eds.), 1995. *Power, Marginality, and African Oral Literature*. Cambridge: Cambridge University Press.

Galtung, J., 1996. *Peace by Peaceful Means*. London: Sage.

Galtung, J., 1986. 'On the Role of the Media in Worldwide Security and Peace'. In T. Varis (ed.), *Peace and Communication*. San Jose, Costa Rica: Universidad para La Paz (pp. 249–66).

Glaser, B., & Strauss, A., 1967. *The Discovery of Grounded Theory*. Chicago: Aldine.

Gondola, C., 2002. *The History of Congo*. Westport: Greenwood Press.

Gourevitch, P., 1998. *We Wish to Inform You that Tomorrow We Will Be Killed with Our Families*. New York: Farrar, Straus and Giroux

Gowing, N., 1997. *Media Coverage: Help or Hindrance IN Conflict Prevention*. Washington: Carnegie Commission on Preventing Deadly Conflict

Habermas, J., 1989b. *The Structural Transformation of the Public Sphere*. Cambridge, MA: MIT Press.

Habermas, J., 1996. *Between Facts and Norms: Contributions to a Discourse Theory of Law and Democracy* (W. Rehg, Trans.). Cambridge, MA: MIT Press.

Hachten, W. A., 1992. *The World News Prism: Changing Media of International Communication* (3rd ed.). Ames, Iowa: Iowa State University Press.

Hagan, G. P., 1995. 'Nkrumah's Leadership Style: An Assessment from a Cultural Perspective'. In K. Arhin (ed.), *The Life and Work of Kwame Nkrumah*. Accra: Africa World Press (pp. 177–206).

Hahn Dan, F., 1998. *Political Communication – Rhetoric, Government and Citizens*. Pensylvania: Strata Publishing, Inc.

Hampson, F., 1996. *Nurturing Peace: Why Peace Settements Succeed or Fail*. Washington, DC: United States Institute of Peace Press

Hendy, D., 2000. *Radio in the Global Age*. Cambridge, UK: Polity Press.

Hermann, T., 2001. 'The impermeable identity wall: The study of violent conflict by "insiders" and "outsiders"'. In M. Smyth & G. Robinson (eds.), *Researching Violently Divided Societies: Ethical and Methodological Issues*. London: Pluto Press (pp. 77–91).

Hilmes, M., 2002. 'Rethinking radio'. In M. Hilmes & J. Loviglio (eds.), *Radio Reader: Essays in the Cultural History of Radio*. London: Routledge.

Hobsbawm, E., 1973. *Revolutionaries*, London: Weidenfeld and Nicolson.

Hochschild, A., 2006. *King Leopold's Ghost: A Story of Greed, Terror, and Heroism in Colonial Africa*. London: Pan Books.

Holzgrefe, J. L., & Keohane, R. O., 2003. *Humanitarian Intervention: Ethical, Legal, and Political Dilemmas*. Cambridge: Cambridge University Press.

Howard, R., Rolt, F., van de Veen, H., & Verhoeven, J. (eds.), 2003. *The Power of the Media: A Handbook for Peacebuilders*. Washington, DC: SFCG. www.xs4all.nl/%7Econflic1/Media_book_nieuw/a_b_contents.htm (accessed on 29 January 2007).

Howard, R., 2002. *An Operational Framework for Media and Peace Building*. Vancouver: IMPACS.

Huyse, L., 2003. 'The process of reconciliation'. In D. Bloomfield, T. Barnes, & L. Huyse (eds.), *Reconciliation After Violent Conflict – A Handbook*. Stockholm: International Institute for Democracy and Electoral Assistance (pp. 19–39).

Ikambana, P., 2007. *Mobutu's Totalitarian Political System: An Afrocentric Analysis*. New York: Routledge.

Inglehart, R., 1997. *Modernization and Postmodernization: Cultural, Economic, and Political Change in 43 Countries*. Princeton, NJ: Princeton University Press.

Jowett, G. S., & O'Donnell, V., 1999. *Propaganda and Persuasion*, 3rd edn. Thousand Oaks, CA: Sage.

Kaid, L., Gerstle, J., & Sanders, K. (eds.), 1991. *Mediated Politics in Two Cultures: Presidential Campaigning in the United States and France*. New York: Praeger.

Katz, E., & Lazarsfeld, P., 1955. *Personal Influence: The Part Played by People in the Flow of Mass Communication*. New York: The Free Press.

Keller, E. B., & Berry, J. L., 2003. *The Influentials: One American in Ten Tells the Other Nine How to Vote, Where to Eat, and What to Buy*. New York: Simon & Schuster.

Keller, E., 2003. *Influentials online: June 2003*. Report available at http://www.roperasw.com

Kelman, H. C. (ed.), 1965. International Behavior: A Social-Psychological Analysis. New York: Holt, Rinehart and Winston.

Keohane, R. O., 2003. Political authority after intervention: Gradations in sovereignty. In J.L. Holzgrefe & R.O. Koehane (Eds), *Humanitarian Intervention: Ethical, Legal, and Political Dilemmas*. Cambridge: Cambridge University Press. (pp. 275–298)

Kincaid, D. L., 1988. 'The convergence theory of communication: Its implications for intercultural communication'. In Y. Y. Kim (Ed.), *International and Intercultural Annual: Theoretical Perspectives*. Beverly Hills, CA: Sage (Vol. 12, pp. 280–298).

Kincaid, D. L., 1993. 'Communication Network Dynamics, Cohesion, Centrality and Cultural Evolution'. In G. A. Barnett & W. Richards (eds.), *Progress in Communication Science Series*. New York: Ablex (Vol. XII, pp. 111–132).

Kirschke, L., 1996. *Broadcasting Genocide; Censorship, Propaganda, and State-Sponsored Violence in Rwanda 1990–1994*. London: Article 19.

Kitson, F., 1971. *Low Intensity Operations: Subversion, Insurgency, Peace-keeping, Harrisburg*. Penn: Stackpole Books.

Knoke, D., 1990b. *Political Networks: The Structural Perspective*. New York: Cambridge University Press.

Krasner, S. D., 1999. *Sovereignty: Organized Hypocrisy*. Princeton: Princeton University Press.

Krueger, R. A., & Casey, M. A., 2000. *Focus Groups: A Practical Guide for Applied Research*. 3rd edition. Thousand Oaks, CA: Sage Publications Inc.

Latane, B., & Darley, J., 1970. *The Unresponsive Bystander: Why Doesn't He Help?* New York: Appleton-Century-Crofts.

Lazarsfeld, P. F., Berelson, B., & Gaudet, H., 1944. *The People's Choice: How the Voter Makes Up His Mind in a Presidential Campaign*. New York: Columbia University Press.

Lederach, J. P., 1997. *Building Peace: Sustainable Reconciliation in Divided Societies*, Washington DC: United States Institute of Peace.

Lederach J. P., 1996. *Preparing for Peace*. New York: Syracuse University Press.

Lehmann, I. A., 1999. *Peacekeeping and Public Information: Caught in the Crossfire*. London: Frank Cass.

Lindley, D., 2007. *Promoting Peace with Information*. Princeton, NJ: Princeton University Press

Lipshutz, R., & Rowe, J., 2005. *Globalization, Governmentality and Global Politics: Regulation for the Rest of Us?* London: Routledge.

Locke, J., 1947. *Two Treatises of Government*. T. L. Cook (ed.). New York: Hafner.

Mack, A., 2002. *The Human Security Project Project: Background Paper*. Vancouver: Human Security Centre, Liu Institute for Global Issues, University of British Columbia.

McGuire, W. J., 1985. 'Attitudes and attitude change'. In G. Lindzey & E. Aronson (eds.), *Handbook of. Social Psychology*. New York: Random House.

McGuire, W.G., 1986. 'The myth of massive media impact: Savagings and salvagings'. In G. Comstock (Ed.), *Public Communication and Behavior*. Orlando, FL: Academic Press.

McLeish, R., 1994. *Radio Production: A Manual for Broadcasters*. 3rd edition. Oxford: Focal Press.

McNair, B., 1999. *Political Communication*. San Jose: San Jose University Press.

Melone, S. D., Terzis, G., & Beleli, O., 2002. *Using the Media for Conflict Transformation: The Common Ground Experience*. Berghof Handbook for Conflict Transformation. Berlin, Germany: Berghof Research Center for Constructive onflict Management.

Melone, S. D., 1997. 'NGOs, the media and conflict prevention'. In P. Cross (ed.), *Contributing to Preventive Action, Conflict Prevention Network Yearbook 1997/1998*. Baden-Baden: Nomos (pp. 185–202).

Merlingen, M., & Ostrauskauite, R., 2006. *European Union Peacebuilding and Policing: Governance and the European Security Defense Policy*. London: Routledge.

Merton, R. K., Fiske, M., & Kendall, P. L., 1956. *The Focused Interview*. Glencoe, IL: Free Press.

Miall, H., 2004. 'Conflict transformation: A multi-dimensional task'. In A. Austin, M Fischer & N. Ropers (eds.). *Transforming Ethnopolitical Conflict: The Bergh of Handbook*. Berlin, Germany: VS Verlag für Sozialwissenschaften (pp. 67–90).

Miles, M., & Huberman, M., 1984. *Qualitative Data Analysis: A Source Book for New Methods*. Thousand Oaks, CA: Sage Publications.

Morrison, D. E., 2003. 'Good and bad practice in focus group research'. In V. Nightingdale & K. Ross, *Critical Readings: Media and Audiences*. Maidenhead: Open University Press.

Morrison, D. E., 1998. *The Search for a Method: Focus Groups and the Development of Mass Communication Research*. London: University of Luton Press.

Mudhai, O. F, Tettley, W. J., & Banda, F., 2009. *African Media and the Digital Public Sphere*. New York: Palgrave Macmillan.

Murty, B. S., 1989. *The Interntional Law of Propaganda*, Boston: Martins Nijhot Publishers.

Mutz, D. C., 1998. *Impersonal Influence: How Perceptions of Mass Collectives Affect Political Attitudes*. Cambridge: Cambridge University Press.

Nest, M., Grignon, F., & Kisangani, E., 2006. *The Democratic Republic of Congo: Economic Dimensions of War and Peace. Colorado*: Lynne Rienner Publishers.

Newman, S. L., 1984. *Liberalism at wit's end: The Libertarian Revolt against the Modern State*. Ithaca, NY: Cornell University Press.

Olema, D., 1997, *La satire amusée des inégalités socio-économiques dans la chanson populaire urbaine du Zaïre. Une étude de l'oeuvre de Franco (François Luambo) des années 70 et 80*. Thèse de doctorat (Ph.D.) en Littérature comparée générale, Faculté des Études Supérieures, Université deMontréal, 610 p.

O'Regan, T., Balnaves, M., & Sternberg, J. (eds.), 2002. *Mobilising the Audience*. St Lucia: University of Queensland Press.

Paluck, E. L., 2007. *Reducing Intergroup Prejudice and Conflict with the Mass Media: A Field Experiment in Rwanda*. PhD dissertation, Yale University, US.

Perry, R. W., & Maurer, B., 2003. *Globalization under Construction: Governmentality, Law, and Identity*. Minneapolis: University of Minnesota Press.

Philips, J. E. (ed.), 2005. *Writing African History*. Rochester, NY: Rochester University Press.

Pratkanis, A. R., & Aronson, E., 1992. *Age of Propaganda: The Everyday Use and Abuse of Persuasion*. Pennsylvania: Strata Publishing Inc.

Powell, R., 1999. *In the Shadow of Power: States and Strategies in International Politics*. Princeton: Princeton University Press.

Price, M. E., Rozumilowicz, B., & Verhulst, S., 2002. *Media Reform: Democratizing the Media, Democratizing the State*. New York: Routledge.

Price, M. E., 2002. *Media and Sovereignty: The Global Information Revolution and Its Challenge to State Power*. Cambridge, MA: MIT Press.

Price, M. E., Krug P., & United States Bureau for Democracy Conflict and Humanitarian Assistance, Office of Democracy and Governance. 2002. *The Enabling Environment for Free and Independent Media: Contribution to Transparent and Accountable Governance*. Washington, D.C., Office of Democracy and Governance, Bureau for Democracy, Conflict, and Humanitarian Assistance, U.S. Agency for International Development.

Price, M., & Thompson, M., 2002. *Forging Peace: Intervention, Human Rights and the Management of Media Space*. Edingburgh: Edingburgh University Press.

Prunier, G., 2009. *From Genocide to Continental War: The 'Congolese' Conflict and the crises of Contemporary Africa*. London: HURST.

Rawnsley, G., 1996. *Radio Diplomacy and Propaganda: The BBC and VoA in International Politics, 1956–1964*, Basingstoke: Macmillan

Rawnsley, G. (ed.), 1999. *Cold War Propaganda in the 1950s*. Basingstoke: Macmillan.

Reagan, T. G., 2005. *Non-Western Educational Traditions: Indigenous Approaches to Educational Thought and Practice*. 3rd edition. Mahwah, NJ: Lawrence Earlbaum Associates.

Renzi, S., & Klobas, J. E., 2002. 'Developing community in online distance learning'. In S. Wrycza (ed.), *Proceedings of the Xth European Conference on Information Systems*, Gdansk, Poland (pp. 1384–1393).

Richardson, J., 2007. *Analysing Newspapers – An Approach from Critical Discourse Analysis*. New York: Palgrave Macmillan.

Rigby, A., 2001. *Justice and Reconciliation after the Violence*, London: Lynne Renner.

Rogers, E. M., 1995. *Diffusion of Innovations*. 4th edition. New York: Free Press.

Rogers, E. M., & Kincaid, D. L., 1981. *Communication Networks: Toward a New Paradigm for Research*. New York: Free Press.

Sandel, M. J., 1982. *Liberalism and the Limits of Justice*. Cambridge, UK: Cambridge University Press.

Sassen, S., 1996. *Losing Control: Sovereignty in an Age of Globalization*. New York: Columbia University Press.

Schulberg, P., 1996. *Radio Advertising: The Authoritative Handbook*. 2nd edition. New York: McGraw Hill.

Sears, D. O., & Whitney, R. E., 1973. 'Political persuasion'. In W. Pool & W Schramm (eds.), *Handbook of Communication*. Chicago: Rand McNally (pp. 253–63).

Siebert, F. S., Peterson, T., & Schramm, W., 1956. *Four Theories of the Press*. Urbana: University of Illinois Press.

Siegel, P. C., 1998. *Target Bosnia: Integrating Information Activities in Peace Operations: NATO-led Operations in Bosnia-Herzegovina, December 1995–1997*. Washington, DC: Institute for National Strategic Studies, National Defence University.

Signorielli, N., & Morgan, M. (eds.), 1989. *Cultivation Analysis*. Newbury Park, CA: Sage Publications.

Smyth, M., & Robinson, G. (eds.), 2001. *Researching Violently Divided Socieities: Ethical and Methodological Issues*. Tokyo: United Nations University Press.

Snow, N., & Taylor, P. M. (eds.), 2009. *Routledge Handbook of Public Diplomacy*. New York: Routledge.

Stake, R., 1995. *The Art of Case Research*. Thousand Oaks, CA: Sage.

Strauss, A., & Corbin, J., 1990. *Basics of Qualitative Research: Grounded Theory and Procedures and Techniques*. Newbury Park, CA: Sage.

Swarbrick, P., 2004. 'DDRRR: Political dynamics and linkages'. In M. Malan & J. C. Porto (eds.), *Challenges of Peace Implementation: The UN Mission in the Democratic Republic of the Congo*. Pretória: Institute for Security Studies (pp. 166–167).

Taunya, J. N., 2004. 'Public Information and the media: Radio Okapi's contribution to the peace process in the DRC'. In M. Malan & J. G. Porto (eds.), *Challenges of Peace Implementation: The UN Mission in the Democratic Republic of the Congo*. Pretória: Institute for Security Studies.

Taylor, C., 1967. 'Neutrality in political science'. In P. Laslett & W. G. Runciman (eds.), *Philosophy, Politics and Society: A Collection*. 3rd series. Oxford: Blackwell.

Taylor, P. M., 1981. *The Projection of Britain: British Overseas Publicity and Propaganda 1919–1939*. Cambridge: Cambridge University Press.

Taylor, P. M., 2002 'Information warfare and information intervention'. In M. Price & M. Thompson (eds.), *Forging Peace: Intervention, Human Rights and the Management of Media Space*. Edingburgh: Edingburgh University Press.

Taylor, P. M., 2003. *Munitions of the Mind: War and Propaganda from the Ancient World to the Nuclear Age*. 3rd edition. Manchester: University of Manchester.

Taylor, P. M., 2003. 'We know where you are: Psychological operations media during Enduring Freedom'. In D. K. Thussu & D. Freedman (eds.), *War and the Media: Reporting Conflict 24/7*. London: Sage (pp. 101–113).

Taylor, P. M., 2009. 'Public diplomacy and strategic communications'. In N. Snow & P. M. Taylor, *Routledge Handbook of Public Diplomacy*. New York: Routledge.

Thompson, A., 2007. *The Media and the Rwandan Genocide*. London: Pluto Press.

Thompson, M., 2002. 'Defining information intervention: An interview with Jamie Metzl'. In Price and Thompson (eds.), *Forging Peace: Intervention, Human Rights and the Management of Media Space*. Edingburgh: Edingburgh University Press.

Thompson, M., 2005. *Forging War: The media in Serbia, Croatia and Bosnia-Hercegovina*. Revised edition. Luton: University of Luton Press.

Thussu, D. K., & Freedman, D. (eds.), 2003. *War and the Media: Reporting Conflict 24/7*. London: Sage.

Turner, T., 2007. *The Congo Wars: Conflict, Myth and Reality*. London: Zed Books Ltd.

Ugboajah, F. O., 1985. 'Oramedia'. In F.O. Ugboajah (ed.), *Mass Communication, Culture and Society in West Africa*. Oxford: Hans Zell-Saur.

United Nations, 2008. *United Nations Peacekeeping Operations: Principles and Guidelines*. New York: UN Department of Peacekeeping Operations.

United Nations, 2003. *Handbook on UN Multidimensional Peacekeeping Operation*. New York: UN Department of Peacekeeping Operations.

Vlassenroot, K., 2000. 'Identity and insecurity: The building of ethnic agendas in South Kivu'. In R. Doom & J. Gorus (eds.), *Politics of Identity and Economics of Conflict in the Great Lakes Region*. Brussels: VUB Press.

Volkan, V., Julius, D. A., & Montville, J. V. (eds.), 1990. *The Psychodynamics of International Relationships, Vol 1: Concepts and Theories*. Lexington: Lexington Books.

Walters, W., & De Haar, H., 2005. *Governing Europe: Discourse, Governmentality and European Integration*. London: Routledge.

Wasburn, P., 1992. *Broadcasting Propaganda: International Radio Broadcasting and the Construction of Political Reality*. New Jersey: Prentice Hall.

Weaver, D., McCombs, M., & Shaw, D. L., 2004. 'Agenda-setting research: Issues, attributes, and influences'. In L. L. Kaid (ed.), *Handbook of Political Communication Research*. Mahwah, NJ: Lawrence Erlbaum (pp. 257–282).

Weaver, D. H., 1977. 'Political issues and voter need for orientation'. In D. L. Shaw & M. E. McCombs (eds.), *The Emergence of American Political Issues: The Agenda-setting Function of the Press*. St. Paul, MN: West (pp. 107–119) (Reprinted in 1991, D. L. Protess & M. McCombs (Eds.), *Agenda Setting: Readings on Media, Public Opinion, and Policymaking* (pp. 131–139). Hillsdale, NJ: Lawrence Erlbaum).

Weimann, G., 1994. *The Influentials*. Albany, NY: State University of New York Press.

Weis, G., 1959. *Le pays d'Uvira: Etude de geographie regionale sur la bordure occiden-tale du lac Tanganika*. Brussels: Academie royale des sciences coloniales.

White, B. W., 2008. *Rumba Rules: The Politics of Dance Music in Mobutu's Zaire*. Durham, NC: Duke University Press.

Wilby, P., & Conroy, A., 1994. *The Radio Handbook*. London: Routledge.

Wilson, D., 1988. *A Survey of Traditional-Modern Communications Systems in Old Calabar (1846–1982)*. A PhD thesis of the University of Ibadan, Nigeria.

Wolfsfeld, G., 1998. 'Promoting peace through the news media. Some initial lessons from Oslo peace process'. In T. Liebes and J. Curran (eds.), *Media Ritual and Identity*. London: Routledge.

Wolfsfeld, G., 2004. *Media and the Path to Peace*. New York: Cambridge University Press.

Wrong, M., 2000. *In the Footsteps of Mr. Kurtz: Living on the Brink of Disaster in Mobutu's Congo*. London: Fourth Estate.

Yin, R. K., 1984. *Case Study Research*. Beverly Hills, CA: Sage.

Ziemke, E. F., 1990. *The U.S. Army in the occupation of Germany 1944–1946*, Washington, DC: Center of Military History, United States Army.

Articles

Aarts, H., & Dijksterhuis, A., 2003. 'The silence of the library: Environmental control over social behavior'. *Journal of Personality and Social Psychology*, *84*, 18–28.

Aarts, H., Dijksterhuis, A., & Custers, R., 2003. 'Automatic normative behavior in environments: The moderating role of conformity in activating social norms'. *Social Cognition*, *21*, 447–464.

Adelman, K. L., 1976. 'The Zairian political party as religious surrogate' *Africa Today*, *23* (4).

Adelman, K. L., 1975. 'The recourse to authenticity and Negritude in Zaire' *The Journal of Modern African Studies*, 13(1), 134–139

Agostinelli, G., Brown, J., & Miller, W., 1995. 'Effects of normative feedback on consumption among heavy drinking college students'. *Journal of Drug Education*, 25, 31–40.

Aitken, L., 2009. '"First we hold our noses, then we seek justice": The application of the soft approach in the Chapter VII operations conducted in the Democratic Republic of Congo'. *Canadian Military Journal*, 10 (1).

Ajzen, I., 1991. 'The theory of planned behavior'. *Organizational Behavior and Human Decision Processes*, *50*, 179–211.

Ajzen, I., 2002. 'Perceived behavioral control, self-efficacy, locus of control, and the theory of planned behavior'. *Journal of Applied Social Psychology*, *32*, 665–683.

Ajzen, I., & Fishbein, M., 1973. 'Attitudinal and normative variables as predictors of specific behavior'. *Journal of Personality and Social Psychology*, 27(1), 41–57.

Allen, T., & N., Stremlau, 2005. 'Media policy, peace and state reconstruction'. LSE Crisis States Discussion *Paper 8.*

Alleyne, M. D., 2005. 'United Nations celebrity diplomacy'. *SAIS Review*, *XXV*(1), Winter-Spring.

Ansu-Kyeremeh, K., 1992. 'Cultural aspects of constraints on village education by radio'. *Media, Culture and Society*, *14*, 111–128.

Ansu-Kyeremeh, K., 1988. 'Contextual concepts in media-delivered village education'. *Media Information Australia*, *48, 49–55*

Autesserre, S., 2006. "Local violence, National Peace? Post-war 'settlement' in the Eastern D.R. Congo". *African Studies Review*, *49*(3), 1–29.

Ball-Rokeach, S. J., Grube, J. W., & Rokeach, M., 1981. 'Roots: The next generation—Who watched and with what effect?' *Public Opinion Quarterly*, *45*, 58–68.

Baer, J.S., Stacy, A., & Larimer M., 1991. 'Biases in the perception of drinking norms among college students'. *Journal of Studies on Alcohol*, *52*(6).

Berkeley, B., 1994. 'Sounds of violence: Rwanda's killer radio'. *New Republic*, *21*(8–9), 18–19.

Betz, M., 2004. 'Radio as peacebuilder: A case study of Radio Okapi in the Democratic Republic of Congo'. *Great Lakes Research Journal*, *1*, 32–43.

Bogdan, R.C., & Biklen, S.K. 1982. *Qualitative Research for Education: An Introduction to Theory and Methods*. Boston: Allyn and Bacon, Inc

Booth, K. 1991. 'Security and Emancipation', *Review of International Studies*, Vol. 17, No. 4, pp. 313–326.

Bostian, L. R., 1970. 'The two-step flow theory: Cross-cultural implications'. *Journalism Quarterly*, *47*, 109–117.

Botombele (1976). *Cultural Policy in the Republic of Zaire: A Study*. Paris: UNESCO.

Braeckman, C., 1996. *Terreur africaine. Burundi, Rwanda, Zaire: les racines de la violence*. Paris: Fayard.

Bratic, V., 2008. 'Examining peace-oriented media in areas of violent conflict'. *International Communication Gazette, 70*(6).

Burgess. J., Harrison, C., & Maiteny, P., 1991. 'Contested meanings: The consumption of news about nature conservation'. *Media, Culture and Society*, *13*, 499–519.

Burt, R. S., 1999. 'The social capital of opinion leaders'. *Annals of the American Academy of Political and Social Science*, *566*, 37–54.

Burton, F., 1978. *The Politics of Legitimacy: Struggles in a Belfast Community*. London: Routledge

Buzan, B., 1991. 'New Patterns of Global Security in the Twenty-First Century.' *International Affairs*. 67.3. pp 431–451.

Campbell, D., 1994. 'The Deterritorialization of Responsibility: Levinas, Derrida, and Ethics After the End of Philosophy'. *Alternatives: Global, Local, Political*, 19(4), 455–484.

Campbell, D., 2005. 'The Biopolitics of Security: Oil, Empire, and the Sports Utility Vehicle'. *American Quarterly, 57*(3), 943–972

Campbell, D., 2003. 'Representing contemporary war'. *Ethics and International Affairs*, 17(2), 142–164.

Campbell, D. T., & Fiske, D.W., 1959. 'Convergent and discriminant validation by the multitrait-multimethod matrix'. *Psychological Bulletin*, 56, 81–105.

Caracelli, V., 1989. 'Structured Conceptualization: A framework for interpreting evaluation results'. *Concept Mapping for Evaluation and Planning. A Special Issue of Evaluation and Program Planning*, 12(1) 45–52.

Chan, K. K., & Shekhar, M. F., 1990. 'Characteristics of the opinion leader: A new dimension'. *Journal of Advertising*, 19(3), 53–60.

Chen, H.T., & Rossi, P.H., 1987. 'The theory-driven approach to validity'. *Evaluation and Program Planning*, 10, 95–103.

Childs, H. L., 1937. 'Public opinion and peace'. *Annals of the American Academy of Political and Social Science*, 192, 31–37

Cialdini, R. B., & Goldstein, N. J., 2004. 'Social influence: Compliance and conformity'. *Annual Review of Psychology*, 55, 591–621.

Cialdini, R. B., 2003. 'Crafting normative messages to protect the environment'. *Current Directions in Psychological Science*, 12(4), 105–109.

Cialdini, R. B., Kallgren, C. A., & Reno, R. R., 1991. 'A focus theory of normative conduct: A theoretical refinement and reevaluation of the role of norms in human behaviour'. *Advances in Experimental Social Psychology*, 24, 201–234.

Cialdini, R. B., Reno, R. R., & Kallgren, C. A., 1990. 'A focus theory of normative conduct: Recycling the concept of norms to reduce littering in public places'. *Journal of Personality and Social Psychology*, 58(6), 1015–1026.

Clapp, J.D., Lange, J.E., Russell, C., Shillington, A., & Voas, R., 2003. 'A failed norms social marketing campaign'. *Journal of Studies on Alcohol*, 64, 409–414.

Cosmas, S., & Sheth, J., 1980. 'Identification of opinion leaders across cultures: An assessment for use in the diffusion of innovations and ideas'. *Journal of International Business Studies*, 11, 66–73.

Craig, D., 1996. 'Communitarian Journalism(s): Clearing conceptual landscapes'. *Journal of Mass Media Ethics*, 11, 107–118.

Cronbach, L.J., & Meehl, P.E., 1955. Construct validity in psychological tests. *Psychological Bulletin*, 52(4), *281–302*

Davis, J., 1989. 'Construct validity in measurement: A pattern matching approach'. *Concept Mapping for Evaluation and Planning. A Special Issue of Evaluation and Program Planning*, 12(1), 31–36

De Villers, G., 1998. 'Identifications et mobilisations politiques au Congo Kinshasa'. *Politique Africaine*, No. 72, pp. 81–97.

Dillon, M., 2002. 'Network Society, network-centric warfare and the state of emergency'. *Theory, Culture and Society*, 19(4).

Dillon, M., 2007. 'Governing terror. The state of emergency of biopolitical emergence'. *International Political Sociology*, 1(1).

Dillon, M., & Reid J., 2000. 'Global governance, liberal peace, and complex emergency'. *Alternatives: Social Transformation & Humane Governance*, 25(1), 117.

Dillon, M., & Reid, J., 2001. 'Global liberal governance: Biopolitics, security and war'. *Millennium Journal of International Studies, 30*(1), 41–66.

Donaldson, S.I., Graham J.W., & Hansen, W.B., 1994. 'Testing the generalizability of intervening mechanism theories: Understanding the effects of adolescent drug use prevention interventions'. *Journal of Behavioral Medicine, 17*(2), 195–216.

Duffield, M., & Waddell, N. 2004. 'Human security and global danger: exploring a governmental assemblage'. Department of Politics & International Relations, Lancaster University. www.bond. org.uk/pubs/gsd/duffield.pdf (accessed on 2 May 2007).

Dugan, M., 1996. 'A nested theory of conflict'. *A Leadership Journal: Women in Leadership: Sharing the Vision, 1*, 9–19.

Dumont, J., 1989. 'Validity in multidimensional scaling in the context of structed conceptualization'. *Concept Mapping for Evaluation and Planning. A Special Issue of Evaluation and Program Planning, (1)*, 81–86.

Eich, E., Macauley, D., & Ryan, L., 1994. 'Mood dependent memory for events of the personal past'. *Journal of Experimental Psychology: General, 123*(2), 201–215.

Einhorn, H. J., & Hogarth, R.M., 1986. 'Judging probable case'. *Psychological Bulletin, 99*(1), 3–19.

Ellis, J., 2000. 'Scheduling: the Last Creative Act in Television?'. *Media, Culture & Society, 22*(1), 25–38.

Ellis, S., 1989. 'Tuning in to pavement radio'. *African Affairs 88*, 321–30

Esan, O., 2004. 'African media and the new partnership for Africa's development (NEPAD) agenda for africa's emerging democracies'. *African Media Review, 12*(2), 41–56

Featherstone, A. B., 1999. 'The limits of conflict resolution'. Article presented at the International Studies Association Annual Convention, Washington DC, Februrary 16–20.

Flynn, L., Goldsmith, R., & Eastman, J., 1996. 'Opinion leaders and opinion seekers: Two new measurement scales'. *Academy of Marketing Science Journal, 24*(2), 137–147.

Foucault, M., 1995. *Discipline and Punish: The Birth of the Prison*. York: Vintage Books.

Fraser, N., 1990. 'Rethinking the public sphere: A contribution to the critique of actually existing democracy'. *Social Text, 25/26*, 56–80.

Friedland, L., 2001. 'Communication, community, and democracy: Toward a theory of communicatively integrated Community'. *Communication Research, 4*, 358–391.

Fujita, K., Henderson, M., Eng, J., Trope, Y., & Liberman, N., 2005. 'Spatial distance and mental construal of social events'. *Psychological Science, 17*, 278–282.

Fujita, K., Eyal, T., Chaiken, S., Trope, Y., & Liberman, N., 2008. 'Influencing attitudes toward near and distant objects'. *Journal of Experimental Social Psychology, 44*, 562–572.

Fujita, K., & Han, H, A., 2009. 'Moving beyond deliberative control of impulses: The effect of construal levels on evaluative associations in self-control conflicts'. *Psychological Science, 20*, 799–804.

Fujita, K., Henderson, M., Eng, J., Trope, Y., & Liberman, N., 2005. 'Spatial distance and mental construal of social events'. *Psychological Science, 17*, 278–282.

Fujita, K., Trope, Y., Liberman, N., & Levin-Sagi, M., 2006. 'Construal levels and self-control'. *Journal of Personality and Social Psychology, 90*, 351–367.

Galtung, J., 1998. 'Peace Journalism: What, why, who, how, when, where. Paper presented in the workshop, "What are journalists for?" TRANSCEND, Taplow Court, UK, September 3–6.

Galvin, P.F., 1989. 'Concept mapping for planning and evaluation of a Big Brother/Big Sister program'. *Concept mapping for evaluation and planning. A Special Issue of Evaluation and Program Planning, 12*(1), 53–58.

Gerbner, G., Signorielli, N., & Morgan, M., 1982. 'Charting the mainstream: Television's contributions to political orientation'. *Journal of Communication, 32*(2), 100–127.

Geschiere, P., & Jackson, S., 2006. 'Autochthony and the crisis of citizenship: Democratization, decentralization, and the politics of belonging'. *African Studies Review, 49*(2), 1–7.

Goldstein, C.S., 2008. 'A strategic failure. American information control policy in occupied Iraq'. Military Review. March-April 2008, 58–64.

Goldstein, N., Cialdini R., & Griskevicius, V., 2008. 'A room with a viewpoint: Using norm-based appeals to motivate conservation behaviors in a hotel setting'. *Journal of Consumer Research*, *35*, 472–482.

Granfield, R., 2005. 'Alcohol use in college: Limitations on the transformation of social norms'. *Addiction Research and Theory*, *13*, 281–292.

Griggs, R., 1997. 'Geostrategies in the Great Lakes conflict and spatial designs for peace'. Center for World Indigenous Studies. http://cwis.org/hutu3_1.html (accessed on 13 December 2007).

Hagan, G., 1991b. Nkrumah's Cultural Policy. In Arhin K. (Ed), *The Life and Work of Kwame Nkrumah*. Accra: SEDCO 3–26

Haines, M., & Spear, S., 1996. 'Changing the perception of the norm: A strategy to decrease binge drinking among college students'. *Journal of American College Health*, *45*, 134–140.

Hur, K. K., & Robinson, J. P., 1978. 'The social impact of Roots'. *Journalism Quarterly*, *55*, 19–21.

Huckfeldt, R., & Sprague, J., 1987. 'Networks in context – The social flow of political information'. *American Political Science Review*, *81*, 1197–1216.

Howard, A., 2001. *From Refugees to Forced Migration: The UNHCR and Human Security*. 2001. International Migration Review 35 (Spring 2001): 7–32.

Huysmans, J., 2004. 'A Foucauldian View on Spill-over: Freedom and Security in the EU', *Journal of International Relations and Development* 7(3): 294–318.

Jackson, S., 2007. 'Of "Doubtful Nationality": Political manipulation of citizenship in the D. R. Congo'. *Citizenship Studies*, *11*(5), 481–500.

Jackson, S., 2006. 'Sons of which soil? The language and politics of autochthony in eastern D.R. Congo'. *African Studies Review*, *49*(2), 95–123.

Jackson, K., & Trochim, W., 2002. 'Concept mapping as an alternative approach for the analysis of open-ended survey responses'. *Organizational Research Methods*, *5*(4), 307–336.

Kallgren, C. A., Reno, R. R., & Cialdini, R. B., 2000. 'A focus theory of normative conduct: When norms do and do not affect behavior'. *Personality and Social Psychology Bulletin*, *26*, 1002–1012.

Katz, E., 1957. 'The two-step flow of communication: An up-to-date report on an hypothesis'. *Public Opinion Quarterly*, *21*, 61–78.

Keenan, T., 1987. "The 'Paradox' of knowledge and power: Reading Foucault on a bias". *Political Theory, 15*(1), 5–37.

Keith, D., 1989. 'Refining concept maps: Methodological issues and an example'. *Concept Mapping for Evaluation and Planning. A Special Issue of Evaluation and Program Planning 12*(1), 75–80.

Keohane, R. O., 2001. 'Governance in a partially globalized world.' *American Political Science Review*, *95*, 1–13.

Keohane, R., 2002. 'The globalization of informal violence, theories of world politics, and the "Liberalism of Fear"'. *Dialogue IO*, *1*, 29–43.

Kincaid, D. L., 1979. *The Convergence Model of Communication*. East-West Communication Institute Paper Series 18, Honolulu, Hawaii.

Kincaid, D. L., 2000a. 'Mass media, ideation, and contraceptive behaviour'. *Communication Research*, *27*(6), 723–763.

Kincaid, D. L., 2000b. 'Social networks, ideation, and contraceptive behavior in Bangladesh: A longitudinal analysis'. *Social Science and Medicine*, *50*(2), 215–231.

Kincaid, D. L., 2002. 'Drama, emotion, and cultural convergence'. *Communication Theory*, *12*(2), 136–152.

Kincaid, D. L., 2004. 'From innovation to social norm: Bounded normative influence'. *Journal of Health Communication*, *9*, 37–57.

Knoke, D., 1990a. 'Networks of political action: Toward theory construction'. *Social Forces*, *68*, 1041–1063.

Krause, K. & Williams, M.C., 1997. 'Preface: Toward critical security studies'. In: Krause K and Williams MC (eds) *Critical Security Studies: Concepts and Cases*. London: UCL Press, PP vii–xxi

Krug, P., & Price, M. E., 2002. 'A Module for Media Intervention: Content Regulation in Post-Conflict Zones'. In M. Price & M. Thompson (Eds.), *Forging peace: Intervention, Human Rights and the Management of Media Space* (pp. 148–174). Edinburgh University Press. Retrieved from http://repository.upenn.edu/asc_papers/146

Kyrke-Smith, L., 2007. 'Information Intervention and the case of Kosovo: Realising the Responsibility to Protect'. *Knowledge Politics Quaterly*, *1*(1).

Lapinski, M. K., & Rimal, R. N., 2005. 'An explication of social norms'. *Communication* Theory, *15*(2), 127–147.

Larimer, M. E., & Neighbors, C., 2003. 'Normative misperceptions and the impact of description and injunctive norms on college student gambling'. *Psychology of Addictive Behaviours*, *17*, 235–243.

Larner, W., & Walters, W., 2004. 'Globalization as governmentalization', *Alternatives: Global, Local, Political, 29*(5), 495–514.

Larner, W. & Walters, W., 2004a. '*Introduction: Global Governmentality: governing international spaces*', pp. 1–20 in Wendy Larner and William Walters (eds) *Global Governmentality*. London/New York: Routledge.

Larner, W. & Walters, W., 2004b. '*Globalization as Governmentalization*', *Alternatives: Global, Local, Political 29*(5): 495–514.

Larrinaga, M. D., & Doucet, M. G., 2008. 'Sovereign power and the biopolitics of human security'. *Security Dialogue, 39*, 517–537.

Lasswell, H. D., 1928. 'The function of the propagandist'. *International Journal of Ethics*, *38*(3), 258–68.

Levy, M., 1978. 'Opinion leadership and television news uses'. *Public Opinion Quarterly*, *42*, 402–406.

Liberman, N., & Trope, Y., 1998. 'The role of feasibility and desirability considerations in near and distant future decisions: A test of temporal construal theory'. *Journal of Personality and Social Psychology, 75*, 5–18.

Lindley, D., 2004. 'Untapped power? UN Public Information Operations'. *International Peacekeeping*, *11*(4), 608–624.

Lipschutz, R.D., 1992. 'Reconstructing World Politics: The Emergence of Global Civil Society'. *Millennium, Journal of International Studies* 21(3), 389–420.

Lunt, P., & Livingstone, S., 1996. 'Rethinking the focus group in media and communications research'. *Journal of Communication, 46*(2), Spring 0021-9916/96.

Malkasian, C., 2006. 'The role of perceptions and political reform in counterinsurgency: The case of Western Iraq, 2004–05'. *Small Wars and Insurgencies*, *17*(3), 367–394.

Mano, W., 2005. 'Scheduling for rural and urban listeners on bilingual Radio Zimbabwe'. *The Radio Journal – International Studies in Broadcast and Audio Media, 3*(2), 93–106, doi: 10.1386/rajo.3.2.93/1.

Marquart, J. M., 1989. 'A Pattern Matching Approach to assess the construct validity of an evaluation instrument'. *Concept Mapping for Evaluation and Planning. A Special Issue of Evaluation and Program Planning*, *12*(1), 37–44.

Marshall, R., & Gitsudarmo, I., 1995. 'Variation in the characteristics of opinion leaders across cultural borders'. *Journal of International Consumer Marketing*, *8*(1), 5–22.

Masoka, H., 2006. 'How can the Fourth Estate be sustained in the DRC'. In Open Society Initiative for Southern Africa (OSISA)'. *OPENSPACE, The Media: Expression and Freedom*, *1*(5).

http://www.osisa.org/files/openspace/1_5_p75-79_hubert_tshiswaka_masoka.pdf (accessed on 02.05.07).

McLeod, J. M., Daily, K., Guo, Z., Eveland, W. P. Jr., Bayer, J., Yang, S., & Wang, H., 1996. 'Community integration, local media use and democratic processes'. *Communication Research*, *23*, 179–209.

McLeod, J. M., Scheufele, D. A., & Moy, P., 1999. 'Community, communication, and participation: The role of mass media and interpersonal discussion in local political participation'. *Political Communication*, *16*, 315–336.

Melone, S. D., Terzis, G., & Beleli, O., 2002. *Using the Media for Conflict Transformation: The Common Ground Experience*. Berghof Handbook for Conflict Transformation. Berlin: Berghof Forschungszentrum für konstruktive Konfliktbearbeitung.

Metzl, J. F., 1997a. 'Information intervention: When switching channels isn't enough'. *Foreign Affairs*, *76*(6), 15–20.

Metzl, J. F., 1997b. 'Rwandan genocide and the international law of radio jamming'. *American Journal of International Law*, *91*.

Nabudere, D. W., 2006. 'Towards an Afrokology of knowledge production and regeneration'. *African Renaissance Studies: Multi-Inter-and Transdisciplinarity,1*(1), 7–32.

Neal, P., & Paris, D., 1990. 'Liberalism and the communitarian critique: A guide for the perplexed'. *Canadian Journal of Political Science*, *23*, 419–439.

Neighbors, C., Larimer, M. E., & Lewis, M. A., 2004. 'Targeting misperceptions of descriptive drinking norms: Efficacy of a computer-delivered personalized normative feedback intervention'. *Journal of Consulting and Clinical Psychology*, *72*, 434–447.

Nisbert, E., 2005 'The engagement model of opinion leadership: Testing validity within a european context'. *International Journal of Public Opinion Research, 18*(1).

Nkrumah, K., 1973a. *Revolutionary Path*. London: Panaf Books.

Nuruzzaman, M., 2008. 'Liberal institutionalism and international cooperation after 11 September 2001'. *International Studies*, *45*, 193–213.

Olema, D., 1984. 'Société Zaïroise dans le miroir de la chanson populaire'. *Canadian Journal of African Studies, 18*(1), 122–30.

Paluck, E. L., 2009. 'Reducing intergroup prejudice and conflict using the media: A field experiment in Rwanda'. *Journal of Personality and Social Psychology*, *96*, 574–587.

Paluck, E. L., & Green, D. P., 2009. 'Deference, dissent, and dispute resolution: A field experiment on a mass media intervention in Rwanda'. *American Political Science Review*, *103*(4), 622–644.

Payne, K., 2005. 'The media as an instrument of war'. *Parameters: Journal of the US Army War College*, *35*(1), Spring.

Peeler, C. M., Far, J., Miller, J., & Brigham, T. A., 2000. 'An analysis of the effects of a program to reduce heavy drinking among college students'. *Journal of Alcohol and Drug Education*, *45*, 39–54.

Perkins, H. W., & Berkowitz, A. D., 1986. 'Perceiving the community norms of alcohol use among students: Some research implications for campus alcohol education programming.' *International Journal of the Addictions*, *21*(9 & 10), 961–976.

Perkins, H. W., Haines, M. P., & Rice, R. M., 2005. 'Misperceiving the college drinking norm and related problems: A nationwide study of exposure to prevention information, perceived norms, and student alcohol misuse.' *Journal of Studies on Alcohol*, *66*(4), 470–478.

Peters, J. D., 1989. 'Democracy and American mass communication theory: Dewey, Lippmann, Lazarsfeld'. *Communication*, *11*, 199–220.

Peter Katzenstein (ed.) 1996. *The Culture of National Security: Norms and Identity in World Politics*. New York: Columbia University Press.

Plaisance, P., 2005 'The mass media as discursive network: Building on the implications of libertarian and communitarian claims for news media ethics theory'. *Communications Theory, 15*(3), 292–313.

Powell, R., 2004. 'The inefficient use of power: Costly conflict with complete information'. *American Political Science Review, 98*(2), 231–241.

Power, S., 2001. 'Bystanders to genocide'. *The Atlantic Monthly*, September.

Price, M. E., 2000. 'Restructuring the media in post-conflict societies: Four perspectives: The experience of intergovernmental and non-governmental organizations'. *Cardozo Online Journal of Conflict Resolution, 1*, 31.

Price, M., 2000. 'Information intervention: Bosnia, the Dayton Accords, and the seizure of broadcasting transmitters'. *Cornell International Law Journal, 33*, 67–112.

Reno, R., Cialdini, R., & Kallgren, C. A., 1993. 'The transsituational influence of social norms'. *Journal of Personality* and Social Psychology, *64*, 104–112.

Rimal, R. N., & Real, K., 2003. 'Perceived risk and efficacy beliefs as motivators of change: Use of the risk perception attitude (RPA) framework to understand health behaviors'. *Human Communication Research, 29*(3), 370–399.

Russell, C., Clapp, J. D., & DeJong, W., 2005. 'Done 4: Analysis of a failed social norms marketing campaign'. *Health Communication, 17*, 57–65.

Salawu, A., 2006. 'Essence and strategies for development communication'. *An Encyclopaedia of the Arts, 3*(1), 42–50.

Schatzberg, M. G., 1993. 'Power, legitimacy and "democratisation" in Africa'. *Journal of the International African Institute, 63*(4), 445–461.

Scheufele, D. A., & Shah, D., 2000. 'Personality strength and social capital: The role of dispositional and informational variables in the production of civic participation'. *Communication Research, 27*, 107–131.

Schiffman, L. G., Dash, J. F., & Dillion, W. R., 1975. 'Interpersonal communication: An opinion leadership/opinion seeking composite approach'. *Marketing in Turbulent Times and Marketing, the Challenges and the Opportunities: Combined Proceedings Series, 37*, 228–232

Schultz, C. G., & Neighbors, C., 2007. 'Perceived norms and alcohol consumption: Differences among college students from rural versus urban high schools'. *Journal of American College Health, 56*, 261–265.

Schultz, P. W., Nolan, J., Cialdini, R., Goldstein, N., & Griskevicius, V., 2007. 'The constructive, destructive, and reconstructive power of social norms'. *Psychological Science, 18*, 429–434.

Shah, D. V., McLeod, J. M., & Yoon, S. H., 2001. 'Communication, context and community: An exploration of print, broadcast and Internet influences'. *Communication Research, 28*, 464–508.

Smith, P., & Trope, Y., 2006. 'You focus on the forest when you're in charge of the trees: Power priming and abstract information processing'. *Journal of Personality and Social Psychology, 90*, 578–596.

Snow, N., & Taylor, P. M., 2006. 'The revival of the propaganda state: US propaganda at home and abroad since 9/11'. *The International Communication Gazette, 68*, 5–6.

Squires, C. R., 2000. 'Black talk radio: Defining community needs and identity'. *Harvard International Journal of Press/Politics*, 5.2, 73–96.

Squier, S. M., (2003). Communities of the air: Introducing the Radio world. In S. M. Squier (Ed.), *Communities of the air: Radio century, radio culture* (pp. 1–38). Durham, NC: Duke University Press.

Taylor, P. M., 2002. 'Strategic communications or democratic propaganda'. *Journalism Studies, 3*(3), 437–441.

Taylor, P. M., 2008. 'Strategic communications and the challenges of the post 9/11 World'. *Journal of Media and Information Warfare, 1*, 9–17.

Teddy, D. J., Hogg, M. A., & White K. M., 1999. 'The theory of planned behaviour: Self-identity, social identity and group norms'. *British Journal of Social Psychology*, *38*(3), 225–244.

Tellis, W., 1997. 'Introduction to case study'. *The Qualitative Report*, 3(2). July.

Thakur, M., 2007. 'Demilitarising militias in the Kivus (eastern Democratic Republic of Congo'. *African Security Review*. *17*(1), 51–67.

Trochim, W., 1985. 'Pattern matching, validity and conceptualization in program evaluation'. *Evaluation Review*, *9*(5), 575–604.

Trochim, W., 1989. 'Outcome pattern matching and program theory'. *Evaluation and Program Planning*, *12*(4), 355–366.

Trope, Y., & Liberman, N., 2000. 'Temporal construal and time-dependent changes in preference'. *Journal of Personality and Social Psychology*, *79*, 876–889.

Trope, Y., & Liberman, N., 2003. 'Temporal construal'. *Psychological Review*, *110*, 403–421.

Ugboajah, F. O., 1979. 'Developing indigenous communication in Nigeria'. *Journal of Communication*, *29*(1), 40–45.

Ugboajah, F.O., 1986. 'Communication as technology in African rural development'. *African Media Review*, *1*(1), 1–19.

Valkenburg, P. M., Semetko, H. A., & de Vreese, C. H., 1999. 'The effect of news frames on readers' thoughts and recall'. *Communication Research*, *26*(5), 550–569.

Varadarajan, L., 2004. 'Constructivissm, identity and neoliberal (in)security'. *Review of International Studies*, 30, 319–341.

Vlassenroot, K., 2002. 'Citizenship, identity formation & conflict in South Kivu: The case of the Banyamulenge'. *Review of African Political Economy*, 93/94, 499–516.

Weaver, D. H., 1980. 'Audience need for orientation and media effects'. *Communication Research*, 7, 361–376.

Wechsler, H., Nelson, T., Lee, J.E., Seiberg, M., Lewis, C., & Keeling, R., 2003. 'Perception and reality: A national evaluation of social norms marketing interventions to reduce college students' heavy alcohol use'. *Quarterly Journal of Studies on Alcohol*, 64, 484–494.

Weimann, G., 1983. 'The strength of weak conversational ties in the flow of information and influence'. *Social Networks*, 5, 245–267.

Weimann, G., 1991. 'The influentials: Back to the concept of opinion leaders'. *Public Opinion Quarterly*, 55, 267–279.

Weldes, J. et. al. 1999. 'Introduction: Constructing Insecurity'. In Weldes, J. et. al., (Eds.) *Cultures of Insecurity: States, Communities, and the Production of Danger*. London; Minneapolis, University of Minnesota Press.

Werch, C. E., Pappas, D. M., Carlson, J. M., DiClemente, C. C., Chally, P. S., & Sinder J. A. 2000. 'Results of a social norm intervention to prevent binge drinking among first year residential college students'. *Journal of American College Health*, 49, 85–92.

Whitman, S., 2003. 'Balancing act. An insider's view of the Inter-Congolese Dialogue'. *African Security Review*, 12(4).

Williams, L. E., & Bargh, J. A., 2008. 'Keeping one's distance: The influence of spatial distance cues on affect and evaluation'. *Psychological Science*, 19, 302–308.

Wilson, D., 1987. 'Traditional systems of communication in modern African development: An analytical viewpoint'. *African Media Review*, 1(2), 87–104.

Wilson, D., 2008. 'Research on traditional communication in Africa: The development and future directions'. *African Communication Research*, 1(1), 47–59.

Zanotti, L., 2006. 'Taming chaos: A Foucauldian view of UN peacekeeping, democracy and normalization'. *International Peacekeeping*, 13(2), 150–167.

Zanotti, L., 2008. 'Imagining democracy, building unsustainable institutions: The UN peacekeeping operation in Haiti'. *Security Dialogue*, *39*(5), 539–561.